Wm. A

Lieuten

U.S. M

Arlington, Virginia U.S.A.
2005

AGENT FOR THE RESISTANCE

TEXAS A&M UNIVERSITY
MILITARY HISTORY SERIES

35

AGENT

FOR THE

RESISTANCE

A Belgian Saboteur in
World War II

By Herman Bodson

Edited by Richard Schmidt

Texas A&M University Press
College Station

The paper used in this book meets the minimum requirements
of the American National Standard for Permanence
of Paper for Printed Library Materials, Z39.48-1984.
Binding materials have been chosen for durability.

Library of Congress Cataloging-in-Publication Data

Bodson, Herman. 1912–
    Agent for the Resistance : a Belgian saboteur in World War II / by
Herman Bodson.
        p.   cm.—(Texas A&M University military history series : 35)
    ISBN 0-89096-607-9
    1. Bodson, Herman, 1912– .   2. World War, 1939–1945—
Underground movements—Belgium.   3. World War, 1939–1945—Personal
narratives, Belgian.   4. Guerrillas—Belgium—Biography.   I. Title.
II. Series: Texas A&M University military history series : 35.
D802.B4B58   1994
940.53'493'092—dc20   94-25762
    [B]   CIP

To the memory of my best friend,
Jan Van der Borght,
Engineer, U.Lv.

who, under German torture, died
in the Arlon Jail
so that Group E of Service Hotton
could continue the good fight.

Also,
To the memory of all
Brussels Free University
graduates and students
who were made victims of their
commitment to Freedom.

Contents

Illustrations

Preface

Some forty years after the events I am about to relate, I started to write an autobiography for my children. This first writing has now evolved into an autobiographical account of one period of my life, the years 1932 to 1945—the war in Europe. At first I wondered how I could possibly remember so many events, so many dates, so many minute details. It was an interesting retrieving process. It did not occur simply, but was a long and often painful search that has taken me four years to complete.

The process started with some vivid images, very precise scenes shrouded in the mist of long ago. The chronology was there, exact sequences, but without reference. While writing, I felt the need for accuracy and read intensely on war history, making notes of all that related to our fight. From there came dates, places, even times of actions on which I could rely. I organized my memories and put them in context. I separated the now historically known facts from what I did not know at the time. Throughout the process, my memory freed details I could not at first remember, details hidden in some dark and sealed niches of my brain.

Some events which I remembered well I did not at first write down, as I voluntarily suppressed them from my recollections as being too tragic or too cruel to be passed along. I came later to recognize this as dishonest, vis-à-vis myself and potential readers. The story did not represent my involvement but some other, more likeable fellow's. By refusing to convey some images of my past, I camouflaged the real me and my story fell short on veracity. At that point I made the decision to acknowledge the unpleasant aspects of my life as I was propelled by historical events into action. I came to realize that for all these years since the end of World War II, I had tried to obliterate part of my past. I had to confess I had been less than honest in only being willing to remember what I could live with.

Writing such a book as an experience in honesty has meant the liberation of the mind. At last, all is clear, all is out. I am whole. I have accepted the knowledge that in fighting against cruelty and violence, I myself have been cruel, harsh, and violent. I have accepted having been a killer, a man responsible directly and indirectly for the deaths of others. I have come to learn to live with the past as well as the present—to live with the memory of a friend who died so that I might live, as well as with the vision of a train plunging into a river valley with six hundred human beings aboard. Mine is not an easy story, but these images must be remembered.

It is a story of friendships and freedom; about men who generally had not been trained for war, but who did not hesitate to enter into a very personal conflict; men who fought long and hard and died for their convictions.

I write about the friendships that allowed the underground movement to be born and survive. I write about the friendships that enabled men of different nations to join together and pool our resources and efforts to destroy a monster whose driving ideas were domination by force and universal slavery.

In 1961 I came to the United States with a scientific background acquired in French-speaking Belgium. My knowledge of the American language is still limited. I wish to recognize the tremendous help given by my editor Richard Schmidt, writer, poet, and history buff. Not only did he translate my "Franglish," he spotted many unclear areas, refined my ideas, and enriched my language. Without his help, this story would never have reached the status of a publishable book. Along the way I gained a true young friend.

I became a writer to tell of events that had not yet been written about, to convey a message. I wish these pages to be a message of hope.

Introduction

The Belgium of my youth was a wonderful place to study, to work, to be; a small yet diverse country of great plains and gently rolling land, mountains, lakes, rivers, canals, where seashore bordered sand dunes called vacationers and citizens alike to a climate that was never harsh, though often rainy.

Belgium, a land rich in resources: hard workers, fertile land, coal, industry, prosperity and a long tradition of master craftsmen and fine workmanship dating as far back as the Middle Ages.

That was Belgium before the war. The Great War. WW II.

My name is Herman Bodson. I grew up a product of that world view, a city boy taught to love the countryside and its villagers, its farmers and hill people. At that time they were easy to know and easy to like. As a child, it seemed that closeness to nature brought out courage and respect for others, for the morals of the heart. As a young man I discovered that mountain people differed from their bottom land neighbors in this main respect: they were gentler, more honest and readier to help, a consequence of the harder lives they lived.

In the towns of old Europe life moved faster than in the country, but still flowed on at an agreeable pace.

Walking to an open air market with my mother was delightful. So much to see, to taste. Stands, erected by categories of merchandise: vegetables, cheeses, meats, fish, stood artfully displayed. Most were locally produced and there was great diversity.

We lived with the fruits of the season. There were few imports, few exotics. Fruits and produce from distant lands were available only in premiere stores and at high cost.

People walked to do their buying, their purchase wrapped in twisted screw of newspaper carried under their arm to their homes to prepare good meals with fresh produce. If there was a great distance between home and market, one could take the streetcar, but most walked. Few cars existed and the air was agreeable to breathe.

More importantly, as people were not isolated in their cars, we met on sidewalks to inquire as to each others well being and to say hello. It was as if we lived in a conglomeration of contiguous villages, sharing the feeling of belonging. Life had a humane quality. The neighborhood bakeries provided fresh, tasty smelling warm bread for our breakfasts and eventually, beer and bread were delivered to the door in horse drawn delivery vans. Milk was delivered in small carts drawn by dogs.

Vendors loved their animals and treated them as work companions. In winter, when the icy streets were salted, the dogs sported leather booties.

Our streets were full of pushcarts and vendors selling fried potatoes, escargots and mussels cooked over charcoal. From May to November, flowers of the season were sold from large woven willow baskets at streetcar and bus stops. In winter, the roasted chestnut vendors appeared.

From inside our houses we heard the calls of the different trades' people: knife sharpeners, attic cleaners and those who bought old bones, bottles and clothing. In summer, some came selling waffles stuffed with flavored ice creams. Another attraction were the organ grinders. Some with small monkeys entertained children in expectation of coins being tossed from upper story windows. Such was life in the city of Brussels in the early 1930's and the quiet pleasures of a people living in a country too small to afford much arrogance.

To fully grasp our heritage, it is necessary to go back briefly through our history to Caesar's conquest of Gaul. Belgium was a part of that empire, which was later dismembered by the Merovingians and the Franks. Still later we became part of the Duchy of Burgundy, then Spain, then Austria, then France. With the defeat of Napoleon at Waterloo (only 20 miles from Brussels) the territory passed in turn to the Dutch and finally, in 1830 to independence. Belgium, a young state whose people have suffered and labored under many masters, was shaped by many influences and in the process inherited a treasury of many cultures. But most important, its inhabitants are the sons and daughters of a people resistant to domination and centuries of the experience of rebellion.

Spain, in the mid-1600's, in order to subdue the protestant Dutch, passed through Belgium avoiding the shorter, but much more difficult road over the Ardennes and Vosges mountains. The allied armies of the Grande Alliance fought in Belgium to defeat Napoleon. The Germans in WW I attacked neutral Belgium on their way to France. The geographical features of Europe promoted these incursions onto our territory for Belgium sits at a crossroads, a turning point, seemingly in everybody's way on their march to someplace else.

For these same reasons, we also became a great commercial center ideally located on the important trade routes linking the east to the west and the north to the south. This brought importance to places like Bruges, Ghent and Antwerp, which is the third largest harbor of Europe. The Spanish character of Brussels' old center and the influence of the French are marked in both Liege and Brussels and in the flexibility of the Belgian people, our acceptance of foreigners and our traditionally indomitable character.

AGENT FOR THE RESISTANCE

CHAPTER 1

▼

Darkening Skies,
the Prelude to Violence

In the waning days of August, 1932, in the Hertogdom of Luxembourg, Charles De Groot and I were setting up camp. It was about six o'clock in the evening, and Charles, a classmate of mine, was hammering tent pegs as I busied myself with cooking dinner, our only substantial meal of the day. Lunch had been a snack retrieved from our bicycle bags and eaten quickly along the way. All that summer the weather had been warm with only occasional rain, and we were now returning from our summer vacation to begin our sophomore studies in chemistry at Brussels University. Our bicycle tour in France and Switzerland was near its end.

As we busied ourselves with our tasks, a tall, dark-haired young man approached us asking if, perhaps, he could pitch his tent near ours. Yet another student hurrying back to home and school. He was an engineering student at the Louvain Catholic University; his name, Jan Van der Borght. Upon learning that Charles and I attended Brussels University, a nonsectarian, freethinking institution, he was quick to point out that he attended Louvain for reasons of convenience and not of faith. His family lived in Heverlee near Louvain, close enough for him to commute. His father, a high school teacher, could not afford to send Jan to Brussels and the school more suited to their philosophy. As we spent that evening together, we talked amicably of our trip experiences, our student life, and our young ideals. We liked what we discovered in each other so much that before retiring for the night we agreed to travel together until our paths diverged toward our own homes. Charles would depart first toward Tirlemont where he lived. Another short day would bring Jan and me to Louvain where he would turn off to Heverlee, and I would continue another thirty miles to Brussels. It was during those first few days on the road toward home that I began to appreciate Jan's presence, his clear thinking, and his political and philosophical ideas so close to my own. We had read and explored in similar directions, covering a lot of common mental ground.

At Tirlemont, as planned, Charles left us and we continued to Louvain where Jan invited me to spend the evening with his family. In Heverlee, he lived in a modest house, tastefully appointed. Art and books were displayed without ostentation, the books obviously read. That evening, in long conversation, Mr. Van der Borght, Jan, and I compared our ideas of the world.

In the Europe of 1932, events in Germany were a focal point of many a discussion. Most of us had read *Mein Kampf,* the first volume in the mid-1920s and the second in late 1927. The prose of Herr Hitler was not great literature, but what he was attempting to impart to the German people was not meant to entertain. It touted a new, yet altogether old sensibility, a déjà vu: German racism dressed in new clothes and new social overtones; hatred of the Jews, hatred of the masons, hatred of the church, the Hapsburgs, and even the Prussians. It was not prose meant to unify or calm a dissatisfied Germany, a Germany facing bankruptcy. Hitler's repeated calls for expanding the German military might, for *Lebensraum,* with no suggestion as to what lands were to be conquered or what was to be done with those already occupying those lands, was simply frightening madness. The man who wrote the first half of his book in jail as a political prisoner in 1922 had, by 1926, risen to political power. His only serious opponents seemed to be the German communists, his strongest collaborators and supporters, the social democrats. In the beginning it was clear to us that he did not have much success in the German north, and it was equally clear that he was making great progress in the south. In the recent elections of 1932, Hitler, for the first time, had run for the position of head of state, and although he had not won against the old World War I hero Marshal Paul von Hindenburg, who rallied his votes from the Catholics and the trade unionists, he did garner 30 percent of the votes, enough to deny Hindenburg a majority.

What none of us understood at the time was the appeal of Hitler's views regarding an Aryan race and its superiority. Ideas of superior races had long been discredited by serious anthropologists, and yet here he was advocating those same ideas. He was believed by many in Germany, especially among the working classes, jobless and not. Even more extraordinary than the ideas expressed in *Mein Kampf* were those in the pamphlets of the National Socialist Workers' Party, as the Hitler movement was then called. Outside Germany few had actually seen the party's meetings. They were superbly organized and took place within a grand *mise-en-scène* of organized hysteria and emotional exaltation inflaming the lowest gut reactions. The man was a genius of gesture, cliché, and the sensibilities of his audience. In the German press we read some of his perorations—empty of substance and appealing to the basest instincts. This spiritual and political vitriol seemed to work magic on those Germans who simply could not get out of the hole into which their defeat in World War I had plunged them.

Hitler, as he promised to do in *Mein Kampf,* gave the adolescent youths of his followers uniforms and assembled them into groups to parade at his meetings. The older youths he also provided with cudgels to act as his police at the meetings, and we came to pity those who dared to speak out.

Thus our conversation moved in and around the events of the time, throughout that long evening in August, 1932, in Heverlee.

When I arrived home, classes were to begin in only a few days. What a year it turned out to be, in retrospect! My second university year in sciences included all the basic general subjects: geology, mineralogy, crystallography, botany, biology, and physics, to name but the majors. I studied with confidence. My trip to France had been marvelous, and more. For the first time in my life, I had discovered in Jan Van der Borght one I believed to be a true friend. Someone I would come to trust and to whom I would feel free to confide my most intimate secrets and thoughts, someone who would understand and pardon my mistakes. And our friendship did indeed grow into unconditional, reciprocal, and unlimited confidence and devotion. As Aristotle believed friendship one of the virtues and the Greeks and Romans built altars to friendship, so Jan and I were friends. That which we discovered in each other, we nurtured, protected, and honored.

Rich in this new relationship, we began our second university year, Jan in Louvain and I in Brussels. There was no time to see each other. Isolated as we were by distance and work, we could communicate only occasionally by telephone.

September eventually yielded to July with neither of us seeming even to notice the changing seasons, so busy were we with our studies. In the same way, 1933 became 1934. A camping trip that Jan and I had planned for that summer was canceled when my dad formed the idea that it was time for me to perfect my knowledge of the German language, "the enemy's tongue," as he called it. My summer would be spent in a German-speaking territory, arranged by a former employee of my father, a Herr Madert, who had resettled in Saarbrücken, the land of his origin. The Saar, a disputed area near Lorraine and Luxembourg, had been given to France after World War I as part of the German war reparations. Even before my exams were over, it was arranged. I would spend two months in a little town near Saarbrücken as the guest of a German high-school teacher who would tutor me. Thus evaporated any plans to camp leisurely in the Ardennes that summer.

In July I completed my exams. I had felt prepared, but the results were above my wildest expectations. I was close to the top of my class and had been awarded my bachelor of science. Within the week I readied myself for a summer of intensive German studies and, as I was soon to discover, industrial pollution.

When I arrived in Saarbrücken, I found myself in a European Pittsburgh, an industrial valley of steel plants and machinery construction, the town being a commercial center serving an industrial area. Before joining my tutor, who happily lived out in a small rural town where the air was more breathable and life less frantic, I spent two or three days with Mr. Madert becoming oriented.

The tutor's family was large, including seven children my age and younger. They lived in a spacious house on a hill away from the main street. Mornings were spent being tutored and studying. In the afternoons, the older children, some of their friends, and I bicycled in the countryside, providing yet another opportunity for me to perfect my language skills.

My lessons took place in the tutor's study. After an hour's lecture, Herr Professor sat in his armchair, smoked his pipe, and read until the noon meal, while I worked to complete a generous assignment which usually took me the rest of the morning and sometimes part of the evening to complete. Our ritual never varied. The lesson over, Herr Professor would take his incredible pipe—its large furnace of decorated porcelain sitting on the floor and connected to the mouthpiece by a long, flexible stem that passed between his legs—fill it tenderly, and ask me to light the contraption. Then the room would fill with aromatic smoke as I sweated over verb conjugations and the intricacies of the German language.

Each weekend, Mr. Madert had arranged for me to spend one day with his family. One Sunday we all went to Trier, an old Roman settlement built along the old Roman road connecting Paris and Cologne. In Trier there were superb and well-preserved ruins of a theater and vast public baths that, excepting the roof, were nearly intact, including subfloor heating ducts under terracotta tiles.

One week near the end of my stay with the professor, Mr. Madert came and gathered me up for a business trip that would take us through Lorraine and along the Mosel River. We were traveling in his Citroën B-14, one of the early front-wheel drive vehicles. We were driving along the river road passing between terraced vineyards when, suddenly, a rear spring broke and we had to stop. Because having the car towed and repaired would take several hours, Mr. Madert took the opportunity to show me around the many wineries and their aging caves hewn out of the limestone walls of the valley. According to custom, we sampled the fare from huge barrels aligned along the carved tunnels. What an afternoon! I became a very happy young man blessed by the broken spring.

We saw little Hitler-inspired activity in Saargebiet, because that was then French territory and his followers could not openly be active there. However, in Trier, as well as in the Mosel valley, we saw many Brownshirts parading wearing the swastika armbands. With summer of 1934 at its end, I returned to my home in Brussels by rail, taking the train from Saarbrücken to Nancy and from there the Geneva-Brussels express. I was sporting a German haircut very similar to that which became the fashion in the United States in the mid-1960s and known as a flattop. By then I was able to hold a decent conversation in German and write Gothic script, and Dad said I even looked like a *Boche*.

A few days remained before classes resumed, and I took the opportunity to visit Jan in Heverlee. We talked of books, French anarchists, and the role of violence and change, noting the past as we searched the future for our own future. We were young, still so very young.

When we returned to school that fall, we would both be entering into the depths of our chosen subjects and were excited. Vacation was over and we were back to work, but work with a difference. We would study in the lab from 8:00 A.M. to 6:00 P.M., five days a week, interrupted only occasionally by classroom work. I relaxed a little and could, thanks to the course load being reduced, afford some evenings for outside activities. Walking home from school, I sometimes took a little detour and spent some time on a park bench in the marvelous Forêt de Soignes near the university, relaxing among the large beeches. In the fall, particularly, it was fun to watch the squirrels gamboling about, running after each other, preparing for winter by gathering the delicious triangular little beech fruits. Sometimes I would join the harvest, filling my pockets.

It became my custom to reserve Wednesday nights for discussions at a club called The Black and the White. It was a debating society that had adopted an excellent format. An orator would speak on a subject as controversial as possible. The podium would then be made available for rebuttal, questions, or answers pro and con, providing lively evenings. Needless to say, fascism, Germany, and international politics often figured on the agenda.

I also became active in a university group called Le Libre Examen, which concerned itself primarily with philosophical debates on the ethics of the university, freedom of expression, and antidogmatism. Basically this was an anti-Catholic attitude which sometimes went too far for my liking. I believed then as I do now that there is a place for religion, that people should be allowed to choose their beliefs and, as we say in Belgium, be allowed "to chew altar candles" if they so desire. In retrospect, I believe that joining those two groups were two of the best decisions I ever made. The discussions contributed much to my development by exposing me to many contradictory opinions, by helping me sort my feelings and encouraging me toward independent thought, and by requiring me to assert myself in taking to the podium to defend my views.

In January, 1933, a political bomb had been dropped when Hitler became the new chancellor of Germany. No one knew at the time how or why President Hindenburg, then nearly senile, had made his choice, especially after he had reportedly declared following a 1932 meeting with Hitler, "That man a chancellor? I'll make him a postmaster and he can lick stamps with my head on them." But apparently, Franz von Papen, a minister in the German government, had been hard at work for months influencing Hindenburg until he finally gave in. In February, just days after Hitler's nomination, the Communist Party was declared illegal and forbidden to hold meetings or demonstrations. By the end of the month, the Reichstag burned to the ground, temporarily leaving no place for the assembly to meet, and the communists were blamed. It was not so much the disappearance of the Communist Party that troubled Jan and me as the fact that Hitler could so easily suppress a well-established party and deny the right of free expression. We resented this brazen abuse of power. Future months only reinforced our dislike of these new German political changes, the disappearance of German democracy, and the birth of Nazism.

Hermann Goering, the Prussian minister of the interior, soon organized the arrest of over four thousand leaders of the Communist Party. Then Joseph Goebbels organized new elections. The Nazis garnered 288 seats, as opposed to 251 for all opposition parties combined, and the die was cast. The Nazis had a majority and soon the minorities learned that they had rights no more. Hitler opened the new assembly hall in Potsdam and, on March 24, 1934, by a vote of 441 to 94, the assembly granted Hitler emergency powers for the next four years. Nearly all of the socialists voted with him, with only the few communists still at large voting against him. Germany, believing itself in need of a savior, proclaimed the Messiah had arrived. This Messiah was to be called the *Fuehrer*, meaning the leader, but in *Mein Kampf* Hitler had defined the Fuehrer as "the man who gives experience to the divinity, that is enshrined by his people."

Gottfried Feder, the editor of the party's newspaper, said of the Fuehrer, "He must have a somnambulistic feeling of certainty . . . in the pursuit of his goals he must not shirk from bloodshed or even war." The German cult of nationalism had become the state religion.

During the same year in England under the Labor Party's leadership, Britons acceded to German arguments and agreed to disarm. How was it possible to maintain a nation with twice the population of France with such meager forces as one hundred thousand? asked the Germans. Should Germany not at least have parity of armament?

In March, from England, Prime Minister James Ramsey MacDonald came forth with his plan for the disarmament of France. He proposed equal armies for France and Germany of two hundred thousand each (at this time the French army numbered half a million), the difference being that Germany was to have a brand new army with modern equipment, while France would keep its obsolete matériel from World War I. Germany was not allowed an air force, although France and England could maintain five hundred planes each.

At home around the dinner table, the conversations fell back on the international situation in an ever-widening circle. Dad would pass me published remarks in the English parliament by Winston Churchill, the former first lord of the admiralty during World War I and a senior member of parliament, asking me to read the speech and tell him what I thought.

I read. Why are we giving in when the government of Germany has been replaced by a grim dictatorship? I reflected a short while and answered that the man was right, and certainly was not afraid to tell his country what he thought. He had an interesting attitude, so different from that of most of the English and French leftist government spokesmen, who seemed to give in and allow Hitler to do as he pleased.

Dad looked intently at me and said, "When you face violence—political violence such as in Germany—you simply cannot respond with niceties; you cannot deal honestly with dishonesty."

Clearly the official British attitude made it easy later for Hitler to repudiate the disarmament clauses. Soon Germany left the League of Nations, making a farce of all its previous agreements. Hitler's word was broken, then and there. His message to the world was clear. Leave Germany alone. No more dictates. We will do as we please. Throughout 1933, we read the papers with an ever more discerning eye.

During these years, distantly entrenched in isolationism, the United States paid little attention to far-away Europe. American sons were forever asleep under the poppies of Flanders and the fields of Verdun and Argonne, but other concerns more directly occupied American minds.

In 1931, the Japanese had occupied Mukden and taken the Manchurian railway. In 1932 they landed north of Shanghai. By 1933 they had taken the entire province of Jehol and occupied the north of China to the Great Wall. We need coal, they said. In 1933, Japan also left the League of Nations. Each for itself, while the rest of the world wallowed in the total disintegration of all the efforts and goodwill that had followed the previous world war.

Before my third year of study was out, another blow fell and I remembered *Mein Kampf* again: "German Austria must return to the Fatherland." It was clear that in Austria a schism was growing between the left and the right, the left supporting the status quo and the right favoring Nazism. For the left it was a peace obsession, peace at all costs. Equally clear from the press was that the Austrian *Heimwehr*, the army, favored Hitler.

Theoretically, Austria was within Mussolini's sphere of influence, yet before the first crocuses were in bloom, it was announced that Hitler and Mussolini had signed a secret protocol. Why secret, we wondered? Soon after, Mussolini paid his first visit to the Fuehrer who would soon become his master, his cunning master.

Returning to Italy, Mussolini told Foreign Minister Galeazzo Ciano, as the press reported it, "You will see. Nothing will happen." Dad and I were in agreement that this assessment would prove mistaken. Mussolini had fallen victim to Hitler's bluff and duplicity and like others was being swept along and, eventually, away.

At the same time, Hitler was dealing with internal problems within the *Schutzstaffel*, the infamous new force known to the world as the SS, which was under the direction of Ernst Roehm. The army—that is, the old German army—was afraid of Hitler and considered the SS, already three million strong, a dangerous competitor for power.

The European press followed events in the German political arena closely and, for the most part, the facts were known to all. However, those facts were open to wide interpretation. Two main sets of differing opinions appeared and, depending on the reader's background, ideology or ideals, seemed to gather people at the polar extremes. Leftists became more liberal, more pacifistic, even more communistic, while rightists moved toward fascism and the center disappeared altogether.

Roehm, out of the mass of the SS, had created units called the SA, for *Sturm Abteilung* or shock troops. They were elite troops, a virtual Hitler guard, and more. This group would blindly execute all of Hitler's orders, including murder, no questions asked. It was perceived by the Reich that the SS was a little too leftist inclined and deviating from the rightist party line. Having earlier dropped the "Workers" from the National Socialist Workers' Party, it now seemed that the word "socialist" was there only to fool the democrats. An announcement was made that a certain Heinrich Himmler would take control of the SS immediately, while Hitler went to Munich and arrested Roehm. Simultaneously, all other SS leaders were arrested under Hitler's orders in the south and Goering's in the north. The purge was over in less than two days. It is estimated that five thousand to seven thousand were arrested and executed. The purge brought the party troops into total obedience. This news came to Belgium by way of the communist press, while the rightist press kept mostly silent.

Jan and I often read and discussed the articles in the *Red Flag*, the Belgian communists' paper. Disregarding the habitual sloganeering and the Marxist dialectic, we found it an excellent source of information on events in Germany. It indicated that there were still some active leftists in Germany, although most certainly in hiding and in contact with our ultraleftists. Daily, the German government appeared more and more like a dictatorship ruling by terror and murder and reeking of blood. We read that the government had opened camps to intern the opposition and that common criminals were being removed from the jails to make room for political prisoners awaiting judgment.

In July, 1934, Austria was back in the news. In an aborted coup in Vienna, the Austrian Nazis revolted against the socialists. Chancellor Engelbert Dolfuss, who acted with vigor to put down the revolt, was shot and left in his office to bleed to death as the coup was stopped. Mussolini, alerted, sent a division to the Brenner pass on the Austrian border. Hitler recoiled and ordered his supporters to calm down.

That summer I had planned to go back to Germany to perfect my knowledge of the language, but because of the unrest in Austria I had just about decided to stay home. However, Italy's near intervention and its calming effect reassured me of my safety and I went, spending eight weeks in the Eiffel, a volcanic area near the Belgian border. I stayed near Stadtkyll and Prüm in the village of Frauenkrone ("Virgin Crown"), so named because it had been built and rebuilt on the ruins of an old abbey dedicated to the Virgin Mary. I traded my labor for the hospitality of a local farmer. As so often happens in Europe, much of the village was built of materials from the tumbled-down abbey walls, providing an oasis of real charm in the austere, volcanic landscape. Many of the houses had large vaulted basements connected by stone passageways and corridors, very convenient for visiting on rainy days. In the house where I lived, sauerkraut was prepared and pressed under boards and lava rocks in a superb renaissance baptismal font salvaged from the ruins.

These honest people with whom I stayed were Christian Social Democrats and they were interested in what we in Belgium thought of Germany. Throughout 1934, Hitler continued pushing his way up. Although many did not like what they witnessed, they were clearly exasperated by the economic rut they had been in for so long. Still, I soon discovered that no one in this small village had any sympathy for the rising Nazi party; but they were farmers and traditionally were suspicious of change.

Occasionally we would go to the next town, Stadtkyll, where one saw many young men and some adults in the Brownshirts' uniform. All were then unarmed. All were members of the local Nazi party.

The local authorities were still neutral at this time, but the Nazis, trying their wings of oppression, were intentionally creating conflicts within the neutral elements of the population. No one was yet parading, as happened later. However, even in 1934, one could see changes coming over their *Vaterland*.

One weekend, in Stadtkyll, we had imbibed a little Mosel wine and were happily touring the city loudly singing a socialist anthem until Brownshirts in all sizes and shapes came out of the woodwork, forcing us to stage a hasty and prudent retreat. Within a few days, they came calling on me at Frauenkrone. They knew that I was Belgian and, at first politely, made it clear to me that as a foreigner I had better stay out of their affairs and mind my own business or . . . the "or" was never elaborated upon, but was clearly understood. Officially they had no power, but intimidation often worked. As I listened to their threats, my farmer host and his three stout sons approached and the discussion grew hotter. Then one of the Boches tried a show of force. In short order the discussion degenerated into a brawl and then a fight. It was one of the shortest fights I've ever witnessed. The city clowns in their brown shirts were no match for the farmer and his sons. As that became apparent to them, cowardice surged and they fled in all directions, but not fast enough for one who was grabbed by the shirt and seat of his pants and thrown fifteen feet through the air onto the manure pile, which, he was told, was his deserving place. They did not come back; but then perhaps I still don't know the rest of that story. For me, it was time to go home, return to school, and finish my master's.

On the way I stopped to visit Jan. Summer had been glorious, warm and quite dry and his Heverlee garden proved an inviting place to converse over drinks. Mr. Van der Borght, although younger and slightly more conservative than my father, was equally concerned about what we perceived as the on-coming menace.

In December of that year our radio stations and newspapers were filled with the Italian news as Italy launched an attack on Abyssinia from its colony of Somaliland. By January, 1935, the news highlighted the Saar plebiscite: 93 percent of the voters voted to rejoin the *Vaterland,* and thus Germany reclaimed an area rich in coal, iron, and steel without a fight. Yet another feather in Hitler's cap. And yet another blow to the former victors' alliance that now gave in to Hitler's demands in what appeared to be becoming a habit, a pattern, a fatal affliction of miscalculation.

Against this backdrop, we began to hear reports that Germany was slowly and patiently rebuilding its air force. Prototypes were being built in new factories and pilots were being trained in Russia. "Air glider" associations sprouted like milkweeds. In the many provinces of the Reich, public sub-scriptions were opened to purchase "civilian" airplanes for all of these associations. Meanwhile in England, Churchill's impassioned pleas and the Tories' wise counsel to reinforce the Royal Air Force and strengthen air defenses went unheeded, thanks to the defeatist attitude of both the Liberal and La-bour parties. How could they ignore the Roman adage: *Si vis pacem, para bellum* (If you wish peace, prepare for war)?

Or Churchill's equally to-the-point quote of an unknown author's poem about a train disaster:

> Who is in charge of the clattering train?
> The axles creak and the couplings strain;
> And the pace is hot, and the points are near,
> And sleep has deadened the driver's ear;
> And the signals flash through the night in vain,
> For death is in charge of the clattering train.

By March of 1935, Germany, in complete abnegation of the Treaty of Ver-sailles and all subsequent agreements, officially announced the creation of the new German air force and the introduction of compulsory military ser-vice. France responded by increasing its term of mandatory military service to two years. French communists, furious with their leader, Maurice Thorez, declared that they would not tolerate the working class being drawn into a so-called war in defense of democracy against fascism.

The government responded through Leon Blum. The workers of France would resist Hitler's aggression.

In Belgium, our neutrality forced us to silence and our officials observed a strict attitude of no comment. The United States, which had long since washed its hands of European concerns, still looked west, toward Japan and China.

These latest German violations of the Treaty of Versailles, which had put an end to World War I, brought England and France to the point of challenge to the Germans. To "settle" their differences, the Stressa conference was called in Italy under the auspices of the League of Nations. It was estimated that Germany had at this time already achieved air parity with England, but despite this fact, England still opposed sanctions. Churchill railed that the conference had become a "region of words."

"Words? Are words going to stop a fool? A violent lunatic? A murderer?" he asked.

After this conference, Hitler seemed encouraged to pursue his rearmament and to disregard even more of his previous agreements. Next he moved the rebuilding of the German navy up the agenda—this time with the help of Britain! Britain and Germany signed a new agreement allowing the Reich to build a navy exceeding the limits set at Versailles, then set at four battleships not to exceed ten thousand tons each and six cruisers not to exceed the same tonnage. The fact that Germany had already broken the old treaty by building the *Scharnhorst* and the *Gneisenau,* each twenty-six thousand tons, went unremarked. This new agreement between England and Germany (no one else was consulted) specified that the German navy would not exceed half of the naval strength of Britain. With this agreement, Germany achieved three goals: it divided the most committed allies, France and Britain; gained a decent navy; and gained yet more prestige for Hitler.

The Germans immediately put two new ships under construction. Evidently the plans had already been drawn for the *Bismarck* and the *Tirpitz,* each fifty-six thousand tons. These were to be ultramodern and superior in armament and speed to anything the Allies had. The largest British ship did not exceed thirty-six thousand tons. This development created a furor in the Baltic states where it was rightly perceived as a threat to their security. But more, the agreement allowing Germany to increase its troop strength to half that of the French army was calculated in numbers of men only and Germany had a different concept, the armored division. Starting with three units, each furnished with the most modern equipment, they built tanks that French weapons could not stop. The only one who immediately saw the importance of these new panzer divisions was a colonel in the French cavalry named De Gaulle, who later was promoted to general and served at their headquarters, but for the moment his advice was ignored.

As before, I stayed in contact with Jan. I had agreed to help him during the summer of 1935 to collect geological data for his final dissertation. For this purpose, he had chosen the most geologically complex region of the Ardennes, near Salmchâteau, where a distant relative on my father's side, Gustave Jacques, owned and operated quarries. We devoted our days to collecting and assembling data and specimens, but our evenings we spent comparing world views. By the end of our stay there, we had come to the common conclusion that neither communism nor fascism offered much appeal.

During the six weeks that Jan and I spent in the Ardennes, we camped on the land of Gustave Jacques, brother of General Alphonse Jacques of World War I fame and himself a veteran of World War I intelligence. He offered not only his hospitality but his help in Jan's project. He was a miner and well acquainted with the geology of the area. When we were preparing our evening meal, it was not unusual for Gustave to appear with a gift of a bottle of wine from his well-stocked cellar.

During this Ardennes summer with Jan our friendship matured and came to fullness. Although each would normally be considered a loner, we took comfort in each other's company around our evening fire, amidst intense discussions and the as yet unspoiled enthusiasms of our young lives. Unbeknownst to us, we were losing the innocence of the better times, the calm twenties, the years which followed the "end of all wars." However vaguely in the future we saw the conflict coming, we knew we would have to choose a side and make a stand. We wondered what we would do and how best to prepare ourselves for the bleak time approaching.

One evening, as we cooked our meal, Gustave came to greet us with his usual calm and gentleness. He inquired of our meal and returned home, soon to reappear in our camp, hands concealed behind his back. One hand came forth offering a dusty bottle of Burgundy that he thought would agreeably complement our meal. He insisted that we uncork the venerable flask to make sure of the integrity of its contents. He tasted. We tasted. And then he declared that it might be starting to turn and that maybe this bottle, now revealed in his other hand, might be the better. We repeated the sampling. This time he declared the second bottle to be fine. He wished us *bon appetit,* leaving both bottles with us. The Burgundy put us in a euphoric mood that allowed us to make the jump, to liberate ourselves of reserve, and to speak freely and openly of our deepest feelings as friends, allies, confidants.

In September, Jan graduated and took employment as a coal mine engineer near Mons as I returned to school. I had by then gained some visibility among the student body. Probably because of my involvement in the Libre Examen group, I was asked to serve as the secretary-treasurer of our student union and I accepted. The academic year of 1935–36 was the centennial year of the university and great festivities were planned. Each year in November, we honored the founder of our institution, Theodore Verhaegen. He had been a liberal, anti-Catholic Freemason and had founded the Brussels Free University to counter the influence of the Louvain Catholic University. Hence "Saint Verhaegen Day" had evolved into a day devoted to poking fun at Catholics.

A parade of floats representing various departments wound its way through the downtown streets. I conceived the theme of the chemistry float using what I had come to believe about Germany and Belgian politics. On the float, a large retort distilled swastikas and other fascist symbols, while the distillate emerged as little Rexist puppets. Rex was a new Belgian political party which incorporated Nazi ideas in its stated beliefs while denying Nazi affiliation. Its leader and our Belgian quisling was Leon Degrelle, born in Bouillon, the city of Godefroy, the first crusader. Each time I engaged a Rexist in conversation I found only one train of thought: unhappiness, dissatisfaction, racial prejudice, and above all, an overriding sense of bitterness and willingness to use force to get rid of any politician considered dishonest or worse yet, stupid. No matter how much Rexists denied any sympathy for Nazism and rebelled at the suggestion that their beliefs aped national socialism, I knew that in time they would reveal their true nature. And in time, they did.

Being fluent now in German and keen to maintain my fluency, I bought and read the German newspapers. One thing became clear. While in the past various papers contained differing opinions, now they all sang the same song. The old, humorous though conservative *Spiegel,* the democratic *Der Muenchener Zeitung,* and the Christian Democrat *Kölnischer Zeitung* of the early 1930s had all died and been resurrected under common leadership. This leadership, as we learned later, was Goebbels and the now infamous *Propaganda Abteilung,* the organization responsible for creating public opinion, telling the government's lies, stuffing the German mind, and creating fear in opponents outside Germany.

Before 1935 was over, elections in Britain brought the Conservatives to power by a landslide. Campaigning on a "No War! No armaments!" platform, they won by a majority of 247 seats. Stanley Baldwin, the isolationist, became the prime minister for the third time in his long career. Soon his foreign secretary, Samuel Hoare, proposed the Hoare-Laval pact. In short, it amounted to this: Italy, hard pressed by sanctions as it fought in Abyssinia and leaning toward a German alliance, could be brought into the Allied camp by conceding to it part of Abyssinia. The idea was proposed to the League of Nations and was supported by England and France. Italy was to receive a fifth of Abyssinia and withdraw from the rest. But the plan backfired when the League voted down the proposal and Hoare, having embarrassed his government, was forced to resign and was replaced by Anthony Eden on December 22.

On January 20, 1936, King George V died, and as England mourned its great monarch, Italy regained control in Abyssinia, soon occupying all of what is now Ethiopia and moving decisively into the German camp.

Der Muenschener Zeitung on May 16 published an interesting article about the British way of life and the kingdom's unwillingness to go to war. The article commented on the weakness of British men, material, and morale, and concluded with, "Today all of Abyssinia is irrevocably, fully, and finally Italian alone. This being so, neither the League of Nations nor London can have any doubts that only the use of extraordinary force can drive the Italians out of Abyssinia. But neither the power nor the courage to use force is at hand." Here, at last, we felt the Germans made a serious error. At that time one did not tweak the tail of the British lion with impunity. As spring of 1936 approached, the tone of the British press indicated an important change of opinion taking place. For the first time, Britain appeared to be contemplating war against the German and Italian tyrannies. Use of force was spoken of more openly, even among some of the clearly convinced pacifists. Unhappily, the aging Baldwin was comfortable believing in the huge isolationist majority that had placed him at the helm five years previously.

On March 7, Hitler announced to the Reichstag that he intended to reoccupy the Rhineland and deny one more clause of the Treaty of Versailles. As he spoke, thirty-five thousand German soldiers entered all of the main towns on the left bank in the demilitarized zone.

The French, ready to act, waited for the British to join them in pushing the Germans back. They waited in vain. Baldwin, unwilling to commit his country to war, did nothing. And the French, left standing alone, retreated.

If France had acted decisively then, I believe it would have been the Germans who would have retreated. But once again, Hitler's bluff proved successful. Another feather in his cap.

French Premier Pierre Flandin said in the British press, "If you can, with the support of all the little nations that look for your guidance, act now, you can lead Europe. You will have a policy. All the world will follow you and thus prevent war. It is your last chance. If you do not stop the Germans, it is all over . . ."

A British lord replied that the Germans were after all only going into their own backyard. Later, Churchill said he believed this view to be representative of much of British opinion. This belief was also shared by the *Muenchener Zeitung.*

Thus, Germany reoccupied the left bank and immediately began to fortify the area. Soon there would be no way for the French to reenter the zone to push the invaders back across the Rhine. The French and we in Belgium viewed these events as another step toward yet another possible invasion.

In mid-July, Germany announced that it had signed a pact with Austria, agreeing not to influence any more the affairs of Austria and not to give support to the Austrian National Party. Five days later, the Austrian National Socialists intensified their Nazi agitation. We wondered if Germany was preparing to attack across their common border.

In October, I started a doctorate at my alma mater in the study of surface tensions for the European Bureau of Standards. My laboratory, of necessity, was in a darkened basement. Darkness was needed to avoid deterioration of the light-sensitive chemical compounds employed in my research. It was ironic to both Jan and me that at one of the darkest moments in European history, when the world needed all the light it could get, he and I spent our days in darkness; he in the coal mine and I in my lab. This was not without influence on our morale.

November brought the revelation by German minister Konstantin von Neurath of the newly signed Anti-Commintern Pact between Italy and Germany, declaring Russia their common enemy.

Each year I filled out my student deferment papers and each year, almost as a matter of course, they were approved. In return, upon completion of my studies, I would automatically be enrolled in an officers' training school. However, early in 1937, I learned that my deferment had been rejected and that I would be conscripted in August. With renewed efforts, I worked as hard and as fast as I could, hoping to encounter no problems with my research and to complete my thesis before the conscription date.

Jan was now engaged and would soon be married. I rejoiced for him although I had also learned of a sad reality. During his army physical, it was discovered that he was diabetic and would need to take daily insulin injections to keep his illness at bay. The army rejected him.

It was also in this period that the world became aware of the deep deterioration of the civil order in Spain. Communists and anarchists were fighting the rightists. For months they had been resorting to murder and assassination to further their cause. A rightist military coup was in the making. The climax of this political unrest occurred with the murder of Sotelo, the leader of the conservatives. In response, the army, acting under the leadership of a certain General Francisco Franco, rallied the church and the conservatives to action and Spain's civil war began. Soon, leftists from many countries entered Spain to fight under the banner of the International Brigades, while fascists and Nazis entered to fight on the side of Franco. It would prove to be a long, bitter, and especially cruel war. Theoretically a Spanish war, it was in fact a thinly disguised international conflict confined to Spanish soil.

In Britain, as had happened earlier at the death of George V, government was at a standstill as Edward VII abdicated and the nation awaited the coronation of George VI on May 28, 1937.

Every sign out of Germany indicated that its armed forces were growing and that its war machine was being outfitted and completed. Pictures in the German press of military parades frankly displayed new matériel: more tanks, more planes, more guns.

As my thesis was being printed in August, I reported for my induction physical. My country was calling, the enemy was known, his views were known, and I looked forward to serving. The only possibility of not being enslaved was to fight. I was ready, as was every loyal Belgian. We had had the experience of German occupation during World War I and by now knew the Nazis would be worse.

During the physical, the army doctors discovered something that I had known all along, that the vision in my left eye was severely impaired. This defect proved reason to preclude me from entering an artillery officers' training school with the rest of my classmates and I was assigned to the Medical Corps, where I would have no hope of achieving officer rank. Only medical doctors and pharmacists could become officers.

I entered boot camp in August, 1937, and, in September, was granted a short leave to return to Brussels to defend my doctoral thesis. It was with pleasure that I visited my parents to inform them that I could now properly be addressed as Dr. Bodson. I was twenty-four years old.

In late October, boot camp complete, I was sent to serve in the main military hospital in Brussels. Being a chemist, I was assigned to count pills in the pharmacy, but not for long. A pharmacy captain from the laboratory discovered my background and had me reassigned to his department. There I worked with doctors and pharmacists and was treated like a professional without regard to my rank of private.

During the year that I served there, events in Europe moved us ever closer to conflict. In Spain the war escalated dreadfully and thousands were dying. In Austria, the Germans were successfully putting intense pressure on Austrian Chancellor Kurt von Schuschnigg to force him to accept Arthur von Seys-Inquart, chief of the Austrian Nazi party, into his cabinet. As the new minister of the interior, Seys-Inquart would have control of the state police and the worm was in the apple.

In England at the end of the month of February, 1938, Anthony Eden resigned as foreign minister and was replaced by Lord Halifax. In Germany, Hitler became commander in chief and called Schuschnigg to Berchtesgaden. There he pressured the Austrian chancellor to join the Reich, but the chancellor resisted, offering instead to hold a plebiscite on the issue, knowing that the Austrian majority would reject it. By March, Hitler had decided to invade. As commander in chief, he knew his orders would be obeyed. On March 11 the invasion began. On March 13 Hitler entered Vienna. Austria was annexed and made a part of the Third Reich. Mussolini, himself now a German vassal, kept his mouth shut. In Czechoslovakia the situation also became critical. Hitler had for months been active there. In February he had addressed the Reichstag saying over ten million Germans lived in two states adjoining their frontiers—it was Germany's duty to "protect and rescue them . . . To give them general freedom, personal, political and ideological." The intent was immediately clear. Under the pretext of protecting German minorities abroad and within the context of the *Mein Kampf* declarations of the need for *Lebensraum,* the expansion of Germany would proceed. It became evident to me that economics were also at issue here. Czechoslovakian mineral resources were many and abundant, among them coal, bauxite, iron, and uranium, in addition to the big Skoda works, one of Europe's greatest arsenals.

The conquest of Austria placed the German armies at the Roumanian border. Had the Third Reich an eye on the Roumanian oil fields? In case of war, landlocked Germany would have a great need for oil. It appeared that Hitler was assembling what was later to be called the Axis Alliance, an alliance capable of launching and sustaining all-out war.

In July of 1938, my military tour completed, I returned home. Near the end of my military service I had been actively and successfully searching for a job. In early August I joined the staff of Etablissements Van Der Heyden, a company involved in the sale of chemicals and laboratory equipment. I was in charge of instrumentation and laboratory design and installation. As part of my training with this company, I revisited Germany, going to Merck in Darmstadt and Hellige in Freibourg.

After a few days in enemy territory I was able to witness the depth of changes, the enthusiasm of the Germans for the Fuehrer. Everybody who spoke, spoke of him and of his achievements. The others kept silent. But there was no doubt. He carried the German majority.

Four months later, I was recalled to duty. Belgium, alarmed and still neutral, recalled most of its forces under what was called a "reinforced peace status," a euphemism for mobilization employed so as not to offend the Germans. Thus I was soon back in the hospital laboratory, this time as a sergeant with the heavy responsibility of organizing the Belgian army's blood bank. We also were charged with preparing massive quantities of antityphoid vaccine to reinoculate all returning personnel.

As we prepared for war, so did Czechoslovakia. It partially mobilized and entrenched its forces behind a strong line of fortifications. On January 30, 1939, speaking at the Reichstag, Hitler referred to Czech mobilization as "intolerable provocation" and by May, his preparations were made for the attack, although "not without German general staff resistance," commented the foreign press. (The German generals argued that the force required to break through the Czech front would dangerously weaken their French front.) Intense European diplomatic initiatives attempted to persuade Hitler to look only toward the German-speaking Sudeten minorities and to leave the rest of Czechoslovakia in peace. The problem militarily was that the Czech fortifications protecting the country were in the German-speaking territory and these the Czechs in no way wished to cede away.

September, 1938, had seen Foreign Minister Neville Chamberlain in Germany visiting Hitler to discuss the matter. At first, the Czechs could not believe this to be true. They had not even been consulted. Soon after his return to London, the French paid Chamberlain a visit which resulted in the French and English accusing each other of selling the Sudetenland to Hitler without consulting Prague. The Czechoslovakian government had, however, already secretly agreed to a German plan that would have ceded the disputed area to Germany on the condition that it have an independent administration and relative autonomy, but this was not the German wish. Germany wanted to use the Sudetenland as a springboard toward conquest of all of Czechoslovakia and, as we had good reason to suspect, more. While Chamberlain was in Germany, Sudetenland radio, which was controlled by German Nazis, demanded the area's return to the *Vaterland*. In fairness, it must be noted that according to previously signed treaties, Britain was under no obligation to defend the Czechs' territorial integrity, although the French were. Unable to reach a Franco-British agreement and feeling that Hitler should, but might not, show some sign of restraint, the British unilaterally mobilized their navy on September 28.

It seemed impossible to believe that the only thing on which the French and English did agree during this period was that there should be no consultation with the Czechs! Hitler, at least temporarily, had managed again to create deep dissension between these allies.

He then sent two clear messages to the Czechs. First, they must evacuate the Sudetenland, and second, this was the last territorial claim he had to make in Europe. In hopes of avoiding conflict and possibly driving a wedge between the ever more closely associated Germany and Italy, England called for a conference of the three countries to be held in Munich on September 29. Russia and Czechoslovakia were excluded, as was France. At the conference it was decided that the Sudetenland would be evacuated and that an international commission would be established to determine the new Czechoslovakian border.

When the results of the Munich conference were known, the German general staff was shocked. The Fuehrer had once again been right, which only served to strengthen their belief in his genius and godlike intuition. It seemed he had it all figured out. He was the greatest political and military genius. The greatest leader! The Fuehrer! Or so the German press brayed to the world. Hitler the hero! Hitler the chief! Hitler the legend and he "who gives experience to the divinity!" Those who before had conspired to destroy him now lay low and in fear.

On September 30, the resigned Czechs agreed to the Munich decisions, but they wished to register their protest before the world against a decision in which they had no part. In his resignation speech, President Eduard Beneš said simply, "The new state must adapt itself."

That same day, the Poles sent an ultimatum to Prague demanding the district of Teschen, thus severing themselves from their American, French, and British friends. Reaction to this in England was violent. Said Churchill, "There will always be two Polands, one struggling to proclaim the truth and the other growing in villainy." Public opinion was greatly divided. First Lord of the Admiralty Duff Cooper resigned. For three days England debated its foreign policy and in the end, a shaken Chamberlain offered to resign, but his resignation was not accepted. A year before, writing of Chamberlain's foreign policy, Churchill had said with premonition, "By this time next year we shall know whether the Prime Minister's view of Herr Hitler and the German Nazi party is right or wrong. By this time next year we will know whether the policy of appeasement has appeased or whether it has only stimulated a more ferocious appetite." It was my experience at the time that most of those in Belgium who had lived through the First World War were in agreement with Churchill that appeasement had failed, and many of us hoped for his return to power.

The year 1939 was also the year that the Spanish Civil War ended in the defeat of the Republicans. With the help of both Italy and Germany, Franco had come to power. Both had jumped at the opportunity to field-test their weapons on Spanish soil. Five Italian divisions had rolled through Spain. Italian U-boats had sunk tonnage headed toward the beleaguered Republicans. German bombers had destroyed Guernica. Franco, promising to repay Germany by supplying it with food, mercury, and wool, was now the fascist military dictator.

On March 15, Germany announced its invasion of Czechoslovakia. The Czech government, trying to avoid what seemed to them a futile resistance, called for no resistance. For Germany, it was a piece of cake, but the peace-loving Chamberlain, for all his candor and illusory hopes, was not to be cheated or passed for a fool. The attack provoked a radical change in his attitude toward Hitler. Almost too late he asked publicly, "Is this in fact an attempt to dominate the world by force?" Perceiving the probability of a German enterprise against Poland, Chamberlain declared that Britain would stand firmly behind the guarantees it had given to Poland. The French would do the same.

In Germany, with Czechoslovakia conquered and Hungary an ally, the way to Poland lay open. Mussolini also had an interest in the Balkan states and in maintaining a strong presence in the Mediterranean, if only on the surface to counteract the French. His real intentions remained unknown until April 7 when he attacked and conquered Albania, opening the way to Greece.

On April 27 Britain introduced military conscription, a courageous act of probable political suicide for those governing in still peace-loving England. About this same time, Chamberlain and the conservatives ceased their attempts to attract Russia as an ally. They had little confidence in the Russian army and the discussions ended.

Also ended was the British diplomacy of appeasement toward Germany. The new diplomacy extended guarantees to Poland and Roumania, "regardless of whether we could give an effective help," said Churchill, speaking for the British. At the same time, a new alliance with Turkey was forged.

On April 28 Hitler unilaterally declared that the naval agreement he had signed with England was null and void and further, denounced the German-Polish Non-Aggression Pact of 1934. The fate of Poland was sealed.

In Russia, Maksim Litvinov was replaced by Stalin's right-hand man, Vyacheslav Molotov. It appeared that Russia had also abandoned the idea of a western alliance in favor of organizing an eastern one against Germany. It seemed that Russia would not fight for Poland. This belief was expressed in the German press in an article saying that Litvinov's resignation was extremely serious for the future of Anglo-French encirclement.

With the departure of "the Jew Litvinov," the tone of the German press changed. Instead of attacking Bolshevism, it turned its sarcasm toward the multiparty democracies and went so far as to offer goods credits to Moscow.

On May 22, Germany and Italy signed the "Pact of Steel," conferring on Italy the sphere of influence that included Albania and the Balkan states.

As discussions between Russia and the western allies broke down and the effort to build a common alliance against Germany failed, Bulgaria and the Baltic states faced the grim prospect of domination either by Russia and the communists, which they feared, or by the Nazis. Predictably, on May 31, Estonia and Latvia signed a nonaggression pact with Germany. Once again Hitler's diplomacy had scored a substantial victory in preventing the formation of a large coalition against his interests.

In June the Belgian government, firmly committed to neutrality, rejected the demand for a Franco-British-Belgian staff meeting.

It appeared to us that the months of German-Russian discussion were paying off. The balance of power was tilting toward the Reich. In August, we would learn from Soviet Tass of the signing of a pact between the two countries.

In the Baltic, only Lithuania would remain within the German sphere of influence and that only to provide Germany with a Baltic port. Hitler's thus far successful policy of "one at a time" continued: first you negotiate with one enemy to eliminate the other, then you fall back on the first.

September 1, 1939: Germany attacked Poland, annihilating the Polish air force and crossing the borders with armored divisions. France and England declared war on Germany. Germany responded on September 3 by conducting a small air raid on London. World War II had begun. On September 5, in a newly formed war cabinet, Churchill was called back into government as first lord of the admiralty.

For us this was great news. Now, in London, in a position of power, was a great man—a man of courage, integrity, and vision; a champion of freedom and one who never had believed Hitler; a man unafraid to speak his mind as we had seen, even at the peril of ruining his own political career.

The slaughter and dismemberment of Poland proceeded quickly and methodically. Attacked on three sides by Germany and two weeks later on the fourth side by Russia, it stood little chance. In one month it was all over. Thirty-five million people were subjugated and enslaved; later, many were murdered. On September 28, the Germans and the Russians met at their respective lines and signed a treaty partitioning Poland.

As time progressed, it became clear to us in Belgium from the news from England that England was bracing for a long war, while news from France indicated that the French had decided, wisely, on a defensive war.

Our hope, and we needed it to survive, was in the British navy, supported by a reasonable air force and the bulldog stance of their leader.

"It is a curious fact about British islanders, who hate drill and have not been invaded in nearly a thousand years, that as danger comes nearer and grows, they become progressively less nervous; when it is imminent, they are fierce; when it is mortal, they are fearless," wrote Churchill.

In Brussels, Jan and I awaited what we believed to be the inevitable attack on Belgium. Depressed by his stay at the mine, by the darkness that surrounded his work, Jan had found another position, in Vilvorde, a Brussels suburb, where he now worked in the Chamebel metal fabrication plant. We were convinced that Germany would simply go around the defenses of the Maginot Line and cross Belgium on its way to Paris and European domination.

CHAPTER 2

▼

Moving toward the Fray

As war flared around us, business in Brussels continued uninterrupted. Law clerks scurried from court to court, and street vendors polished their wares. City and country workers ostensibly continued to work and play as they had always done. Aside from the many men in uniforms and the somber faces, we could pretend all was normal. But times were not normal. Conversations around family dinner tables or on streetcars or sidewalks all turned sooner or later to evaluating our situation and making guesses at the future: a future which looked bleak, gloomy, and depressing no matter how optimistic one tried to be.

War would come by sea. The small but very modern German navy chose as prey the British navy and was clearly intent on breaking Britain's superiority at sea, while Britain quietly moved troops onto the continent to help in the defense of France. As we neared the end of summer, surprisingly, nothing indicated imminent German attack. If we could make it to the coming winter, we thought, we would have a respite until good weather returned. It was a nerve-wracking period. We listened intently to the radio news, read newspapers, and bought more foreign papers, French and British, as well as German. The tone of the British press moved another several degrees from its former attitude of pacifism at all costs toward resistance to the German aggression. Although it was an ill-prepared Britain that had declared war, the nation meant business and had started to rearm and to publish that fact. The Royal Navy sailed the sea lanes armed and at the ready. This comforting change from the pre-Munich era was provoked by a German attack in October, 1939. A German U-boat had succeeded in penetrating the defenses of Scapa Flow bay and had sunk the H.M.S. *Royal Oak*, pride of the British navy. This daring attack gave propaganda ammunition to the British government and helped turn public opinion toward an active war against Hitler.

As cold weather returned to the Belgian capital, the flower merchants at the streetcar stops gradually yielded to pushcarts selling warm french fries and hot chestnuts. The last fall-flowering white chrysanthemums announced All Saints Day and the traditional cemetery pilgrimage. With the advent of cold weather, vacations and outings came to an end, and the season for concerts, theaters, and movies began.

Often on a Sunday, I would travel to Vilvorde and spend time with Jan and his wife Fernande. He was happy with his new job and his health and spirits were improving. He too believed spring would bring more German provocation and probably an invasion of our land. We talked at length about the Belgian communists and Rexists. The former, as usual, followed Moscow's orders and tried to depict the Germans as friends now that Germany had made a pact with Russia. The latter were actively trying to embarrass the government, showing more and more sympathy toward the fascists. It was ironic to see these two extreme political parties showing sympathy for Belgium's old enemy.

At the army medical laboratory we prepared for war. Vaccines were in full production. Collaboration with the Pasteur Institute was established. They had the only facilities for antitetanus vaccine production and would be of great help in the anticipated fight against infections from dirt-contaminated wounds. We also actively organized the army blood bank by collecting, treating, and storing a wartime blood supply.

As the chestnut vendors reappeared, we heard of Britain's success in avenging the sinking of the *Royal Oak*. The British navy found one of Germany's ultramodern war ships, the *Graaf Spee,* and blockaded her in a Uruguayan estuary, preventing her escape. In response the Germans blew her up.

The end of the year in sight, Saint Nicholas dutifully brought gifts and toys to the good kids on December 6 as we prepared for Christmas and the new year. But it was hard to summon enthusiasm for the festive season. How could we visit family and friends and honestly wish them a happy New Year when clearly it would not be that for most Europeans and probably not for us either? Our land offered the Germans easy access to turn the Maginot Line. The previous world war would probably repeat itself and we could not stop it. A new Charlie Chaplin movie, *The Dictator,* in which Chaplin for the first time would break film silence, was being heralded around the world.

We in Belgium, however, learned that the movie, being offensive to Hitler, would be banned from our theater screens lest it provoke German ire. Time passed slowly as the relatively mild winter faded away. The chestnut merchants went home and we hoped soon to see the baskets full of spring blooms: narcissus, daffodils, jonquils. In March, Finland signed an armistice with Russia, something the Finns are still proud of today. Their little army had for months held the Russians at bay.

In April, the British navy sank a German troop transport that was illegally using Norwegian waters to sneak back into the Baltic Sea. The same day England mined the waters at Narvik, a northern Norwegian harbor, from which, in winter, the Germans had been transporting Swedish iron ore. Norway was duly informed of the allied action on April 8. At the same time, without warning, Germany began a massive attack on Norway and invaded Denmark. Both were easy prey for the German sledge, especially with the help in Norway of the grand-scale perfidy of the traitor Vidkun Quisling, who gave the world a new word, and his pro-Nazi men. Surprise, precision, and ruthlessness were the tools of the Germans. But the battle for Norway also provided an occasion for the British navy to show her power and superiority—so much so that in the end the Germans had gained Norway but had practically lost their navy. All they had left were U-boats. However, the Germans, now close to the vast Göllivare iron ore fields, would have all the iron they needed, transferred in summer through the unfrozen Baltic, in winter through the rebuilt Narvik harbor and the Norwegian coastal waters. It was anybody's guess what Germany would do about Sweden. By April 29, the resistance in Norway had practically stopped and the king and government embarked for Britain. The country was all but left to its conquerors, aided by traitors trained by Quisling who had aped the Nazi movement for years. But not entirely. Soon, a superb underground began to take shape and act.

Having seen what the Germans had done to Poland, how quickly they conquered Denmark and Norway, the kind of armament they had, the discipline of their troops, and above all, their two-pronged attack using panzer divisions supported by a very good air force, we were frightened. Our government, still resolute in its neutrality against all odds, elected to fight only if necessary. Our worst apprehension became our reality. The Germans, in for the big kill under the principles of a philosophy we could never adhere to, would soon be at the gates.

As a young man raised in a world of hope and peace, I shuddered to think of my ideals shattered, my wants denied, my values destroyed.

From the pacifism of my youth, events would lead me down unexpected paths. At first, I believed my part was to take care of the wounded and the sick, to alleviate pain and to provide comfort. This I would do with determination and devotion because our cause was pure and I believed that our nation was in grave danger of being unjustly attacked. I would work for the protection of human rights and freedom. I did not belong to an inferior race, nor did I agree with the use of violence for domination. I was ready to resist with a clear conscience and the desire to do my best to maintain a decent world in which to live. With these high ideals and passionate thoughts, I went to bed on May 9, as did many of my countrymen.

CHAPTER 3

▼

Short Journal of a War Medic

May 10, 1940

5:00 A.M. Awakened by the sound of bombs and the noise of antiaircraft batteries, I turn the radio on. The enemy moves toward us on a front extending from the north of Holland to south of Luxembourg. The attack was begun at 2:00 A.M. with extensive aerial bombing and advancing motorized units. They say it is the first phase of the conquest of France. As we anticipated, the Germans are attempting to turn the Maginot Line by attacking through Belgium. All men eighteen to thirty-five are mobilized for our defense. A total blackout is in effect. Massive numbers of enemy paratroopers are dropping behind our lines in many locations, with the largest concentrations behind the Albert Canal.

6:00 A.M. I make my way to the laboratory at the hospital. The streetcars are filled with men on their way to their assignments. Many carry backpacks. Little conversation is offered. Serious faces, tense with preoccupation. At the hospital, ambulances are lined up delivering casualties, mostly from the military airports near Brussels. The laboratory, long prepared for this eventuality, has called in its supplementary manpower and prepares to move from Brussels to Ostend on the coast. This low area behind the coastal sand dunes can be flooded at high tide by opening a number of the many locks on our canals as well as special floodgates. Historically it has often offered safe haven to fleeing Belgians. (It is an area extending from the south of Nieuport to France, passing Ypres and Dixmude. During World War I, the front stabilized there for four long years and was not overrun.) We will move jointly with the personnel and material from the Brussels Pasteur Institute, departure scheduled for 12:00 P.M. on May 14. Once in Ostend we will reorganize and work with the rear-echelon hospitals. Working in haste, we pack, move, and load. German armored divisions are moving across the difficult Ardennes terrain opposing our best border troops, the Chasseurs Ardennais, who, according to the radio, are offering stiff resistance.

The Germans are also on the move north of the Ardennes under command of General Von Rundstedt. They move forward on our primary line of defense, the Albert Canal, which joins the Meuse River to the Schelde north of Antwerp. In yet another assault, Germans attack Holland and move quickly through that flat country. By afternoon, the British and French are crossing our southern border to establish a second line of defense, while a second French army moves inland from the Atlantic coast toward Holland. Near Louvain, a combined British and French force takes position toward the Meuse at Namur to connect with the French guarding the Maginot Line south of Luxembourg to the Swiss border. Behind the Albert Canal, German paratroopers capture and secure two bridges and subject our forces to a double assault on their front and rear guard. Everywhere there is intense aerial bombardment. The Germans are the masters of the skies, having annihilated our air force on the ground. Few escaped. Those who did are unable to return. The runways are cratered concrete rubble. In the Netherlands, the Hague is under attack and the government paralyzed, but the plot to capture Queen Wilhelmina has failed. Faint hope in a dark hour.

Rotterdam is destroyed. We struggle against panic.

May 11
Our news is incomplete and confusing. One thing only is clear: we are attacked in force along the entire line of our defense in a new method of warfare. German units speeding toward us, German paratroopers behind our lines, German mastery of the skies, all major roads bombed. In the Ardennes it appears we are holding our ground, but under intense pressure. We are constantly machine-gunned from the air. Clear weather favors the enemy. From Liège, a reporter observes rural populations entering the city by the thousands. Many refugees tell of German fighters attacking traffic on the roads, hundreds of vehicles disabled, the number of deaths and casualties huge. The government repeatedly exhorts us to stay calm and to listen only to officially confirmed news. During this second day of war, enemy troops have penetrated forty miles into Holland with little opposition.

The hospital is filling rapidly; our surgeons have worked thirty-six hours without stopping. Casualties are high and demand for blood is acute. Our reserves dwindle rapidly. The staff, unable to keep up this pace, asks for Red Cross backup. Our blood supply cannot be replenished until we reach Ostend. The packing and loading continues. All of our trucks are civilian requisitions. Some come supplied with drivers, others not. I put some men to work painting large white circles with red crosses on green canvas to be attached to the roofs of our trucks in hope this will deter fighter attacks on the road. During a short rest over lunch my thoughts are with my former classmates, most of them at the front. Late in the afternoon an order comes to accelerate our preparation for the move toward Ostend. Our bacteriologists are already moving a load of precious live cultures and are expected back late in the day.

As evening approaches, I manage a quick visit home. Mother is boiling old bedsheets and dyeing them black to cover the windows. The streets are without light. Streetcars move with their headlights covered except for a narrow horizontal slit. Dad tells me that as in 1914, he and mother will remain at home for the duration. He expects it to be another four years in hell. Under the influence of his somber vision, I return to my duties. Mom and Dad both wish to come and see our column move out of the hospital. I promise to call them as soon as I know the date and time.

May 12

5:30 A.M. Our national broadcasting station broadcasts nonstop. It reports that our army engineers have destroyed all the bridges over the River Meuse and have erected temporary pontoon bridges to handle military traffic only.

Reports from the Dutch government indicate that German paratroopers have seized all locks and waterworks. The plan to inundate all of south Holland has failed. Germans have passed the north of the Meuse and are moving toward Amsterdam. From the Ardennes, heavily armored enemy divisions have penetrated the line and are moving toward Liège and the Meuse River. The French hastily prepare for the expected assault on their retrenched line.

At the laboratory, preparations for moving are progressing, but it has become evident that we will not be able to go before May 14. Our civilian truck drivers complain about the military food. One disappears. I am searching for talent among my men and find two experienced truck drivers. I also volunteer and am put in charge of a six-ton truck carrying two heavy electric generators. In the afternoon, the government officially announces that French and British troops have taken prearranged positions along the River Dyle toward Namur and along the Meuse. They will try to protect Belgian forces retreating across the Meuse. The Albert Canal is lost. The troops defending the canal are in retreat toward Antwerp and Louvain. Liège and Namur are holding. We are very tired. What took two men to move earlier, now takes four. The day's end news is that the French are on the island of Walcheren, in south Holland, engaging armored enemy forces barely sixty miles from here.

May 13

The last empty trucks arrived this morning and we set about finishing the task assigned to us. The news is bad and worse. Germans, already deep inside Holland, are closing on our northern border. They have bypassed Liège and attacked Namur. The Ardennes are completely in their hands and their advance units already face the French along the Meuse. Belgium is under attack by five armored divisions that have crossed the Ardennes, each with six hundred tanks and twelve thousand men.

Most of our Chasseurs Ardennais have retreated safely over the Meuse near Dinant and Huy. No news from our men on the Albert Canal. Prisoners? Dead? So much uncertainty. We will leave tomorrow morning hoping that our red crosses will save us from German fighter attacks. Traveling at night is out of the question; there is too much destruction. All main roads are cratered or destroyed and side roads must be used. Traffic is reported to be heavy, with civilians complicating the problem. This evening I send a message home, letting my family know that we leave tomorrow at 8:00 A.M. My friend, the young pathologist Dr. Delporte, is to travel with me. I will rely on his dry humor to ease the tensions of the trip. Late in the day I am given the command of two corporals and forty-six medics as well as the civilian truck drivers. A few hours of rest and we will move.

May 14

Again awake at 5:30 anticipating a hard day. The night has passed calmly. We will be on the road throughout the day and lunch will be very much in doubt. I strongly recommend the men eat heartily at breakfast. Our departure is delayed. Time ticks by. Mom and Dad are here. We are thankful that my sister Nelly has been safe in Argentina since 1938. Mother's eyes are wet. Pretending I am needed elsewhere, I cut the visit short. Two rapid kisses and I send them home. God only knows what is in store for us.

From the little news available this morning, I gather that the situation is particularly critical in the northern area of the French town of Sedan where the Germans seem to be concentrating their panzers.

At last, just before noon, we are on our way. The news we heard yesterday about road conditions was all understatement. We move slowly through throngs of civilians, most headed south toward France; on the same roads military traffic moves north toward the front.

Leaving town, we saw mostly British military. Now we see mostly French. Damaged or abandoned vehicles of all kinds, farm wagons, farm carts, drays, cars, and trucks litter the roadside ditches and fields. One can read the terror on civilian faces: most of the living survived fighter attacks. Here and there we pass a section where such actions took place. Dead bodies are sprawled in green fields.

German aircraft fly low above us in mock attack. But for now, they respect our red crosses. Some of their planes are equipped with a kind of whistle attached to the wings that makes a terrifying noise. The effect is nerve-shattering.

By late afternoon we reach Ostend. It is nearly empty. We reach the sea wall and easily locate the large hotel that has been requisitioned for our use. The sky is surprisingly calm. Only a few planes from England fly over on their way to the front. As we move into the assigned building, we discover that a hot meal is waiting for us, a very welcome amenity to our tired and raw-nerved people. The staff allocates the fourth and fifth floors as the men's quarters. Superb rooms with baths. It sure beats the army barracks! I pick a room in front with a direct view toward England. Toward hope.

Later, in darkness, I again listen to the radio. The French, unable to oppose the German armor, cannot resist the German push against Sedan. The road to Reims is open. In Belgium, the Germans are across the Meuse River at Dinant. Our troops are ready to fight for Antwerp. The British are holding from Wavre to Louvain. Brussels is safe, at least for the moment. It is late, I need sleep. Tomorrow portends another day of surprises, no doubt.

May 15

I wake my men at 5:30, take a shower; breakfast follows. Small pleasures to be enjoyed as long as they may last. I am tired but well. We are not to unload. The situation is so unstable that we expect new orders. So we wait and we wait. We certainly welcome the rest, but are troubled and tense. How could we be otherwise?

The front seems to be stabilizing from Holland to Namur and along the Meuse. The battle rages toward Sedan. Having nothing to do, we sit, talk, and wander aimlessly along the sea wall and beach. The weather is superb, clear skies and gentle breezes. Throughout the day the sky is filled with Spitfires speeding toward the front or returning to their British bases. In early afternoon we are mute witness to a dogfight between a Stuka and a Spitfire. The Stuka is finally hit and plunges into the channel waters. As the day goes by we listen for late news. The most intense activity at the front is reported in France to the south toward the Oise River. In a quiet café on a small side street, I treat myself to two dark Rodenbach beers. There I hear that the Dutch have capitulated. Queen Wilhelmina and the government have departed to exile in Britain. I toast to their safe journey. The Rodenbachs raised my spirit a notch, the news lowered it by two. I do the sensible thing and go to bed and restlessly try to catch some sleep. What awaits?

May 16

Reports from France tell us that the Germans are pushing hard into the Sedan area. Advance units have already reached Montcornet, sixty miles behind the Sedan front. A fifty-mile gap exists through the French lines. Farther north, the French are evacuating the island of Walcheren. The Germans have achieved complete occupation of Holland in only six days. Their might and organization astounds us and further increases our fears. A second day passes without new orders. We again walk the beach and listen to the news from Brussels, Paris, and London. The Brussels news is the most complete about the front. Starting south of Louvain, at Limal, the Germans have pushed westward. Their most forward positions now nearly reach the Samber River. In France, they move toward the Oise River. The direction of the German push is aimed at Soissons just twenty miles farther. They are also reported to be no more than twenty miles from Brussels. In the afternoon I have my first conversation with the head of the Pasteur Institute, Dr. Jules Bordet, a Nobel laureate for his discovery of the sero-reaction test which provided for the early diagnosis of syphilis. He is a friend of Dr. Octave Gengou, a former professor of mine. Dr. Bordet is in the company of his wife. As we sit on a bench by the sea wall facing the channel, I note that she, like her husband, is petite and poised. This is the first opportunity for conversation between us since we've departed Brussels. Dr. Bordet has from the beginning impressed me with his extraordinary calm and soothing attitude toward others. In his wisdom, he faces the world's absurdity head-on. To him, these current events are just the latest expression of human folly, only the latest outburst of its periodic collective violence.

Later, having absorbed the nurturing sunlight and his good counsel, I feel soothed; more able to accept the unavoidable events ahead.

May 17

Under cover of night, the German armored divisions have moved to the very doorstep of Brussels. They are also approaching Saint Quentin in France. Brussels radio is still on the air, but for how long? Still our new orders do not arrive, nor do new supplies. Our cooks do marvels with what they have and so we wait. In late afternoon, Dr. Delporte joins me for a beer.

May 18

I believe the capital to be occupied. Brussels radio is off the air. Mid-morning, London confirms. Brussels is overrun. In France the front moves west, seemingly not toward Paris but in the direction of the coast, toward Abbeville and the Somme River. It appears to be a German attempt to encircle the armies still fighting in Belgium and simultaneously trap the British. Paris confirms German panzers advancing rapidly toward the Atlantic coast.

At four in the afternoon our orders arrive at last. Move out. Destination Angers. Angers? On the Loire River? Three hundred miles south! I suggest we requisition one of the gasoline trucks so as to have our own supply. It is difficult to get gas at pumps and soon may be impossible. The idea is approved and I am to be responsible for its distribution. The staff decides we will travel under the cover of night. Departure is set for 10:00 P.M. Many career officers and reserve-officer scientists travel with their families in their own vehicles interspersed between our red cross–bearing trucks. I do not like the arrangement and question if it is even proper. Before leaving, I appropriate from the kitchen a twenty-pound tin of military biscuits that I place well-hidden in my truck, along with a five-gallon jug of water. Better safe than sorry. At 10:15 P.M. we are on the move, learning to drive at night without the benefit of lights. Delporte peers into the darkness, looking for the ditch that parallels the road so that he can help me stay on the pavement. Even at fifteen miles an hour, it is challenging. It is near midnight when we cross the French border. Except for us, the roads are deserted.

May 19

Cloud cover deprives us of the little light we might have had. Progress is slow. At 2:00 A.M. we stop to rest and to refuel the vehicles. It is decided to try to reach Saint Omer, approximately forty-six miles south of Dunkirk and east of Boulogne. At 6:30 A.M. we reach our destination and park our convoy around the town's large central market. People are curious and inquire who we are. Although we are south of the war zone, people are wary, wondering; above all, concerned. We breakfast on cold leftovers brought from Ostend. I, like the others, try to rest in my vehicle. From the little news we gather here and there, it seems that our reaching Angers may be in question. The front is not stable and there are reports of Germans everywhere. The most certain news concerns Arras. The Germans are fighting hard there and seem to be gaining. If Arras is taken, the enemy will be only thirty miles from Abbeville. What will happen to us if our column is captured? At least we have not seen or heard the German air force scourging the roads in this area. Departure time is fixed for 9:00 P.M. We will try to reach Abbeville on the Somme and maybe push even farther, trying to reach Reims on the Seine River.

9:00 P.M. We inch through the darkness.

May 20

Fatigue and tension take their toll on our band of adults, children, and army men in the assortment of cars and transports. Our bodies are depleted, our nerves uneven, our eyes bloodshot. Delporte and I try to find something to say just to keep ourselves awake. During one refueling stop, some officers try to bribe me for gas. I refuse any distribution. Without a written order from Dr. Devester, head of the laboratory, the answer is no. I know there are problems finding gas at pumps, which are mostly closed at night, but I have my orders. Is the army obligated to move families in private cars? Fear erodes decency in many. Around 4:00 A.M. we think we hear the noise of battle to the east of us. We keep going, trying to be prepared for what lies ahead. At 6:00 A.M. we at last approach Abbeville and stop in the small town where the streets are already filled with anxious people. A motorized German reconnaissance unit had been there just an hour before asking for the road to Etaples, a small town on the coast.

Some of our trucks are stopped for refueling. Others, without waiting, push south. We will have to catch up with them as we go.

Looking down the road a little north of Abbeville, Delporte and I notice a large building, its doors flapping in the wind. We decide to investigate. As we stand on the sidewalk peering inside, the floor seems to be at least four feet down. All that we can see at first is dim light filtering through dirty windows at the far end of a corridor. As our eyes adjust, we realize that we are looking down a long alley bordered on both sides by huge oak kegs. Delporte first notices a faint noise that we soon identify as liquid escaping from the large casks. Then and only then do we notice that the floor is flooded; the breeze has prevented us from smelling and identifying the scent. Calvados. Applejack. Brandy! A metallic noise clanks eerily through the long, dark chamber. A closer look reveals a soldier's body floating face down in the liquor, military canteen rasping against the stone wall. This German I like. Pickled. Dead. After ten days of war, we have encountered the enemy. A tank man of a kind, with helmet and goggles, in an encounter with death so unexpected and gross that we burst into tension-releasing laughter at the tragicomic sight. What a way for the conqueror to go, drowned in spirit far away from home.

As we leave Abbeville, the citizens urge us to cross the bridge quickly as it may soon be blown up. Our convoy crosses and we decide to continue in daylight, trying to move closer to Rouen. About midday the staff announces that we will have a hot meal around four in the afternoon. We push on a little farther until exhaustion forces us to rest. We will take to the road again at 9:00 P.M. In early afternoon in a small roadside village I look for news and inquire as to where I may be able to listen to a radio. A friendly house offers me what I am looking for and some welcome beverage. I am left free to tune in to whatever I can. I hear Paris and London. Brussels remains silent. From reports, the battle is said to be raging around the Schelde and Antwerp area. In France, all seems to be quiet on a line from Sedan to Cambrai. Arras is still holding but under increased pressure from a main German force. It seems safe for us to continue south. We are definitely out of the German zone of action, having slipped through a keyhole.

4:30 P.M. A hot meal in a school cafeteria. Each of us leaves with a large snack wrapped for the road. The French people are amiable. Are we not all dealing with the same misfortune?

9:00 P.M. On the road. Sixty miles to Rouen.

Midnight. We have just crossed the Seine and are in Rouen which is calm and mostly asleep. We can see the spire of the famous Gothic cathedral faintly lit by moonlight toward the east.

May 21

1:00 A.M. South of Rouen, on our way to Lisieux, the sky is clearer and the small, dim moon allows us to navigate. We resume moving after refueling. The commanding officer, Dr. Devester, has decided that we will drive until 6:00 A.M., then stop and decide what to do next.

2:00 A.M. The space between vehicles has been increased for security. The enemy is moving behind us. At 3:15, we pass through Lisieux on our way to Argentan which we reach at 4:30. At 6:00 A.M. we stop in Alençon as the town is awakening. By 8:00 A.M. I have refueled our vehicles and again I look for a friendly house where I can listen to the news. It is clear that the Arras area offers a challenge to the Germans. It is a vital road center and a good capture. There may be a reason for the French to fight so hard there. Do they have a plan? In Belgium, our troops are holding the Schelde from Antwerp to Ghent and Oudenarde. The British hold south of there, concentrating toward the coast. As long as Arras is holding, the Germans cannot turn north and again attack our troops from the rear.

Brussels radio comes back on the air, the familiar voices of our announcers gone, replaced by new ones telling us that all is well, the town is calm. Soon we will be totally liberated from the French and the British.

Liberated!

We are to have confidence in the German soldiers, says the announcer; they are our friends. They will protect us from the British imperialists and the decadent French democracy. Propaganda Abteilung. No doubt.

5:00 P.M. The staff again manages to provide a hot meal, this time in a nearly deserted French army barracks. This French menu is better than the Belgian, a hearty stew with lots of meat, potatoes, and lentils. Some of our men, unfamiliar with lentils, do not like them. What do they expect, I ask, steaks, french fries, mayonnaise? Perhaps dessert?

10:00 P.M. On the Angers road moving toward the Loire. We are deep in France as we bypass Le Mans, well-known for the European Grand Prix. The moon is brighter, the road easier, the sky calm. If not for the uniforms, the fearful faces, and the war, it would be a night favoring romantic adventures.

May 22

On our way to Angers, we follow the Sartre River valley. The road turns narrow and curving. We are forced to slow down again.

5:00 A.M. Angers. The town is still very much asleep. We stop and take a little rest. The staff searches for the Catholic University Medical School where we are to serve. At 10:00 A.M. we receive our orders to move to the facilities at the university. Men without rank will be quartered at the French army barracks nearby, within walking distance. Officers will live in the town's hotels. I settle in and again search the radio dial for news. There is very little from the front. Arras still blocks the enemy's progress. As for as Belgium, the situation is chaotic. After lunch and organizing the men's quarters, rest is in order. Showers are welcomed. Many are washing clothes.

May 23

There is no way to avoid the 5:30 reveille. War or no war, the army has its rules.

8:00 A.M. We are at the university after a short march with the men. We are told not to unload. All needed material is at hand at the university to accomplish what is intended—to help the French army by preparing and offering them antitetanus vaccine. The Pasteur Institute has eight inoculated horses from which serum will be used to prepare thousands of doses. The large horse trailer will be driven to the city slaughterhouse, where the animals will be put to sleep in order to retrieve their blood. We will need to unload one panel truck to obtain the necessary ampoules.

For a few days at least, we are virtually free in a city not lacking interesting vistas or monuments, but the disquieting quiet of the town preys on our tiredness. We are apprehensive. What comes next is anybody's guess. The staff grows concerned. Having noticed unfavorable reactions from some of this city's people, we will need to be on our guard. The last thing we wish is to be the source of an incident. It is clear that some people consider us fugitives; soldiers of an army that has not been able to protect France, men of a country that since last summer has resisted offers to join the Allies in a common defensive cause. The fact that we are members of a medical unit is ignored.

Within our group, there are many petty dissensions. Dr. Devester wishes all necessary personnel to stay in the barracks unless they have reason to be about. Dr. Bordet opposes this idea and proposes that the men be allowed, in organized groups, to march in formation through the town and be allowed to look at the monuments and other points of interest. His view finally prevails, but is accepted with reluctance.

My orders for the day are to organize these city tours. The men staying in the barracks will entertain themselves with sports and gymnastics. I am to take a first group out this afternoon. Morning is devoted to unloading the little equipment that the university does not offer by way of preparing the vaccine.

2:00 P.M. With twenty-three men and a corporal I march to the imposing château of King René, to whom the throne of France was offered in the thirteenth century; he refused it. My reason for going there first is that the site is on the city outskirts. The walk through the suburbs will allow us carefully to monitor the city's pulse. All goes well on our way there. We admire the sights along the River Maine and have a good look at the castle and its outside walls behind the well-maintained moats. The uniqueness of this construction, erected on top of ninth-century remnants, lies in its massive round towers and unusual masonry: blocks of cream-colored stones interlaced with bands of black shale. It is an incredible thirteenth-century work that comes to us nearly intact and illustrates the value of not being in an army's path, for it has remained untouched by the destruction of war.

As all seems to go well, I decide to walk closer to the city proper in order to show the men two churches. First we visit Saint Maurice Cathedral, an eleventh- to thirteenth-century construction of Romanesque style with some early Gothic elements. Next we pass the Byzantine-style Trinity Church which is located in the old medieval center of town. We walk along narrow streets bordered by stone houses dating to the seventeenth century. We have successfully toured through town and back to the barracks without having been subjected to any unpleasantness. Tomorrow I will embark on the same tour with the other platoon.

Later we hear that the situation in the north has taken a turn for the worse. Although the march toward Paris envisioned by some has not yet taken place, the Germans, exploiting the Sedan bulge to their advantage, have turned their panzers west, toward the coast. The maneuver is clear: isolate the remaining forces in Belgium and block the retreat of British forces. It is curious that Arras still resists. The French have little or no armor to oppose the onslaught and the British armor is light and inferior to that of the Germans. In another arena, British and Belgian troops tenaciously defend the River Lys. The Chasseurs Ardennais, reorganized, harry the invaders a second time.

May 24

Last night was our second in the extraordinary calm of Angers. What a contrast to previous days.

8:00 A.M. I depart for the château with my second group. About 11:00, close to Trinity Church, an aristocratic French cavalry lieutenant insults us without reason. Dr. Delporte, who accompanies us, cannot intervene before one of my men loses his temper and punches the officer in the face, knocking him out and bloodying his nose. Were it not for the honest intervention of two French military police, we could be in a very precarious position. They testify in our defense, but outings are canceled. The men are confined to barracks, allowed only intramural activities, except after dinner when they may visit one of several little cafés close to the military facilities. At least they can enjoy a beer or a glass of Anjou wine.

May 25

The Germans are achieving great success and it is only a matter of time before they are in complete control. Belgians and British still fight hard defending the Lys River. On the lower Schelde, Belgians stand alone. It is said that there are British at the harbor cities of Boulogne and Calais, but they have not made contact with the enemy yet. The battle for Arras gains new intensity. Eight French divisions are in retreat to the south and out of Belgium. The lack of Allied mobility is against us, as the Germans gain control with their motorized units.

This evening the men are again allowed out to the cafés. The rosé d'Anjou proves to be intoxicating to our beer drinkers. One of my men staggers in front of a passing car and is killed. The first casualty of our unit is a casualty of stupidity, in the quiet of Angers.

May 26
All attempts to receive Radio Brussels now prove unsuccessful. London news is rare and only when one combines it with news from Paris does a picture emerge. It is clear that the Germans are on the offensive with renewed vigor. Arras still holds, but the Germans push west of it. The pincer is closing and there is no longer a chance for French divisions to retreat south. No sizable force will make it out of Belgium.

May 27
Intense fighting still rages in Flanders around the Lys River. A fool's errand? It is clear that sooner or later we must succumb to their larger and better-equipped forces.

May 28
Belgium has capitulated, but King Leopold III has refused to join the government in exile. He wishes to be taken prisoner with his army. So it is over. Belgium is lost. Our government has suffered the fate of Norway's and Holland's.

The British forces, protected by our combatants on the Lys, have, for the most part, reached the Atlantic coast, to a place called Dunkirk. There is no more news.

CHAPTER 4

▼

Sojourn in France

The bright sunny day could not dispel our somber gloom. I was not the only one unable to appreciate the sunshine. Men from the laboratory, drivers who had been requisitioned along with their trucks, reacted the same way. Our thoughts turned homeward to family and friends who were fighting at the front. Some we already knew we would never see again. We thought about the civilians maimed and killed along the roads during the exodus from the killing fields. My dad's voice still echoed in my mind, "It will be another long one, four years in hell." We Belgians were not alone, but still, we were now just another victim listed among the recently occupied nations. Any plans of resistance protected by inundations, as in World War I, were far behind us now.

The French still fought against impossible odds; the British expected another attempt on their island. And the rest of Europe, from Sweden to the Baltics?

I felt isolated among the soldiers, with whom I had little in common. It was only at the laboratory that I could converse with the officers whom I had befriended: Delporte, Captain Nicaise, and Dr. Bordet, among others, all working on the vaccine. I learned that the head of our unit, Dr. Devester, had departed for Toulouse where the headquarters of the Belgian Medical Corps had relocated. Many of our young men aged eighteen and older had been evacuated from Belgium and brought together in camps around Toulouse with the intention of training them there for war. Belgian capitulation meant everything was illuminated under a new, crueler light. The future of more than two hundred thousand young men was to be decided in accordance with German dictates.

Lille was under attack on three sides. The French were attacked on the road from Graveline to Dunkirk. The chaotic entanglement of the British and French forces was being sliced into ever smaller pockets of resistance. It was clear that even our staff was confused about the situation along a front constantly moving without apparent continuity. The situation was critical for the Allied forces. Back at the barracks, new orders were expected as soon as Dr. Devester returned from Toulouse.

For several days nothing happened. Then the front from Arras to Alsace stabilized, although the action was fierce in the Arras area and around Dunkirk. On June 2, Dr. Devester came with the orders: the main lab, after having finished the vaccine, should go south, passing through Toulouse. There we would receive orders to quarter in the area. Our medical personnel were needed in the camps where our young men had been concentrated in overcrowded, inadequate facilities, where food was lacking. The situation had the potential to become serious indeed. The French government asked for our assistance. Gasoline would be provided. In a week our task in Angers should be over and the vaccine delivered to the French Red Cross.

On June 6, Radio London gave an extensive news bulletin allowing us to assess the magnitude of the British effort around Dunkirk. It was reported that between May 27 and June 4 a total of 338,000 men had safely been evacuated from Dunkirk harbor and from several beaches. Among them were fifteen thousand French. This crucial announcement was followed by a speech that Churchill had delivered on June 4 before Parliament:

Even though large tracts of Europe and many old and famous states have fallen or may fall into the grip of the gestapo and all the odious apparatus of Nazi rule, we shall not flag or fail. We shall go on to the end, we shall fight in France, we shall fight in the seas and oceans, we shall fight with growing confidence and growing strength in the air, we shall defend our island, whatever the cost may be, we shall fight on the beaches, we shall fight on the landing-grounds, we shall fight in the fields and in the streets, we shall fight in the hills; we shall never surrender, and even if, which I do not for a moment believe, this island or a large part of it were subjugated and starving, then our empire beyond the seas, armed and guarded by the British fleet, would carry on the struggle, until, in God's good time, the new world, with all its power and might, steps forth to the rescue and the liberation of the old.

To comprehend now the effect such a speech had upon us, upon men defeated, men still fighting, upon men as yet unwilling to accept defeat and ready to resume the fight against all odds, requires a deeper listening. For it reached deep within us, pushing away despair and renewing the courage of many in the occupied lands. We were not alone. We were made stronger even if temporarily crippled and powerless. That indomitable man was calling for our help from inside our jails and we took heart.

Only hours after Churchill's speech, the Germans began a new offensive, a new phase of operations. Since they now claimed Belgium, they were able to consolidate their forces in the south for an all-out push toward Paris. The first attack was on Amiens toward Soissons. Of the British forces in France, only a few remained: the First British Armored Division and the Fifty-first Highland Division pulled back from the Maginot Line. Both of these, incorporated into the French Tenth Army, survived the powerful punch of the best German troops, among which were six panzer divisions. In only five days the enemy moved from the Somme River to the Seine, from Rouen to Vernon. By June 8 the French Sixth Army above Soissons was pushed south of the River Aisne, which the Germans then crossed. It was agony to think of those poor souls.

Orders arrived to fill the tanker truck and we prepared for departure south toward Toulouse. The farther south I was to travel, the more depressed I felt about the increasing distance between me and my fallen country. I discussed my sorrow with Delporte who, as a career officer, was more inclined to dismiss such feelings and to follow orders. Our job was to take care of the health of the youngsters interned in camps, he reminded me. I had to admit his point, but the dense veil of the unknown that the Germans had thrown around us remained baffling.

The Germans had reached the Marne River on June 11, the day before we got on the road to Toulouse. We arrived there on June 15 without any problems, traveling in full daylight on roads mostly empty of traffic. In the evenings we stopped and ate anywhere we could: schools, army barracks. We gathered news and listened to the radio as we went.

On June 14 the Germans entered Paris and French spirit plummeted. Two days later, as we were waiting in a Toulouse suburb for our next destination to be decided, we learned that the Germans had reached the Loire and the French had retreated below Orléans. On the eastern French front, the Maginot Line had been easily and quickly breached from the rear through Dijon and Besançon. Germans were at the Swiss border. The French government reestablished itself in Tours. To shorten their communication lines, the Germans had crossed the Maginot Line through Colmar, in Alsace.

On June 17, General De Gaulle spoke on Radio London: "France is not alone. She has a vast empire behind her. She can unite with the British Empire, which holds the sea, and is continuing the struggle. She can utilize to the fullest, as England is doing, the vast industrial resources of the United States."

So spoke the young French general who carried with him the honor of France; a young general who, as a cavalry colonel, had predicted the new type of German war: motorized units supported by panzer divisions.

At the same time we also learned that French Marshal Henri Pétain headed the new cabinet in Tours. The French people thought and said that with Pétain, the hero of World War I, at the helm, things would change for the better. Personally I did not share in their optimism. No one person could reverse this situation. France simply had nothing modern with which to oppose the mighty German armies. At Toulouse we were given orders to go farther south and settle in a village at the foot of the central Pyrenees Mountains, Les Cabannes.

We arrived there on June 19, establishing ourselves as best we could. The men found a place to quarter in a large, empty house. The officers and I obtained quarters in private dwellings in and around the village.

On June 23 it was announced that France had capitulated. Pétain had signed an armistice with Germany. German troops would occupy all conquered land and be permitted to move along the Atlantic to take possession of a fifty-mile coastal zone as far south as Spain. They had succeeded in securing all French harbors facing England. The French navy, having abandoned these, was now spread among Toulon on the Mediterranean, North Africa, and other French possessions such as Martinique. France was divided in two, an occupied zone to the north and along the Atlantic coast, and a free zone south and west toward Switzerland, Italy, and the Mediterranean. The Pétain government established itself in Vichy in the volcanic central region.

As far as we were concerned, once bivouacked in Les Cabannes, we had not much to do. I spent my days touring the country in search of food, driving to headquarters in Toulouse with staff members, or taking outings to the mountains in my free time. In my time off, I even went patrolling the Spanish border with the French gendarmes' border unit looking for contraband. It was a tedious experience. More exciting was a trip with smugglers to the small principality of Andorra, but I paid for the excitement with total exhaustion. These men did not follow roads, but, like goats, jumped from rock to rock in impossible places that the gendarmes would never reach.

Vivid in my mind even now are the numerous trips made with our doctors to the different camps where our young Belgian men were behind barbed wire. The camps, built to hold Spanish freedom fighters of the 1937–38 civil

war, were primitive, with totally substandard hygienic conditions, and the
food provided was wholly inadequate in quality and quantity. The effects of
malnutrition showed readily. Luckily the weather was balmy.

During the long days spent in the Pyrenees we had ample opportunity to
listen to the news and read the French press. Many things previously misun-
derstood or not known became clear. In the last weeks of the campaign the
French had suffered not only military defeat, but also internal divisiveness.
Their chief of the army, General Maxime Weygand, a Catholic conservative,
adversary of all politics and of the parliamentary regime, was in favor of a
cease-fire to save the lives of his soldiers. The premier, Paul Reynaud, wished
to continue the fight in the colonies and would have liked to join Britain. The
position of the president of the Republic, Albert Lebrun, was not clear—but
was unimportant since he had virtually no power in France. Minister Pierre
Laval had tried to form his own government in Bordeau and favored yet
another solution: France must choose sides and join Germany, the winning
side.

Now both Laval and Pétain, together in Vichy, played the collaborators'
game. Such was the situation in the summer of 1940. The local population
of Les Cabannes was hospitable and resigned. They were still in their country, but without contact with the enemy. Only later did they suffer from the
Vichy government's collaboration with the Nazis; only later did they feel the
lack of food, the lack of goods, for everything that was manufactured, produced, or grown went to the winning side, to a Germany at war. Much later,
they too suffered occupation like the rest of France, when the enemy felt
insecure due to an organized resistance and feared an Allied landing. The
Pétain armistice did not spare France the pangs of the conquered, the pangs
of physical and spiritual hunger.

The fate of the French navy, the fourth largest fleet in the world, was still
undecided. The British government, concerned about the possibility that the
French fleet would be used by the Germans or the Italians, asked the British
admiralty to act. In early July, 1940, all French ships in British ports were
taken under British control. For the most part, the vessels did not offer resistance except for the *Surcouf,* which had to be seized by force. Many French
seamen volunteered for service to Britain. In 1942 the *Surcouf* perished in
Allied service. In North Africa, French ships refused to surrender or to sink
themselves. There was only one solution, reluctantly adopted: destroy the
French navy before it could side with the Italians or block the Mediterranean, so vital to British supply lines. This was started at Oran and continued
at Mers-el-Kebir. All French ships in those ports were destroyed or severely

damaged. Only the *Strasbourg* evaded destruction to join the remaining fleet
at Toulon. Two other modern units, the *Richelieu* and the *Hermès*, were destroyed at Dakar. A French aircraft carrier and two destroyers were immobi-
lized at Martinique. Thus came to an end the illustrious French navy built
by Admiral Jean Louis Darlan, whose grandfather had perished at Trafalgar.
That very fact may explain why negotiations for the transfer of the fleet to
Britain had failed. Painfully, the French fleet outside Toulon had been neutralized, but it was also lost to the Allied cause. The rest of the fleet, in Toulon and still under command of Admiral Darlan, was temporarily secure in
this harbor of non-occupied southern France. The sea, at least, would be
secure for Britain, save the menace of the German U-boats still remaining.
The rest of the German navy had been destroyed in Norway. At the end of
July, German diplomatic activity was intense as Hitler tried to obtain no less
than British acceptance of the German domination of Europe.

On the night of July 22, this German idea was simply brushed aside by an
official radio announcement: "Britain will never capitulate to Hitler's will."

It was now more than a month since we had arrived in southern France.
The effects of war were more evident with every passing day. With less and
less success I toured the country in search of food. Potatoes all but disappeared. Sugar and coffee were simply not available. Happily, it being summer, vegetables and fruit were still aplenty. Meat was available with coupons
and at twice the normal price. Our staff was still engaged in the care of our
young men and moves to repatriate them were begun. Our conquerors
voiced a desire to reestablish normal life in Belgium. It was only later that
we understood why: they wanted Belgium to work, to supply their arsenals.
From the German authorities controlling Belgium and the north of France
we learned that they wished our unit to return and, so they claimed, reopen
the Pasteur Institute to help maintain public health. Parleys were exchanged
between Toulouse and German headquarters in Brussels. Most of the staff
were reluctant to agree to the German demands, but many of the troops
were willing to go home. I sided with the men, feeling I could be of more
use at home than wasting time in a friendly but foreign land. There was
nothing I could do in France, artificially divided and politically disrupted. At
home I had friends, a nation—at least united, although small and not free.
Could "free" France expect to be so for long? Besides, I had a growing desire
to see what could be done to help the cause of liberation, perhaps to organize
an active subversive movement. Naturally all was blurry and vague from that
distance, but my mind was set. I would not accept the enemy's dictates; I
would not tolerate German "idealism."

By mid-August, our orders were to move north using gas allotted by the Germans. Our military status was changed to civilian on our last day at Les Cabannes. Our departure was marked by spontaneous manifestations of goodwill from the French villagers. They brought fruit and vegetables for the enlisted men's kitchen and invited those of us billeted in their houses to dinner.

On the French roads our progress was rapid as we traveled along nearly empty stretches, now with a clearly reduced traffic load. It took us only five days to reach the "demarcation line," the northern limit of unoccupied France. There our column was stopped by the German military that we were meeting and seeing in action for the first time. I remember this first encounter with the *Feldgrau,* uniformed and very disciplined men of the Third Reich. Their efficiency and politeness were impressive. We were processed, checked, scrutinized to their satisfaction. The outfit was traveling under signed orders from General von Falkenhausen, military governor of Belgium and northern France. Having been demobilized, we all were in civilian attire, dressed in the best our French hosts could provide.

At this border we were given an itinerary to be followed until we reached Brussels. The roads were now busier, with a lot of German traffic, checkpoints, and more checkpoints. The Belgian border was as before with the customs men at work, but supervised by Germans. And finally, Brussels, a changed Brussels buzzing with activity.

Dr. Devester asked us to drive to the military hospital and help unload the trucks, but I had formed another idea. I was now a civilian; my military duties had ceased on the day I received my discharge in France. So, near Mons, after the last refueling, I changed vehicles, taking the wheel of one of the Pasteur Institute's trucks with the agreement of Dr. Bordet. In Brussels I delivered the truck to the institute courtyard and took a streetcar to the Rue de l'Ermitage. Once there I rang the bell, kissed Dad and Mom, and was home. I had so much to tell, so much to learn, and so many things to get accustomed to.

CHAPTER 5

▼

Resisting with Bare Hands

Having been raised a pacifist, never having had any toys resembling a gun, hating the use of force, I was certainly not prepared to become a belligerent person.

I had already realized I could not live with the German philosophy, and now that they had imported it into my country, it was just intolerable. Something had to be done. From there came the thoughts of rebellion, of resistance. But I also realized that thoughts alone would not achieve anything, action was needed. Individual acts, even if possible, would have very little effect against this fantastic war machine well oiled by propaganda. The only logical way to organize would be to form small groups of trusted friends to discuss, train for, and embark on some serious and very dangerous ventures.

It would take time to establish the right contacts, pool resources, and assemble capital. I could not see any other way. I discussed this with my father, who had gained experience in World War I while engaged in information gathering. He advised me well, confirming that I should work only with people in whom I had total trust. He asked me not to involve him unnecessarily—the fewer who knew, the better, said he. This highly clandestine work would not be organized in a day; it would grow slowly like a mushroom out of an underground mycellium.

So we built from scratch, slowly and securely. Starting with small actions, we gained experience. Much thought was given to all the possible ways of harassing the enemy. Our structure in place, we assembled materials. As what we needed was not readily available, we had to find ways to fabricate it ourselves. But, above all, we had to know what was happening in the outside world, to keep abreast of the news the Germans tried to deny us. When they occupied a country, their first task was to close all existing newspapers and

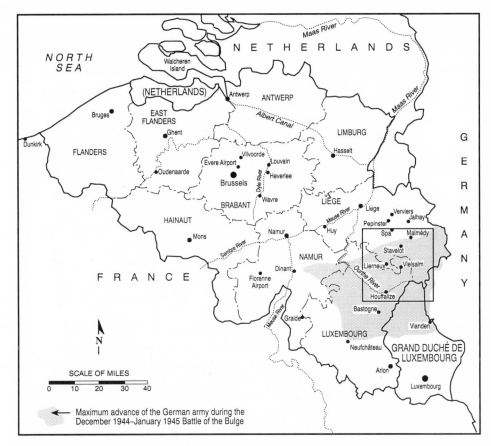

Belgium and Its Neighbors.

reopen them staffed with people willing to work for them. These were fed information distributed by the Propaganda Abteilung in Berlin under the leadership of Goebbels and Fedder, indoctrinating the conquered with their lies.

Returning from my military expedition to France, I decided to introduce a small radio at home to be able to stay in touch with the free world and listen to the forbidden BBC, the British Broadcasting Corporation, from London. That was my first deliberate act of rebellion against the enemy.

What a morale booster it was to listen religiously at seven each evening to the London news reports in French, which always began with the four opening notes of the Beethoven's Fifth Symphony—three shorts and one long, the Morse symbol for V and victory—then "Ici Londres" (This is London) and the news would follow. How I appreciated this link with civilization. It was so unlike 1914 when the occupied Belgians were isolated and could only obtain news, other than German lies, by much-delayed means. Real news eventually reached them only weeks or months later through the clandestine press. But this modern means of communication also had its drawback. From London we could promptly be kept current, but good news in those first years of war was rare while the bad was plentiful. London of course censored the news, though rarely were outright lies broadcast, except as needed to fool the Axis. Radio London never told the exact damage done by German bombing and would even give wrong information to confuse the assailant. Nonetheless, keeping in touch with London was a boost in itself. At least we knew the British were alive and fighting and by summer's end, information began to surface of German troop movements through Belgium, Holland, and the north of France. We also heard reports of intense activity on the coastal canals with massive requisitions of barges and tugs. One moonless night in Ninove, a small Brabant town well known for its match industry, I was awakened by the noise of a large German truck convoy which had stopped in the market square.

Cautiously, I peeked out at the trucks. They were filled with dead German bodies. I could see an arm here, a leg there protruding from under the tarps. Later, all came together when news circulated that the Germans had made a tentative stab at invading England by sea. Midway across the channel, they received a very warm welcome from the Royal Air Force who dropped fifty-five-gallon (Imperial) drums of gasoline equipped with percussion fuses into the water, setting the sea afire around and over the invaders. Many burned soldiers had been seen in Ghent and Antwerp. Some had spoken about their odyssey. However, so as not to alarm British listeners, London kept this off the airwaves. The Germans also did not publicize the trap into which they had fallen, although we made certain the news traveled all over our country. It was a German defeat. It merited publicity.

Soon after this tentative assault on Britain, the Germans began bombing London in what has since been called the Battle of Britain, the Blitz: massive, murderous raids, day after day, week after week, mostly over the capital of the isles. London reported casualties, but beyond that acknowledged no disruption of business as usual. It was part of the game.

At home we were miserable and very anxious. We had heard, if not seen, what the Germans had done to Rotterdam in May and we feared the destruction of London. Throughout, Radio London announced the assaults and never complained. It reported estimates of downed enemy bombardiers and gave accurate figures of lost Spitfires. The figures were staggering and we wondered how they could survive; would the Germans continue despite their own losses? The British never gave casualty numbers, but we knew they must be staggering, too. We suffered for them. We suffered with them.

In October, 1940, Brussels was suddenly filled with airmen of a new sort, Italian-speaking and dark-blue–uniformed. They had come in bombardier squadrons to help the Germans bring the British to their knees. These officers were flamboyant in their garb and covered with braids of gold and flashy insignias. It seemed all the doormen of Europe had joined us for a convention. They invaded our restaurants, shopped for what was left in our stores, toured the city admiring our monuments. We had to accept them on our transportation systems. In Brussels, by German edict, tramway collectors could not ask for fares from men in uniform. However, one day, onto the packed streetcar platform came one of these gold-braided, blue-uniformed airmen. The collector called out, "Fare money, please." When he had collected from the civilians, he pointed to the Italian and said, "Mister, hey Mister." Receiving no answer from the officer, he extended his arm and touched the man's shoulder. "Mister, you have to pay." The Italian turned around saying something we all interpreted as "Military." "Ho, yes! Come on, you must be kidding," said the collector. "You pay, Mister, or out you go at the next stop." There were a few Germans on the car. They laughed. We laughed. And at the next stop, the Italian got off.

Some weeks after the streetcar incident, and thanks to London, we learned that the Germans had lost many planes, and the Italians had lost most of theirs. We also learned that the bombardment of London had practically stopped. Did Hitler think it too costly and not sufficiently effective? We adopted a position of guarded optimism. While the men of the Italian air force were still in Brussels shopping and sightseeing, one noon at the Porte de Namur, a busy intersection leading to Brussels University, students by the hundreds emerged from streetcars on car line sixteen. Each wore a raw piece of straight macaroni decorated with a black crêpe ribbon knot pinned to his or her lapel. To everyone the message was clear: *Requiescat in Pace*, rest in peace, the final words of the death mass. Even though the Germans appreciated the joke, many students found themselves on potato-peeling duty for the rest of the day at Saint John's Hospital, which the occupiers had requisitioned. Small price, good joke. Unhappily, however, that was the final straw for my alma mater. The Germans closed it. The other three universities, including our old political enemy, Louvain Catholic University, opened their doors to Brussels University students. During the war no distinction was made between the freethinkers and the Catholics. We were now all Belgians suffering together and supporting each other. Old quarrels were abandoned, political differences forgotten. Soon the humiliated Italians departed, their crashed planes scattered over the British landscape. They had been victims of flak and of the courageous and able young Britons flying for the RAF.

Throughout, Winston Churchill kept his sense of humor. On October 21, 1940, the day after "Eagle Days" (the worst days of the air raids), he excoriated the Germans with dark humor. Over the airwaves he asked them: "When are you coming? We are waiting for you; so are the fish." He was referring to the German operation Sea Lion, the failed plan to invade and occupy the British Isles.

At the end of September while Brussels and the occupied countries were experiencing their new slavery under the harsh German boot, the French forces stationed in Britain under the leadership of General De Gaulle, with the help of the British navy, had tried unsuccessfully to capture the fortified harbor of Dakar on the east coast of Africa. Unfortunately the weather benefited the Vichy-controlled troops who successfully fought back their incoming countrymen. Little was said from London. The Germans, exploiting De Gaulle's foiled attempt to the fullest, tried to persuade us that French resistance was a farce and that Britain supported the losing side.

Near the end of October and during most of November, Mussolini attacked Greece, penetrating quickly and deeply. In mid-November the Germans launched another intensive and vicious air attack on several British cities and on many east coast harbors as well. The Germans invented a new verb, *Coventrieren,* which they explained as meaning "total destruction," the leveling of an entire city. Poor Coventry. We wondered what the demons would do next. Poor Birmingham, its entire center a heap of bricks and broken concrete; but London continued to report business as usual. "We have suffered, but our efforts will continue at an unabated speed; we are confident in the distant future."

Then winter was upon us, our first winter of the war. It was relatively mild and the food situation tolerable, though barely so. We needed official coupons to purchase the equivalent of fifteen hundred calories a day. Some merchandise was still available and the quality, if not the quantity, was acceptable. With a little imagination the table could still be inviting. Hunger helped our appreciation. Some things were still not rationed, mainly vegetables, excluding potatoes. Carrots, for example, were often available and could be used to make desserts. Carrot pie was perfectly palatable without sugar, thanks to the natural sweetness of those bright roots. For the coldest days of winter I had managed to obtain a twenty-gallon drum of pure, concentrated glucose syrup. Although it did not have the sweetening capacity of sugar, it was a healthy and precious possession. During that first winter I also made a successful pepper substitute by mixing fine poplar sawdust with piperine, a natural extract from pepper. I had located a 250-gram jar of it on the supply shelves of the company with whom I worked. When I returned from France, my former employer, Etablissements van der Heyden, was required by law to rehire me. Through my work I was in contact with laboratories of all kinds—medical, industrial, scientific. I traveled all over the country, technically as a salesman, but with eyes wide open.

Such work, I realized, put me in a privileged position for collecting information. Without any special effort, I had a way to enter enemy installations. If I was alert, I could gather information that could be passed on to a Belgian intelligence network already in place. I now embarked upon rebellion more focused than merely listening to the BBC—subversive work, underground activity. As soon as I found something of value to report, I made contact and passed the information along. I used the opportunities of contact with other labs to meet with former students from my university, knowing they could generally be counted on to collect and assemble isolated bits of information. As most scientific materials used in Belgium were of German origin, my company ran on imports from Germany, but we were limited by importing licenses which were hard to get, unless, of course, the items benefited the army of the occupation. Being fluent in the enemy's tongue, I could discuss these matters with the occupying authorities, who were somewhat blinded by the pleasure of meeting any Belgian who showed interest in their language.

One of the illegal activities made possible by my acquaintances at the German quota office was to change a large amount of Dutch money to aid a Jewish family who had escaped to the Netherlands and were now in Brussels. They could not go to the bank, as the Germans kept track of all foreign currency transactions in order to trace illegals and Jews. This left them without means of subsistence. My German contact asked no questions and was well satisfied at making a little pocket money for his help. Now, however, I was obligated to him. Being away from home, he was lonely and pursued my companionship. I could refuse only so long with trumped-up excuses, until finally I had to accept his invitation to dinner. We met at a German-requisitioned officers' restaurant. Nothing was lacking—meat, pastries, wine, and liquors were all to be had just as before, as if calamity had not befallen us. I was ashamed to be there, of being in the company of the enemy and eating well. What if somebody should know me? Still, I believed the risk to be worth it, especially if I could use the connection to be of help to others. So I spent the evening practicing my German.

The town, so friendly and jovial in prewar days, its people normally so congenial, was now morose and moody. People drew in upon themselves. Smiles were all but a thing of the past. It was everyone for himself; gloom settled over us. Frowning faces abounded. Among the working class, the signs of lassitude were evident. They were robot-like and lacked enthusiasm.

Then there were the Germans, well fed, smiling, alert. Germans everywhere, on our streets, our streetcars, our trains, our roads. As we walked, they rode. The enemy was happy and hopeful. We were miserable and depressed. We could not demonstrate; they marched arrogantly through town with brass bands. We were in our homes by curfew, they walked all night. Our homes were cold, theirs warm. We were restricted in our travel, they traveled freely. We were arrested and jailed, judged by their military courts. Justice became a word of the past, with frequent deportations and summary executions. The masters. The obedient slaves. They human, we but numbers, animals to be herded, counted, or corralled at will.

In 1938 I had installed a new assay laboratory at the National Bank of the Belgian Mint and I now reestablished contact with the head chemist and his assistant, Louis Pierard. We had had several opportunities before the war to discuss the coming situation openly. Trust had been established, though we didn't know in 1938 how it might be tested. One day I met the assistant chemist on a streetcar and he asked if I could visit him in the evening at his home in the Boisfort suburb. His address was Rue de la Hulotte. Hulotte is the name of an European owl. I thought it was a good omen. A nocturnal bird of prey, which I intended to become toward the enemy. Louis did not elaborate. A streetcar was no place for private conversation. I accepted his invitation.

When I arrived at his home I found several men seated around the table. I was asked to swear secrecy about the meeting and, after having done so, was asked if I agreed with resistance to the enemy; if I would consider eventually joining a group engaged in such activity, specifically, as a chemist, an expertise they needed. I looked favorably on putting my knowledge to good use. Except for my host, I knew no one there and knew better than to ask for introductions. But I did ask a few questions and was satisfied with the answers I received from the oldest man in the group. If accepted, I would work with a newly formed group headed by a World War I veteran. They clearly indicated my choice should be made freely. They did not require an immediate answer. I would be recontacted in time by my host, which suited me fine.

Intending to inquire into the origin of this group, I spoke to my dad about it. Soon he reported that the information he had about them was good and he thought I should join. A fortnight later I was contacted again to come to another meeting and be sworn in. So, early in 1941, I began my work in earnest in the underground as a chemist. The movement I worked for, I was to learn later, was the Office Militaire Belge de Résistance, OMBR. I knew only one person by name and a select few others by code names. This system, common to all secret societies and illegal political groups, was closely related to the communist cell style of organization. I was to receive orders from and report only to Pierard, the man from the bank. At least for now.

My first task was a curious one. A dentist had volunteered to donate to the group two pounds of diamond grit, provided we could come up with a valid way to use it to sabotage the enemy's war machine. I was given a small sample and asked to study possible applications. Diamond being by far the hardest abrasive there is, I had to think of a way to use it in a form that could be well camouflaged and used to our maximum advantage.

The Germans, in order to keep their men in the army, had hired Belgians for all kinds of jobs in extramilitary duties: as cooks, hospital attendants, clerks, shop workers. I had to find out if some were working in military airports. The answer was positive. Mechanics' helpers, refuelers, and general maintenance people were used at Evere and other former Belgian military airports.

A small dose of diamond powder in a crankcase would work marvels on delicate engines. The next question was how to find a covert way for volunteers to carry the abrasive without possible suspicion? I decided on aspirin tablets carried in their original containers, using an aspirin formula of my own making: talcum, stearin, and diamond powder. The owner of the powder agreed to deliver the material. All that I needed now was a mold to fit the machine I would use to make up a batch in a small pharmaceutical lab belonging to an acquaintance. The mold problem was presented to my friend at the bank and rapidly solved. I also would need a few hundred empty Bayer aspirin tubes to store the product. These appeared in a few weeks and I was ready to deliver. What could be less conspicuous than a headache remedy in a shirt pocket? The bearer could even swallow one or two to make things look right. They would pass the digestive tract without any problem, though what exotic waste!

The organization would handle the distribution and usage. I know of one result. At Evere, near Brussels, a ground crew including one of our men was asked to prepare a plane quickly to take German staff personnel to Berlin. Changing the oil, he added the contents of a tube, twenty diamond tablets into the crankcase. The plane took off . . . and crashed in a field a few miles away. That made my day and confirmed the advertisement that Bayer works wonders. How many other plane engines were destroyed or damaged I do not know, but no one was ever caught using my strong medicine to cure the German headache.

Despite this small success, the news in early 1941 was all bad. Italians as well as Germans were on the offensive with little opposition from the Allies.

In March, the Germans took Bulgaria and bombarded Belgrade. In April, General Rommel landed in Libya with Italian and German support and attacked in the direction of Egypt. Greece then completely surrendered to the Italians. In May, in the biggest battle in the Atlantic, the German battleship *Bismarck* sailed out of the Baltic and attacked and sunk the H.M.S. *Hood*, prized possession of the British admiralty. The *Bismarck* then disappeared for three days, trying to escape to a harbor in France. A British seaplane found her and successfully disabled her rudder through repeated bombing attacks. While the ship circled helplessly, the Allied navy arrived and finished her with concerted gunfire. The newest and largest German battleship sank into the deep on May 27. Almost simultaneously Germany resumed bombing the British Isles, particularly Dublin, Derby, and London. Germans also claimed to have destroyed totally the Rolls Royce airplane engine factory. To protect their operation in Libya, they started a merciless attack on the island of Malta. In the Atlantic, they concentrated their U-boat attacks on convoys to England from the United States and loss of convoy ships increased to alarming proportions. If the Germans were to be believed, Britain would be without materials within months. England did not deny the situation, but kept hope high and conveyed the same positive message to us.

In North Africa, Rommel piled success upon success as the British seemed to succumb to his superior tank armament.

Because Hitler had signed a pact with Russia, the Belgian communists did not support the feeble efforts of our resistance. Germany was an ally of Russia and communist internationalism seemed to make them forget they were occupied Belgians. Practicing a politic I could not comprehend, they put their political beliefs above the desire to liberate their country. And then on June 22, 1941, Germany attacked Russia on a wide front with two main pushes toward Leningrad and Moscow. We rejoiced.

Listening to Radio London and sometimes to Radio Lausanne, which was also *verboten*, gave us the only credible international news worth listening to.

On June 22, regarding the attack on Russia, Churchill made another of his famous speeches. All who heard him remember his thundering conviction: *"We will never surrender."*

Just after the attack on Russia, I went to Vilvorde for a long conversation with Jan. Our spirits were high. Hitler was committing suicide! At least that was the way we saw his Russian adventurism. Napoleon had made that mistake, securing his downfall in his attack on European Russia. Now Hitler had attacked not only Soviet Russia but, by doing so, Soviet Asia as well. It was by definition futile, as the Soviet republics extended from the Baltic to the Bering Sea and the Crimea. We used this latest news to fuel our hopes.

Jan's wife was expecting their first baby. Jan was in good shape and had regained the healthy complexion he had lost in the mine. His spirit was good and he liked his work at Chamebel. Among the things that were manufactured there were steel boxes. Jan had no idea what they were to be used for by the enemy but I asked him to take note of the company's production. It would be of interest to London when I passed the information along. I brought Jan further into my confidence regarding my growing activity in the resistance and asked him if he would agree to be my tacit backup, if needed. I explained to him what I meant. He would be my confidant, memorizing a very few addresses and code names of people to be contacted if anything should happen to me. He accepted, but made it clear that his help would be limited to that. Expecting a baby, he felt his responsibilities had changed. I fully understood. We resolved that Fernande, his wife, would be kept in total ignorance of our agreement. Invigorated by our talks, I returned home more committed than ever to continuing the fight for freedom. Where once our idealistic exchanges had been abstract, now I clearly saw that ideals required service to the cause of freedom, justice, the survival of reason.

I was convinced that the attack on Russia would be a drain on Germany, keeping forces involved in the east and perhaps relieving the pressure on the rest of us, certainly on England. Both Jan and I understood the need to undermine the Germans in Belgium through harassment. The more troops they had to deploy to keep us obedient, the more thinly stretched their resources.

Marcel Franckson, Jr., son of my father's friend of the same name, was also engaged in resistance with a few of his trusted friends. He was busy collecting arms from the enemy by attacking German soldiers at their love-

Marcel Franckson, Jr. (alias Martial), head of Group D.

making with Belgian prostitutes in the forest north of town. They usually attacked using pieces of rubber hose filled with lead pellets as truncheons and captured mostly pistols, stacking them in secure caches for future use.

Soon I was asked to perform another assignment for the OMBR, one that plunged me into total fear for weeks. I was asked to produce explosives for sabotage, including, if possible, dynamite. A young man who had been doing this in Ghent for the resistance had blown his family and himself to pieces. For the simple explosives, my answer was immediately positive for some were quite safe to produce if one was careful. But as regards dynamite, I had many reservations: the need for a safe place to work, the need for supplies whose origins could not be traced, the special tools required to fabricate nitroglycerine. I would also have to inquire into the many technical questions regarding the manufacture of dynamite before being able to answer.

Luckily I had a former classmate working at the Poudreries Royales de Belgique, a company that had manufactured explosives for the Belgian army and was now forced to do the same for the enemy. I knew I could trust him and approached him. He appeared dubious about my sanity when I put the question to him, however. His first reaction was to tell me I must have gone totally crazy even to think about it. Then he relaxed and said, well, yes, it might be possible, but would be extremely dangerous even in small batches of only a pound at a time. But, yes, it could be done if a person had the proper tools, good solid knowledge, and more than anything else, steel nerves. He promised to create a modus operandi for me and to give me sketches of many of the tools I would need for the work, using wood, rubber, copper wire, and nails. Friction heat and sparks had to be avoided at *all* costs. Once a batch was started, you could only breathe freely after the nitroglycerine had been thoroughly incorporated into the diatomaceous earth, transforming it into dynamite.

I recontacted him in a few days after he had prepared all the information I needed. Discussing the plan with the OMBR, I discovered that the "factory" would be located in the basement of a city school, in the middle of town, a building empty at night and on weekends except for the janitor, his wife, and son, who were acquainted with the plan and in agreement with it. My friend from the Poudreries then provided me with a way to obtain glycerine on the black market, no questions asked, but at black market prices. All was set. Soon, on late weekday afternoons, I would be at the school on the Rue des Capucins hiding in my basement, making various nitrate-based explosives. Dynamite, taking more time, was a weekend job even for one-pound batches.

What I did not know then, but learned only after the twentieth and final pound of nitro was finished, was that the custodian of the school was the OMBR chief! By the time I found that out, however, I could no longer have harmed him for he was in the hands of the gestapo, as I will relate in due course.

In that it was well-known at OMBR headquarters that I spoke fluent German and could be trusted, it was perhaps inevitable that I would next be approached about a spying job. I was asked to draw a complete and accurate plan of the military airport at Florenne, near Namur. The Germans were currently using it for small planes, but had plans to lengthen the runway to accommodate larger and faster planes. Their plans included eliminating acres of valuable forest and they were contacting wood merchants to obtain bids for the timber. The owner of a large dairy nearby was a member of my resistance group and kept an eye on the place from the third floor of his house. He realized that without entering the airport he would never be able to gain accurate information and asked for help. I studied the installation in the guise of a wood merchant equipped with the tools of the trade: tape, logbook, and a fast-acquired knowledge of lumber jargon. I took leave from work and spent two days in the woods being very observant. At night I was hosted by the dairyman and we compared notes.

As the Germans proceeded with their construction, the dairyman, aided by powerful binoculars which we provided, took daily notes of the work in progress. Putting it all together later, I was able to draw quite an accurate plan of the facility. I was given an appointment with an intelligence agent who was part of the chain to London. The appointment was set for two in the afternoon in a downtown café near the stock exchange. I was there early, the plans stowed carefully in my briefcase. As I waited, army trucks arrived to seal off the area for a thorough search. My contact, I learned later, arrived just at that moment and disappeared down a side street to avoid being snared in the net. In the midst of this hornet's nest, with very compromising documents in my possession, I looked rapidly for a way to get rid of my treasure. The Germans had learned a few tricks of their own and one of the first things they did was to make sure all public toilets were sealed, barring places that could be used to flush away evidence. All doors were guarded, forcing all of us to stay in the buildings we were in. Then, one by one, the buildings were emptied and the people sent out to be searched and checked. Adrenaline flowed in my system. My faculties multiplied. My brain raced through my options. I struggled to remain calm.

Opting at last to try to bluff my way out, I finished my drink—hoping it would not be my last—took my identity card from my wallet, and walked straight to the soldier guarding the door. Presenting my card with my thumb over the words *"en sciences,"* I told him in his own language that I was Dr. Bodson and had to be at my medical office for an emergency as soon as possible. Would he permit me to go directly to the head of the search party and explain my case? Impressed by the visible word "doctor" printed on my identity card, he accompanied me to the captain in charge. There I repeated the scenario. The captain, addressed in German, gave but a cursory glance to my identification and agreed to allow me to leave immediately, politely asking if I would travel by streetcar or if I needed a taxicab. I said that due to the delay, I would much prefer a taxicab. He sent for one, apologizing for the inconvenience. In the cab on the way home, my nerves gave out and I crumpled like a wet rag against the leather seat. Stopping the driver after a short while, I paid the fare and continued on foot, hoping the exercise would restore my spent nerves.

Contact was reestablished with the intelligence agent, and I was finally able to give him the full set of plans and information. Shortly thereafter the airfield plans reached their final destination and the Florenne airfield was soon the site of precision RAF bombing. It was blown off the military map for quite a while. Our friend at the dairy suffered only a few broken panes of glass. Thanks to him I would later acquire a few rare pounds of fresh butter that Mother salted for keeping.

While the Germans were engaged deep in Russia, moving toward Moscow and the Urals, the Free French forces fought in Syria against Vichy troops. The battle for North Africa came to a standstill as both sides were exhausted and halted to regroup. The British, aided by Australian resupply efforts, held Tobruk, but were surrounded by Rommel's men.

As the Germans along the Russian front reached the Don and the Crimea, U. S. President Franklin D. Roosevelt declared that Moscow would never surrender. Did he know something we could not? The theater of war now covered all of Europe and North Africa and was rapidly extending into the Middle East.

Before that summer was over, the OMBR again called upon my knowledge of chemistry. I was asked to investigate the possibility of developing an escape method for a car carrying copies of the clandestine monthly paper *La Libre Belgique,* a World War I underground publication that had now been resurrected. Printed in Brussels, it had to be disseminated throughout the country by car. Recently, I had been told, a delivery car had almost been overtaken in a chase between Brussels and Liège by a front-wheel-drive

Citroën gestapo car and had had a very hard time evading capture. The driver had only narrowly succeeded by throwing tire-puncturing devices on the road. The problem with this method was that it left evidence of underground resistance. My job was to design a noiseless, odorless, invisible, efficient "something" to make evasion safer and easier. It took days of pondering the parameters before the idea of a chemical smokescreen germinated in my brain. Was it a possible solution?

How did airplanes write advertisements in the sky? Among those I asked was my former army officer, pharmacist Captain Nicaise. Although he did not know the answer, he had a friend in the air force who might. His friend not only knew the answer, but also offered a free source of the material needed, titanium chloride. It is one of the rare metallic chlorides that is liquid when kept under pressure, but at atmospheric pressure becomes a gas. The compound was sold in steel cylinders. When the chloride came into contact with humid air, it decomposed and combined with the water creating gaseous hydrochloric acid and titanium dioxide, an opaque, white powder. After some experimentation, the engineering phase began. The car was stripped of its rear seat and the trunk partition removed. Two cylinders were installed, one of compressed air, one of titanium chloride, while the trunk was fitted with a flat tank that contained enough water to provide humidity when compressed air was bubbled through it. Into the same tank but above the water level came the titanium chloride and *voilà!* Out of the tank through a large exhaust pipe came the cloud of powder. Experimentation transformed the powder into a dense fog through which one could move but not see, even an inch away, so opaque was the air. We knew it should work and were anxious to put it to a test. We did not have to wait long. During another pursuit, our driver sped toward a sharp curve in the highway and just before entering it, opened both valves. Looking back for his pursuers, the driver saw nothing. The Citroën had continued straight ahead into the fog and collided with a tree. It was totally demolished, its occupants dead. A slight breeze removed the cause of the "accident."

Our group operated, like others, on very safe principles. Each sabotage idea that came to us was submitted to headquarters, discussed, and evaluated. For those found worth pursuing, means of realization were sought. Questions would eventually flow back down the echelons to provide insight and knowledge from the membership. For security, a project was never presented in its totality to members, but was fragmented for technical advice and manufacture. Only at the top did anyone have the complete picture. As a result, the lower echelon at times wondered if there was anybody able to think straight at the top.

But in our work we learned not to ask too many questions. Knowledge can be hazardous to your life. When this project was presented to me I was never told it was for moving bulk copies of *La Libre Belgique*. Only later, after having gained HQ's confidence, did I learn the ultimate destination of the vehicle and its use.

Soon after this project was finished, I was asked if I knew of a way to steal a large German army truck, a ten-ton model with double rear axles. I answered that perhaps I could, but I had to inquire. It would take days before I could give an answer.

Located on our street was a large body shop that before the war had fabricated car bodies to order, to fit deluxe chassis. Now forced to work for the enemy, the shop was doing body repairs and paint jobs on German army cars and trucks. I had known the owner well for many years, having paid him numerous visits to admire his work on one-of-a-kind cars. I approached him one evening at his residence near the shop. Bluntly I submitted the question, confident that I could trust him. He thought it would be possible but said he would have to look at lots of details.

The army delivered the trucks to him with a worksheet and when the repairs were done, an inspector would come and look at the work. Then the unit to which the vehicle belonged would send one or two men to drive it back to where it was needed. These soldiers would come to him with papers to take delivery and he would release the keys. All transactions were subject to paperwork and he needed to keep release forms for all vehicles leaving his place of business. If we could tell him the exact model needed, he would let me know when one came in and the probable finish date. We would need official papers to show his attendant in order for the truck to leave his shop. He would take care not to be present when the operation took place. He could, temporarily, provide original release forms that we could keep for a day in order to forge them for this and possible later projects. His involvement could be hidden if one or two German-speaking men came at the right time with the right papers. His office could then, with relative safety, release the keys in return for the proper forms, which would then be available for the inquiries that would certainly come later. It was primarily a question of precise timing and good forgeries.

Papers with stamps were no problem. We had already brought that to a state of perfection thanks to the personnel of the mint at the National Bank, and their printers and engravers. The most difficult problem was to obtain the necessary uniforms or to find one or two Germans to work with us. The second option was much too dangerous and the idea was quickly abandoned, which left us needing two German-speaking Belgians in German uniforms. The staff decided to proceed and organized the uniform collection. I volunteered to be a German-speaking chauffeur. The rest was organization and timing. It took weeks to prepare the affair. Four of our members ambushed two suitable Germans at night, clubbing and killing them. Their naked bodies were hastily concealed, their uniforms secreted away. This accomplished, I borrowed a set of release papers from the body shop owner and returned them a day later, being now in possession of a forged set. Then the uniforms were altered to fit and disguises provided to change our appearance: wigs, mustaches, glasses. We were now ready, waiting only for the next available truck. As it would take time for the repairs to be done, we would have a few days' advance notice before the final operation. A place to hide the truck had been carefully selected in a large warehouse in a quiet industrial suburb. At the body shop, finished cars and trucks, waiting to be driven away, were parked in the street along the curb. When the moment arrived, a signal was exchanged and the plan put in motion. Our truck driver and I rendezvoused not far away, walked together into the shop, and presented the release papers. Others we signed there and received a set of keys. Out we went— "Guten tag, auf wiedersehen"—and drove away. Concealing the truck and changing back into our work clothes, we returned to our places of employment.

Only after the war did I learn the fate of the truck. Its initial projected use was never achieved. It was supposed to be reinforced in the front and fitted with armor and strong steel arches under the tarp for a proposed attack on a political prison camp at Brendonck near Antwerp. The camp was in the country and protected mainly by a wooden tower equipped with searchlights and machine guns. The idea was to drive the truck through the tower base and force the structure down. For some reason the plan was abandoned, and the truck served only during the liberation of Brussels, after having been repainted and adorned with Secret Army markings.

About the time of the truck theft episode I renewed my acquaintance with a man I had met in Salmchâteau during the summer Jan and I had camped in Gustave Jacques' backyard—Gustave's son Loulou, who was a few years older than I. Recognizing each other and being distant cousins and members of the same resistance organization, we became very close.

As we moved further into what many considered to be an endless and

Loulou Jacques, head of evasion for OMBR.

hopeless war, we realized the odds were increasing against our success, but still we responded to as many of the Germans' terrible actions as we could with even more determined counteractions. Each time we pressured them, they reacted and we counterreacted. The same was true in Holland, France, and the other occupied countries.

In Paris, in the gestapo building on the plush Avenue Foch, a patriot had been arrested and questioned to no avail. His interrogator had devised a system intended to make the man divulge his secrets and then sell out his friends. A flat steel circular band fitted with screw plates was put around the prisoner's head. Pressure was slowly applied in order to break the skull bone into sections. The intention was not to kill, but to torture and induce talk.

Incredibly it did not achieve its intended goal, and the patriot kept his secrets. Not having succeeded, the Germans released their victim and he went home, no doubt followed by agents, whom he managed to lose. Along the way he alerted his friends before going home to die of cerebral hemorrhages.

The French underground shortly thereafter mounted a bold action. They wrote a letter to the chief of the Paris Gestapo and had it delivered one morning at eleven, promising to come at noon and take him prisoner. This, they declared, was to punish the gestapo for the tightening steel torture used on their comrade. There must have been an explosion of laughter in the building at the letter's reception. The Germans justly considered their office a fortress—two armed sentries outside, armed personnel inside. They were secure. But they were wrong. With daring audacity, four Citroën cars screeched to a halt at exactly twelve noon in front of the two sentries, who already lay dead on the sidewalk. The cars' occupants issued forth armed to the teeth and entered the building under the protection of rapidly firing arms, throwing grenades in the corridors as they passed. Capturing the bureau chief, they retreated the same way they had entered and disappeared into the maze of the city, in the middle of Paris, between the Bois de Boulogne and the Arc de Triomphe, in plain daylight. The gestapo chief's body was found a few days later in a coffin, sliced like a leg of smoked ham.

The Germans never used the device again.

Money for the OMBR and other groups was always a problem. It now became a major one. Our men in hiding had to be provided for. Everything had to be purchased at black market prices and our benevolent donors were running out of assets. They had given all they could. New donors were extremely hard to recruit and the OMBR was in a pinch. What came in through collections from friends was limited in supply and quickly used. A plan had to be developed. One of the easier ways to acquire money was theft, so thieves we became.

In Belgium, the postal service operates a postal checking system that works very much like a bank—individual account-holders maintain funds there—but the activity is restricted to fund transfers from account to account within the country. The service is free of charge and handles large amounts of money. The OMBR had among its members an insider in this service who masterminded our operation, the "coup," as we referred to it. Orchestrated under the guidance of our insider to take place on a Wednesday, the slowest day of the week at the checking service, a few initiated people executed the most famous hold-up in the history of the Belgian underground. Eight men under the disguise of postal employees would enter with our comrade-employee at the 8:00 A.M. opening hour. Simultaneously, a large number of patriots would surround the building and position themselves at all street intersections in the vicinity to provide armed protection for the escape cars. As our men entered the building, a truck would back up to a designated dock and deliver several large suitcases that would be brought inside through the service entrance, which would be open at that hour. In addition, two groups of three cars each were needed: one set to pick up the people from inside with their loot; the other two sets to organize relays to move men and money to safehouses. Eight men would be involved on the inside for fifteen to twenty minutes only. Later they could all arrive at their workplaces as usual at nine o'clock. The question of alibi was important, although the largest logistical problem was procuring the necessary weapons and ammunition. Those inside not only had to protect themselves, but also had to maintain calm among the real vault workers and prevent movement in certain parts of the building. The patriots on duty outside and the drivers of trucks and cars also needed protection. Security devices had to be disarmed. Telephone connections would be disrupted at the main exchange by a sympathetic friend, but only for twenty minutes. The extent and complexity of the intelligence required before any reasonably safe attempt could be undertaken was immense.

Weapons were acquired through the intense collaboration of various Brussels underground organizations. Each was promised part of the loot. Some provided people with guns, some provided only guns, which had to be returned later. Still we came up short of our needs if the men outside were to provide armed cover for the escape cars; I was to be one of those armed men. Accordingly, we decided to let the Germans help us.

Again we exploited the German weak point, manpower; citizens of the occupied countries were hired to fill nonmilitary jobs. Members of the underground applied to fill these positions when possible and so gained access to German installations. Thus we had learned through a cook we knew at Le Petit Château barracks that it had a gunshop taking care of nine-millimeter parabellums and ammunition. The underground had kept an eye on that shop for a long while. Now it was time to act. We had learned that in the evening a guard of four was stationed at the shop, but that two usually disappeared into town to have a good time. This was our chance. But how to get into the barracks, into the gunshop, and out again, we hoped with a heavy load? The answer was to use a German staff car and officers' uniforms of the highest possible rank. Along a quiet canal was a route regularly traveled by such prey as they moved officer personnel from a château in the suburbs to the headquarters in town. An ambush was set, the car stopped, its occupants disarmed, undressed, killed, and dumped. The new occupants, now impersonating Germans, secluded the car in a well-concealed garage until action day. As a few Aryan-looking men who spoke German were also needed to play the final scene, I became a German colonel for a few unforgettable hours. I had my own "chauffeur" who was a corporal, and my "secretary" was a captain. We also had a new general staff pennant ready to snap in the breeze.

After a few days we were ready to act. Near dusk we drove off toward the Petit Château barracks and presented ourselves at the gate, demanding, not asking, entrance to check the armory. The doors flew open and sure enough, there were only two guards present in place of the prescribed four. As the colonel, I forced the two into an office where it was not possible for them to see the outside activity and loudly and harshly interrogated the two miserable soldiers while my secretary and chauffeur raided the armory. They loaded twenty-nine parabellums with lots of ammunition into two burlap sacks and transferred them to the trunk of the idling car. My captain then came into the interrogation room and began taking notes, which was the signal for me to know that all had gone well and it was time to depart. We did not prolong our stay with the terrified guards, but made our way out without the slightest problem. We crossed town to our hidden garage twenty-nine guns richer—guns that would arm our friends for the raid on the post office vaults.

A week later at the vaults, the action also went like clockwork, and not a shot was fired. Ten large suitcases of money were handed out through the small service entrance. Several minutes after everybody's departure, the phone lines were reconnected and the first alarm was given.

That same evening, in a classroom of a city school, we were busy counting money—lots of money, nearly fourteen million francs, the largest coup in Belgian underground history, and all for a good cause.

As we neared the end of the count, one of our group came in with a livid face and a copy of the German-controlled paper *Le Soir.* On the front page was an article about our morning action and a list of the serial numbers of the stolen notes. The notes were now useless! All that for nothing! When we recovered from the shock, we checked the list against the notes in our possession. The list was totally false. Not a single note in our possession carried a published number. Later I learned that the head of the postal checking unit was persuaded under pressure by the Germans to give them a list of the serial numbers of the stolen notes. Sensing this was not a common burglars' job, he furnished them with a list that had been totally fabricated in order to protect us and give our loot full market value. As an added bonus, the Germans were now on a wild chase for money that had never been printed.

Much later in the war there was another coup, this one a masterly effort in nonviolent resistance. On November 9, 1943 (not that I remember the exact date, but I still own a copy reprinted after the war), came an outrageous joke in print. *Le Soir* was and still is the leading Belgian evening paper. As soon as the Germans occupied our country *Le Soir* was closed, soon to be reopened under new management. All the old staff quit their jobs, except for one. Immediately, fed by the Berlin news agency, *Le Soir* began its campaign of lies and half-truths. Its circulation fell drastically, but it stayed open. Even biased news is better than no news at all.

In that late fall of 1943, during the long period of waiting for D-day, times grew increasingly hard. Food was rationed down to 650 calories a day (in 1944 it fell to the wartime low of 450 calories a day). Morale was low and the falling temperature in the humid climate of Belgium made the town even gloomier. Mist, rain, and cold penetrated our ever shabbier garments. Mostly, we accustomed ourselves to wet feet. Leather was unavailable and resoling could hardly be had. We tried to prolong our soles' usefulness by gluing old soles, whole or in pieces, onto those getting thin. It was not uncommon to meet people wearing wooden shoes. They reminded me of those I had worn during World War I when I was a young boy of five in the terrible, terrible winter of 1917.

A group of patriots led by a master printer conceived the inconceivable: editing, printing, and distributing a complete but totally false edition of *Le Soir*. With the full cooperation of the newspaper's delivery drivers, they planned to hijack the paper's delivery trucks, empty them of their contents in a distant park, refill them with the pirate edition, and then allow the trucks to continue on their normal delivery routes. We are talking about thirty trucks!

That, however, was but a minor consideration compared to the technical problems. There were not many presses that could be used to print a newspaper and they were of only two types. Each type was easily recognized by the deformations it produced in the printed material. If experts examined it, the special issue had to confuse them. This was done by introducing both types of character deformations into the pirate edition. Later, when the gestapo called in their expert printers, they were unable to reach a consensus about the type of machine used. Their impossible search never led them to the source.

The paper was distributed at the normal time and locations in the afternoon of November 9. When the paper hit, it was a bombshell for the Germans. To Belgians, it arrived like an unexpected fireworks display exploding with hope and humor on a gloomy November evening, two days short of the anniversary of the end of World War I.

The next day, a Wednesday, was stock exchange day in Brussels. *Le Soir* was quoted and traded at the equivalent of seventy-five dollars a copy! Later in 1944, after liberation, a second edition was made and sold to benefit the families of underground members who had been victims of the Nazis.

It is now nearly impossible to convey the humor contained in the text of that paper. Most of it satirized the daily German "War Communiqué." Italians were lampooned as their untrustworthy allies. It ridiculed the Germans in their futile attempt to crush an ever more active underground practicing bolder and bolder acts. It also announced an increase in bread rations thanks to "an abundant crop in Ukraine." Tobacco rationing, it promised, would soon get much better, and two brands would be offered in place of one. Coming soon!—Shit A and Shit B. This was made possible through an intimate collaboration between the Germans and the Belgian League of Equestrian Defecation. Shit A would be of male origin; Shit B, the milder of the two, of female origin. The new smoking material was the product of selected animals: Stalingrad Victor, New Order of Berchtesgaden, Melitopol Rubber, Flattened Hamburg, Morne Plaine (an allusion to the Waterloo battlefield in Victor Hugo's famous description), and Berlin Capitulation. Following was a long list of formalities to be completed in order to secure a small amount of the upcoming brown windfall.

On the society page, there was an article explaining that the Belgian traitor-collaborator Leon Degrelle had been cuckolded by a German officer named Ottokar von Schweinhund. The entertainment section reviewed the movies of the week: *Red October*, a saga of the advancing Russian front; *From El Alamein to Sidi Barani*, with Rommel in the main role; *New Tears*, starring General Speers; a great ballet called *Catastrophe*, featuring the flying fortresses. The theater section contained an item announcing that the Park Theater, closed for remodeling, would open soon with *Rule Britannia*. In the want ads section several tailors advertised cheap "coat-turning." Funeral homes offered sales on coffins. A private individual advertised a large touring car with enough gas to reach the Swiss border. The Belgian attorney general, in London exile, wanted to purchase gibbets and guillotines.

The ongoing, spontaneous generation of jokes was an interesting phenomenon. They would suddenly appear and elate us, make us feel better, and even at the darkest of times generate a smile. Just as suddenly, with the advent of good news, they disappeared as if not needed when our morale had been boosted.

By actively opposing the overwhelming destructive power of the Nazis, resistance members greatly increased their exposure to possible self-destruction. The Germans did not sustain their occupation of our country without feeling even our early feeble blows. They were brutes, but they had brains and they hunted us. Some of us had already been arrested on suspicion; others, gun in hand, were caught in acts of sabotage. The Germans knew we had acquired a few guns. Their men had lost guns to patriot attackers using only bare hands or makeshift weapons. They also knew there was an organized resistance movement and they actively searched it out.

As they devoted more men and more time to the search, the risk to us increased. Reluctantly, we had to recognize that it was becoming advisable to carry a gun for protection during all our actions. Even my pacifist father agreed with that. Ever more dreadful news was circulated about the gestapo's methods of interrogation to extract information from suspects. Horrible, cruel methods opposed to all the rules of decency and law. I never heard of the Paris method being used in Belgium, but they used many others, equally cruel, equally degrading, and very effective. So many people died under interrogation that the Germans changed their methods. Stopping just short of death, they allowed prisoners to recuperate enough for the torture to start all over again.

Some prisoners cracked, letting the pieces go, giving names and places. I do not blame them; it was too much to endure. They let go as an animal act of survival, so enfeebled that they did not even know what they were doing. I like to think I am strong and can tolerate pain, but what I cannot say is that I would be able to withstand such unrelenting torture. As soon as I began carrying a gun regularly, I decided that the last bullet would be for me; that if possible, I would take my life and leave the Germans with a speechless body, a mute witness. Recognizing that perhaps I was not as strong as I might like to believe, I vowed that my personal weakness would never endanger the lives of my friends. More, I would not give the Germans an opportunity to destroy what had taken us so long to build, or be the cause of our losing the little armament that had cost us so much time and pain to assemble. My capture would not interrupt the fight that would only end with the destruction of the beast that was upon us. And by that I clearly meant the survival of intelligence, humanity, civilization.

CHAPTER 6

▼

Protected by a Gun

.

The 1941–42 winter was fast approaching when the great post office hold-up took place. Brussels grew sadder and more somber as cold, gray days returned and the war continued unabated.

In North Africa, Rommel was again on the offensive, trying to eliminate the British presence at Tobruk. He pushed toward Egypt and we again feared a German success that would close the Suez Canal and create even greater problems for Britain. German control of Egypt would greatly lengthen Allied supply lines to India and Australia, dooming Tobruk. The bombing of Malta resumed.

On December 7, 1941, the Japanese attacked Pearl Harbor and two more continents entered the war, Asia and North America. As the significance of these events settled into our thinking, we became frightened; with the entire world now at war, the prospect of total annihilation crouched evilly in the shadows of our minds.

Yet, on the other hand, we realized the industrial might of the United States. The attack on Pearl Harbor had changed the opinion of the American public and allowed the American president to act. But in Europe we feared other factors: would or could the Americans give us their wholehearted support while still protecting their interests in the Pacific and expecting attacks on their own west coast? As we debated these new events, London announced Rommel's retreat from Egypt and into the desert back toward Tobruk, the British in pursuit. Egypt, for the time being, seemed safe again. Although the old year ended in apparent calm, we did not think of celebrating the new. We had nothing with which to celebrate. Our food situation grew increasingly difficult. Food coupons went unused as the stores had no merchandise with which to honor them. The Germans, extended fully along the Russian front, pushed conscription to the limits. Millions were to be fed at our expense. Their factories needed manpower and we, the occupied countries, would deliver our forced labor. Nineteen forty-two was a year of massive deportations.

Fuel was difficult to obtain and the poor, carrying bundles of dead wood from the forests to help alleviate the shortage of coal, were a common sight. At home, to conserve the little we had left in the coalbin, we dressed ourselves in more clothes, and allowed the temperature to drop another few degrees. Although young Belgian and French communists were now actively entering the resistance and our OMBR movement recruited more men, we lacked armament and found that our work was confined to the more and more active field of intelligence. Though some sabotage was possible, it was not without great peril. German reprisals grew steadily harsher and more ruthless. We were caught between the desire to harm our occupiers and the necessity of not endangering the lives of our countrymen. The Germans did not hesitate to use mass deportations or take hostages, whom they simply shot if they could not locate the perpetrators of actions against them. We soon arrived at the conclusion that subversion by destruction was only possible in open country, far away from population centers and always displaying great professionalism—something only a foreign saboteur might have engineered. Our actions, thus limited, concentrated on attacking power lines and on disrupting rail communications by dropping explosives and incendiary devices on passing trains from overpasses. For demolitions, we had a good supply of explosives recovered from unspent or stolen shells, especially army shells from which we could also recover fuses. Supplies of all sorts were in short supply and, once located, their prices were astronomical. Money was a constant problem, and the threat of deportation hung over all our heads. More and more people known to the gestapo were forced underground and had to be fed and supported. Employment for them was out of the question.

Thanks to my own employment, I had access to pyrotechnic materials in the form of phosphorus, sodium, and potassium metals at reasonable prices. I had by now become a trusted member of the OMBR and personally knew the chief, a man in his early sixties and a World War I veteran. Though not a man of great intellect, he was a born organizer and a patriot and as the caretaker of the Rue des Capucins school, he avoided suspicion entirely. His brother was an active member of his staff. They were the Soetens brothers.

As winter deepened, the news of battle lessened as the combatants dug in, resupplied, stockpiled, and prepared for the spring offensive.

At work, conditions were difficult. Stock dwindled away to nothing in some areas, and we could not resupply. It appeared certain that personnel would soon be laid off, and we were asked to look actively for employment. In late 1941, at the request of a former classmate, I had equipped a laboratory created to study war replacement products that could act as war substitutes. The small new company had a good financial backer and I was offered a managerial position, which I gladly accepted. At that moment, anything was better than unemployment, which would mean deportation and direct work for the enemy. I wanted to stay in Brussels and keep active in underground.

Having joined this new company, I soon became responsible for locating stocks of merchandise that it would eventually purchase at vastly inflated prices. We made ersatz toothpaste that we sold to the German army at spectacular profit. In due course it became apparent to me that my friendly classmate and his Rexist backer were clearly working for the enemy and were without conscience, merely using the opportunity to make money. That conclusion did not please me, but had one advantage: I was now working for a collaborator and was thus protected from deportation.

I worked evenings and weekends for the resistance with increased determination to do all I could to undermine the enemy. In addition, my underground group gave me the new responsibility of locating and training a young, intelligent Belgian and persuading him to enter a Belgian pro-German organization as a spy. The organization was a paramilitary outfit recruiting young men just out of school and organizing them into work battalions to help the Germans within our geographical boundaries. Its main activity consisted of clearing bomb-damaged sites and restoring them to working condition. The *Volontaires du Travail* or "work volunteers" dealt mostly with bombed airports, bombed barracks, and other military installations. The young man was introduced to our group staff and under my guidance began to feed us the information we wanted. He also supplied us with their forms, letterheads, personnel lists, organizational details, and whatever else we might need. Through him we obtained superb intelligence on the condition of bombed airports, information that we immediately sent to London. From the stolen documents we duplicated signatures and seals and created documents for our own use. We learned about their stock rooms and garages and could then steal uniforms and even a car and motorcycle which would be used on several occasions, first by the OMBR and later by a sabotage organization called Service Hotton, of which more later.

I acquired a split personality, working by day as the enemy's helper, Dr. Jekyll, and in my free time working to destroy that enemy as Mr. Hyde. It is nearly impossible to describe the confusion of feelings that assailed me during that period. I felt burning shame upon meeting friends who knew for whom I worked; guilt on pay days because of the infamous origin of the money that sustained my life; blameworthiness and self-reproach when entering German offices to discuss business deals; chivalrous patriotism while assembling incendiary devices; pride in using my intelligence to design untraceable stratagems to trick the Germans; and self-esteem when looking back at my achievements in the fight against this occupier. At times I thought myself to be in a temporary situation, that somehow I would find occasion to extricate myself from what was rapidly becoming a nightmare.

With the onset of May, 1942, London and the local press reported new battles in North Africa. Rommel attacked out of his lair west of Tobruk, was stopped temporarily, then resumed his offensive. He conquered the Tobruk fortress and rushed toward Egypt again. Through the summer and early fall the news from North Africa was a litany of attacks and counterattacks; brief periods of calm were followed by vicious assaults until October, when British General Montgomery took command and inflicted on the Germans a defeat from which they did not recover. By November we had reached the turning point. The Allies, landing in French Morocco, nearly destroyed the Axis contingent, forcing the remnants of Hitler's Afrika Korps to retreat into Tunisia.

The French navy berthed in Toulon scuttled itself when it became known that the Germans were occupying all of France. Despite great effort, De Gaulle had been unable to persuade the French navy to join the Allied cause, but at least we knew they would now not join the Axis forces either.

England, hard at work and relatively quiet at home, was fighting U-boats in the Atlantic for control of the sea lanes. Air attacks decreased as the efficient RAF shot down German plane after German plane, while Germany concentrated tremendous effort on the Russian front and the fighting in North Africa. Americans, fighting in the Far East, were, after many losses, slowly regaining a toehold in the Pacific. They also did what they could to help the Chinese—politically divided between the rightist Chang Kaishek regime and Mao's communists, and headed toward civil war. With American help in the Atlantic, the situation at year's end had almost reversed itself and the U-boats, although still there in numbers enough to harass, no longer controlled any sea lanes.

The end of 1942 thus brought provisional good news from the Atlantic, slight hope from the Pacific, and definite proof that Britain had passed from the defensive to a successful offensive in Africa. That demoralizing seesaw desert fight had finally ended with the Americans landing there. But still

Belgian morale was low, and would have been even lower had it not been for an episode in Brussels that punctuated that summer with heroism.

In the spring of 1942, a prominent citizen had been arrested by the gestapo, questioned, and shot. This event made national news. One of the victim's sons was a Belgian air force pilot who had been lucky enough to take to the air in the middle of the bombardment of his air base. He had joined the British and was now a member of a British Spitfire squadron. Knowing of his father's fate, the young airman carefully planned his revenge. One day, in July of 1943, the opportunity to put his plan into action arose. His squadron had been given a mission over occupied Belgium. He took off with his comrades, participated in the mission, and then flew off on his own for Brussels, a city he knew well, since it was his home. His target, the main gestapo building on Avenue Louise, was a six-story-high requisitioned apartment complex with a cream-colored limestone facade facing east, with four large windows per floor. Coming from the west, the pilot was able to see the building from quite a distance as it faced the wide Avenue De Mot and the adjacent Parc de la Cambre. Approaching over the suburban community of Ixelles and flying at rooftop level to avoid early detection, the pilot could easily aim at the building and direct the fire of his wing guns at its base. Continuing his fire while pulling on the joystick, he sprayed the complex from basement to roof with a murderous hail of explosive bullets. He even managed to drop a wreath with his beloved father's name on it on the pavement fifty yards from the building before disappearing into the clouds and speeding back to his field command.

Later, after liberation, we learned that the pilot was Jean de Selys Longchamps. Upon landing, he had been arrested and jailed for having abandoned his squadron. But in those days of radio communication news traveled fast, and two days later he was released with the coveted Distinguished Flying Cross pinned to his uniform.

The gestapo building sustained extensive damage, some of it still evident after the war. To repair the major damage, the Germans recalled all of the contractors who had been involved in the original construction, one of which was the Chamebel company, responsible for the metal windows. Chamebel also happened to be the place where my friend Jan worked; thus he called me on July 22 and reported that he had been asked by his company to go to the building and investigate what had to be done to effect repairs immediately. Would I be interested in accompanying him disguised as a Chamebel foreman? Needless to say, I was very interested. Presses started rolling to forge the false papers I would need, such as a Chamebel employment card and a metal construction union card. I duly became a Chamebel foreman. The next day I toured the bomb site with my engineer. It was unbelievable the damage those little explosives had done. I particularly remember a third-floor office, a major's office. One bullet had entered his mahogany desk and exploded, temporarily adding the major to the plastering job. By the time we arrived he had already been scraped away. How many German agents died that day I was not able to tell, but from the evidence of the damage, quite a few. All the big shots had offices in the front of the building looking out on the Avenue De Mot and the park beyond.

The attack had taken place around ten in the morning while the building was fully lit by the rising spring sun. Not one bullet had hit adjacent constructions. People rushed to the site to look. The Avenue Louise was packed with onlookers, among whom German troopers shouted orders to move quickly on. From mothers with strollers to the elderly, all wanted their part in the scene. Streetcars passing in front were loaded with curious and happy faces. The morale boost for us was immense, for the pilot had demonstrated that the Germans were vulnerable and unable to exercise complete control of the air space. They also could be victims.

The day of the attack was a day of joy. That week, while the news was told around the country, was a week of joy. We were not alone. We were the oppressed, we were the victims, but across the North Sea we had friends, friends who cared and were ready to help.

My company had now developed an ersatz product to substitute for the oil needed in metal-cutting machines and I traveled extensively through Belgium promoting the product in the industrial areas of Charleroi and Liège. On those trips I saw steady deterioration in the working population's health, intense fatigue showing on people's faces, and many undernourished people.

I stayed in close contact with Jan, who, disenchanted with his work at Chamebel, was actively looking for a change. He was unhappy about his health. His diabetes, although under control, was a weight on his mind. He told me of his plans to move to the country, to the Ardennes he had known through me and during the preparation of his university thesis. His idea was to create a small company that would mine sandstone and manufacture grindstones. He had already renewed contact with Gustave Jacques in Salmchâteau and, with help from my father and others, had formed a group of interested investors. He hoped to be able to move to the Ardennes and live in a rural environment at a pace more suitable to his condition, away from the pressures of his German-oriented industry.

Earlier, during that summer, I had learned that my friend Marcel

Jan Van der Borght and his oldest daughter, in Honvelez, 1943.

Franckson, Jr., had left Brussels to escape German capture and was in the Ardennes organizing a resistance group in the Baraque de Fraiture area.

Early in September London gave us extraordinary news, adding to our hopes of liberation. British and Canadian troops had crossed the Strait of Messina and landed in southern Italy, establishing a foothold at Regio in south Calabria. The Germans resisted and soon battles raged. But the Allied forces were determined and soon, reinforced by more troop landings and paratroopers, German resistance weakened and the Allies were on the march north through the heel of the Italian boot. On September 9, the Brit-

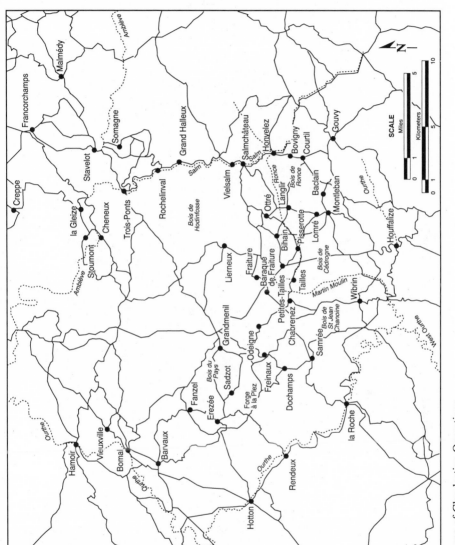

Area of Clandestine Operations

ish First Airborne landed around Taranto and began to progress northward. On September 15 the Allied forces seemed to have gained significant advantage and our hopes rose higher yet. The Allies were in Europe! And the Germans seemed to be offering only enough resistance to allow themselves an orderly retreat. Meanwhile, Sardinia and then Corsica were liberated by the Free French troops who began landing there on October 3, just two days after Naples had fallen into Allied hands.

In southern Italy the former king, with Marshal Pietro Badoglio, had formed a government for liberated Italy. Mussolini had gone north, where the situation had become very confused. It seemed the Italian troops were rebelling and being disarmed by the Germans. A civil war was developing and Italian resistance units began operating against the Germans. In the Balkans, as well as in Greece which had until now been under Italian control, the Germans had to send more of their own troops to take over. This meant that the Germans had to move troops from the southern Russian front, and they soon were on the defensive there also. On October 13, the Italian king declared war on Germany and, most importantly, gave the order for the Italian navy to join the Allied side, which gave the Allies complete control in the Mediterranean. On September 22, a new Allied debarkation had taken place at Bari along the Adriatic, followed by another at Termoli on October 3. Now the Allies were able to push even farther north along both Italian coasts, the Mediterranean and the Adriatic. German resistance stiffened as more troops were brought in.

In the underground, October brought the disturbing news that Marcel Franckson, Jr., and his group had been attacked in the Ardennes in a villa my father had rented for them near Manhay. Luckily, most of them had escaped. My own underground activity was concentrated on two objectives—incendiary devices and establishing more contacts for Loulou Jacques, who was actively building the OMBR escape line. Safehouses were organized in Mons and Liège and people running those in turn organized other safehouses nearby.

Air activity was increasing steadily over Belgium and northern France. Our own industrial sites were now subject to Allied bombings and more raids were crippling Germany. Loulou was kept busier by the week taking care of an ever-increasing number of downed airmen. At work, when in town, I was in frequent business contact with the German purchasing authorities. On occasion German officers would come to our office to discuss deals and I would be called in to translate.

I had been asked repeatedly by the OMBR to look for money and had not been able to generate any, but in early November an occasion presented itself. The Germans had come into our office to conclude a deal and a large amount of cash was stashed in the safe while they went out for lunch with the boss. I had to finish some paperwork so I stayed a little past noon and checked everything before closing the door behind me. Realizing that the safe had not been locked, I carefully inspected the contents: 150,000 francs in large denominations. It did not take long to transfer the bills into my attaché case, being careful not to leave any fingerprints.

I went to a safehouse and left a parcel with urgent orders to transfer it to my organization's staff. Then I ate a quick lunch and was back at the office at my usual time. The bosses, returning from a long lunch, discovered the theft. Everybody was asked, nobody knew. The police were called in, and the wheels of Belgian justice began to turn. Dusting the safe for fingerprints revealed only those of the boss.

He had to admit that the safe had not been properly secured. The absence of safety locks on the office doors was also pointed out by the investigators. I had the impression that the boss suspected me, but as far as the police were concerned it could have been anybody's work, insider or outsider. The police investigation did not shed any light on the case. Two days later I received an unexpected visit from Rex police agents at home. They were looking for me but when Dad answered the door, he talked to them facing the intercom and I was listening at the other end. I disappeared from the rear of the house through the garden to a neighbor's house. From that day, I did not return home, although I stayed in town. Dad inquired as to which prosecutor had been assigned the case. The answer was extremely favorable—the prosecutor was a patriot who could be trusted. I made contact and managed to meet him away from his office, declared the truth, and gave him the opportunity to check that the total amount had been duly transferred to my organization. Soon I learned that the case had been closed for lack of evidence. Nevertheless I still had to be very careful. The day of the theft I was notified that my employment was terminated. I had expected that and could foresee conscription by the Werbestelle into a forced labor assignment. It would be nearly impossible to find a job quickly enough to prevent my deportation.

As if it were not enough to lose my job, more bad news followed. OMBR chief François Soetens had been arrested at the school in midmorning. Late in the afternoon the gestapo returned for his wife and seventeen-year-old

Nom **BERNARD**

Prénoms **HENRI - LUCIEN**

Adresse **HONVELEZ - BOVIGNY**

Carte d'identité No **2567**

Commune de **BOVIGNY**

au

Service des Volontaires
du Travail
pour la Wallonie

en qualité de **CHEF DE CHANTIER**

CERTIFICAT
DE
TRAVAIL

No **1981**

(valable sur la présentation de la
carte d'identité mentionnée ci-contre)

No de Matricule **43.05.713**

Délivré par le chef du camp

d'accueil le **13 - 11 - 43**

SIGNATURE,

REMARQUE IMPORTANTE : Quelle que soit
la durée de validité du présent certificat, le titu-
laire est tenu, en cas de cessation de fonctions,
de le restituer sans délai au S. V. T. W.

Falsified work card in the name of Henri-Lucien Bernard and dated
November, 1943.

son. Mrs. de Neef was released a few days later but father and son were sent
to German concentration camps. The son returned in 1945; François died
in exile.

It was now essential to put some distance between myself and the Germans. A solution was already at hand for that eventuality. Jan, successful in
his new grindstone venture, had moved to Honvelez-Bovigny in the Ardennes and had previously indicated that he would shelter me if need be. I
readied myself for exile and, through Marcel Franckson, Sr., learned that I
could reorganize from Honvelez the group his son had formed but had been
forced to abandon after the Manhay engagement with German police forces.
Another plus was that Honvelez was close to Salmchâteau, where Loulou's
father lived and operated slate quarries. During those days of preparation I
lived with friends, never staying more than two nights in one place. Thanks
to my connections, it was not long before I had false identity papers that
would at least temporarily protect me. I became Henri Bernard (it is wise to

keep your own initials as you may inadvertently carry some old mono-grammed possession).

On December 3, Dad let me know that the Werbestelle summons had arrived. I was to present myself there on December 7 at 2:00 P.M. After much thought and consultation with friends, I decided to accept the German invitation because I now had a plan in place to disappear from view.

How vividly I remember my appointment that December afternoon. I was taken into a German major's office. He addressed me as Dr. Herman Bod-son. He knew I had a chemistry degree, that I had served in the lab at the military hospital, and that I was fluent in German. He offered me a position in a German army hospital lab in Norway—good pay, good food, officer's privileges. I politely declined the invitation, telling him that my military ex-perience had ended the day of my discharge in France. The major's pleasant attitude changed abruptly to Prussian arrogance as he told me I had no choice. As an unemployed worker, I would work for the German war effort, and if not as a chemist, then as a common laborer. He called an attendant who moved me quickly in front of a sergeant's desk. There I was informed that I would receive papers to join the common labor force in Leipzig. Sev-eral forms were filled in and a one-way ticket to Germany was handed to me. Next came coupons for a blanket, a pair of overalls, and a pair of leather work shoes. I was to report on December 12 at 7:00 A.M. to the south railway station. An hour after entering the major's office, I was on the Rue de Namur sidewalk wondering how the major was so well informed. Only one explana-tion made sense: I had been "recommended" by my former employer.

I decided to play the German game to the end and acquired the goods for which I had received the coupons, compliments of the Third Reich. I had learned that the Germans were not checking names at the departure point and I never took the train. My parents anxiously inquired as to my where-abouts two weeks after my "departure" and regularly thereafter. The Ger-mans were unable to provide any information and weeks later finally and brutally told my parents that, as far as they knew, I could have been wounded or even killed by Allied bombs. They had no way of knowing. For the Wer-bestelle I was lost or dead. At least to some, Bodson was dead.

It was time to become the guest of the Van der Borght family in Honvelez and take up my employment as Henri Bernard, a foreman in Jan's quarry. My new identity registration was transferred to Honvelez, and soon I was officially receiving food coupons and paying pension money under my new name. I had become a legal illegal.

In Brussels the Germans' investigation had not stopped. New developments which Dad reported to me were beyond my worst apprehensions. He had received information indicating that the Brussels Gestapo were after me. My picture was appearing on the screen at the Monday morning briefing of agents. The caption read in translation: "Very dangerous communist terrorist, always armed, parabellum 9 mm." I wished I owned such a wonderful weapon, but was happy enough to have a beautiful 7.65 mm FN (caliber. 22) Browning on loan from Loulou. I was also very happy to be well away from the German hunting dogs.

Jan had rented a new house from the local mayor. At that time, it had no water and was located at the top end of Honvelez village. He also rented an old dairy building to house two lathes that were used to shape the stones. The quarry was seven miles away in the valley of the Salm River. As Jan had no car, all errands had to be done on foot or by bicycle. In Jan's house were three bedrooms—theirs, where the little baby had her crib, one for their older daughter, and one for me. As we had agreed, Jan's wife was kept in ignorance of my situation. She knew only that I was trying to avoid the Werbestelle. My arrangement with Jan was that I would work at the shop and the quarry to earn my keep. I could take time off if I had an "errand" to run, but then would work late or on weekends to catch up.

Soon I contacted Marcel, Jr.'s former men and was working hard at rebuilding the group, even enlarging it, as well as at organizing a local escape net using the same men plus some independents. Each of these would in turn spread the word among trusted friends and relatives. I knew the area well enough, having spent many vacations there. Members of Dad's godfather's family were in Statelot, Vielsalm, and Salmchâteau only four miles away. I was not alone. I had excellent old contacts and ready references. Marcel had prepared a complete list of his locals and had even given me the names of all his contacts. Quickly I located an old bicycle that I fixed up for transportation. I could count on Loulou's financial help and was preparing for a second and very different type of underground activity. From Brussels, I knew that a secret army had been formed, an all-volunteer army without uniforms but under Allied supervision, to play a role at the moment of liberation. It existed all over the country and had ways to contact the Ardennes group. But this lay in the future. First I would rebuild a solid group on my own. December flashed by with all this activity.

Even so I gained weight, thanks to Fernande's excellent meals. In the rural Ardennes setting, life was certainly easier than in town. A small garden supplied greens and local farmers had potatoes and grains available, if you knew

*The proper caliber is .32 ACP (ie. Automatic Colt Pistol) designed by John Browning for FN (ie. Fabrique Nationale in Belgium).

them. Stores were depleted of goods here too, but the land still produced the essentials. Meat could be obtained from the local butcher and supplements could be purchased at reasonable prices from farmers. The only missing items were those not locally produced, such as sugar and coffee. Compared to city dwellers and considering the war, we ate like kings. As for the Germans, we saw few of them unless we went to small towns like Vielsalm where there was a local *Feldgendarmerie* and some infantry occupying the former Chasseurs Ardennais barracks in nearby Rencheux.

For news, living in an isolated house, we could safely listen to Radio London. December of 1943 was marked by battles in Italy. The Allies were blocked on their way to Rome by a well-organized German front at a point roughly halfway between Naples and Rome, in the little town of Ortona on the Adriatic. Near the end of the month, on December 27, London announced the sinking of the last unit in the German navy, the pocket battleship *Scharnhorst*. Out of a Norwegian fiord, she had attacked a well-protected British convoy and had been engaged by cruisers and destroyers. The *Norfolk* was hit, but escaped. The *Scharnhorst* then disengaged but was spotted on the radar of the *Duke of York* and was attacked again. The German battleship sank with nearly two thousand men on board; only thirty-six survived. The sea, save the U-boats, now looked good. It was the first time since 1940 that we faced the new year with eager anticipation. At Jan's house we had food and prepared in the warmth of friendship to celebrate the presence of the Allies in Europe. We distantly perceived the possibility of an Allied offensive through France. After three long years of bleak occupation, our hopes were rising. And after the close call in Brussels, I felt relatively secure out in the country.

As for my resistance group, after just weeks in Honvelez I had only good news. All of Marcel's men had responded to my call and a few others had indicated willingness to join. I had ordered three portable sheds to be built at a local sawmill to move, disassembled, into the woods. Word that the group was ready to accept downed Allied airmen was spreading, and we needed somewhere safe for them.

Doing all I could to help my friends and in the process getting quite fit, I fetched water from the communal well a hundred feet downhill from the house, using two buckets suspended from a yoke, and I split wood—tasks that would transform this city dweller into a sturdy rural man. Running errands on long bicycle rides through hilly country completed the transformation. Although I began to consider myself a good outdoorsman, I also realized I had a lot to learn from members of the group. Some were former

Christian Mannie (Kid), spring, 1944, in the Ardennes woods wearing a U.S. Air Force uniform.

Chasseurs Ardennais, others were poachers and hunters. From them I learned how to travel through the woods leaving minimal tracks, and how to interrupt a scent by walking in a brook or river, even if it meant getting wet and cold feet.

At the end of January, 1944, Christian Mannie, spotted by Germans while fighting in Marcel's group, arrived to join mine. He was not alone. Dad had been unable to alert me in time that, via Loulou, he was sending another fugitive, Charles de Greef of OMBR, who had to go into hiding from the ever more attentive German police. For safety, it had been decided that they would leave the train at Salmchâteau, south of Honvelez, then travel on foot from there guided by an escort I provided. They would come to the woods and live in one of the forest shelters we had assembled and camouflaged for precisely such use. When Charles told me he had participated in capturing a German staff car and its occupants' uniforms prior to the theft of pistols at Le Petit Château, I knew I had a fine recruit, a man of courage. Charles had been a former craftsman at the maintenance division of the Brussels tramway company. The Germans had seen him throwing incendiary devices on a passing German train. He was in danger and a great security risk for the others.

I could now count on twenty-one men still able to live on their farms and two in the woods, while I occupied an in-between category. My tasks grew more complicated, as I now had to provide for my two illegals who were totally deprived of official status, and had to put some men in charge of providing food on a regular basis. Mayor Faisant from Bovigny provided food stamps; farmer members of the group provided bread, butter, and meat. I also delegated some work to men who had family connections over the border. Belgium had two counties populated with predominantly German-speaking people, Eupen and Malmédy. In 1940 Germany had declared these counties part of the Reich and the former border was moved around them to the west, close to the Honvelez area.

It was very possible that Allied airmen would bail out over those counties and, although they were officially in Germany, we might be able to bring them out. My recruiters' main task was to contact their families over the border and to organize the first echelon of our escape line. I would be the second, Liège the third, and OMBR the fourth, moving them farther along through Loulou's organization. The men successfully recruited twenty people who would let other trusted ones know. Only the future would eventually reveal the efficiency of our dangerous efforts. Of necessity, these activities took some of my daytime hours, but mostly my evenings under the cover of winter's early darkness. During the day, I worked for Jan at the quarry or at the shop below the house, close to the welcome woodstove.

As I became known in the area, I could even venture through Salmchâteau to the town of Vielsalm where Jan got supplies. One day Jan asked me to get some fuses. He told me there was only one electrical supply store in town, owned by Charles Legros. If Charles did not have what I needed, he would get it in Liège where he went weekly. Two customers stood in front of me when I entered Legros' store and as I awaited my turn, a door at the far end of the shop opened and a woman came in. "Manou!" she said—a nickname by which very few knew me. I went straight to her and explained softly that I had a new identity and she had better call me Henri from now on. I nudged her back to the rear of the shop and we retreated into the kitchen of their house.

Lucienne Legros, Charles' wife, was the former Lucienne Bouarmont, daughter of a successful farmer from nearby Grand Halleux, down the Salm River valley. I had spent several high school vacations in Grand Halleux and had worked for the fun of it on her parents' farm. Of all the Bouarmont kids, she and her brother Albert were the closest to my age and we had become good friends. Having told her of my new identity, I revealed to her that I had had to leave Brussels because of a Werbestelle problem. I told her of my interest in her husband's weekly trips to Liège. As we chatted, the clock struck noon and Charles closed the shop and appeared in the kitchen. Lucienne told him about our old camaraderie but the ever prudent Charles asked how he could be sure I was a bona fide patriot. I suggested a way to prove my contact with the Allies. If he would give me a message I would ask London to transmit it back on the air; it would take two to three weeks to arrange. That would prove my overseas connections. This is the message he gave me: *Le sanglier est le roi des Ardennes* (the wild boar is king of the Ardennes).

On the 7:00 P.M. edition of the news three weeks later, after personal messages for France and Belgium, sure enough, there came Charles' message. Charles had no further questions and enrolled as a supplier for my group, mostly for hard-to-get things. He did marvels. The first thing I ordered was a multiband radio good enough to use in the woods. I also asked him if he could locate a good pair of binoculars. He came back with a pair of Zeiss German navy night binoculars.

Through Mayor Faisant's good offices we had a reasonable supply of food coupons and because the villagers were set in their habit of not eating organ meats, we were well supplied with tongues and livers. There was even enough to be able to can some tongue and send it to my parents. Fernande, Jan, and I shopped in different stores so as not to attract attention. We also learned that stores had an oversupply of infant food of the brand Phosphatine, which tasted delicious and made great creamy desserts. Loulou sent money to support Christian and Charles.

The sky above us grew busier by the day. We began to discern a new type of plane, different from the Lancasters—American B-17 bombers. Hundreds flew over us. The large bomber formations were surrounded by new long-distance fighters as they passed over us almost daily en route to Germany. The German air force seemed to disappear from our air space. Americans flew undisturbed over us, squadron after squadron, toward their enemy objectives. On the return flight, the formations were slow, uneven, marked by planes smoking in distress. Some would probably not make it back to home base.

CHAPTER 7

▼

The Birth of Service Hotton

At the end of February came an urgent message from Loulou. He was coming to see me and wanted a very safe meeting place for the two of us and a friend. The laconic message requested a swift reply to a drop in Liège. Charles Legros carried my answer to the drop, a place where letters, messages, or information could be left for a recipient who would know how to get the documents to their final destination. The system was designed not to divulge the location of either addressee or consignee, part of the network intended to fragment the lines of communication and insure tighter security. A few days later Loulou appeared with a man who had a pronounced local accent. The meeting took place in one of our wooden shelters deep in the woods. Charles de Greef and Christian, with two others called up for the occasion, mounted guard at a distance. Loulou, I could see, was excited. I had never seen him in such a state of euphoria. I could hardly wait for the meeting to start. He explained that in 1942 he had helped the man with him to join the British by moving him across and out of France. Now the man was back. He was an Allied Special Force Mission agent in charge of a certain project in Belgium. His name was Léon Joye. He was a former schoolmate of Loulou and a noncommissioned officer in the Chasseurs Ardennais.

Léon was in Belgium with the mission of organizing sabotage and disruption to take place before and during the liberation campaign, activities Allied HQ deemed necessary for the pending invasion of France and Belgium. Léon was looking for three groups to operate within Belgium: one for each of the borders to be covered, France, Holland, and Germany. Now it was Léon who spoke, slowly, clearly, to the point. He defined the tasks and asked many questions. Taking no notes, he mentally stored the information. When I answered a question, he interrupted frequently to ask pertinent details. He

Léon Joye (alias Therese), parachuted Special Forces agent.

was very interested in all I could tell him about my group and also what I could tell about Marcel's group around Chimay at the French border. He was anxious to contact Marcel and Marcel's father, whose position as a senior railroad engineer was of great interest to Léon. He asked me a lot of questions about my own father's activities, past and present. I told him the little I knew, explaining that we kept our work separate unless reasons dictated otherwise. As the meeting ended, Léon extracted from his pocket a packet of Lucky Strikes! I recognized the package but had forgotten the delicious, sweet smoke of those cigarettes. What a difference in taste from what we could sometimes obtain with our coupons.

Before leaving, Loulou and Léon reaffirmed the absolute secrecy of the meeting for now. It was understood that we should meet again soon, in two or three weeks at the most. Gustave was to be my contact. It was imperative that not a word of Léon's presence in the area be spoken. Under the cover of darkness, they departed through the woods that they both knew better than I, leaving me with my thoughts, hopes, and eagerness to help. Something was in preparation. Were we to be part of it? Would we be able to participate in a tangible way?

I was elated and swelled with pride at having been questioned by this parachuted envoy. Above all, the meeting indicated beyond any doubt that something important was soon to happen. I went back to Jan and Fernande's home, having trouble restraining my enthusiasm, and found sleep only in the wee hours of the morning.

The next morning, as soon as Jan and I were alone, he asked me the reason for the exhilaration I had been unable to mask. I told him I could not divulge the substance of the previous day's meeting, but that it was very good news, altogether too early and too important to talk about. Sorry, dear friend, I had to tell him; for the time being, he would have to trust me. Soon, I said, I hoped to be able to convey to him reasons to rejoice.

A week later we had other reasons to rejoice—not just we three, but all the villagers, all the citizens of occupied Belgium. For the first time, eight hundred B-17s flew over us in formation, mounting a massive raid to the enemy's country. Listening to the radio we learned that the raid had been over Nuremburg. At last. Their turn to be *Coventriert!* London said there had been practically no Luftwaffe intervention, but the losses had been serious nonetheless due to numerous antiaircraft batteries.

Spring was almost upon us. I felt it in the air. I sensed it would be the time for great happenings and perhaps a turn in this long war.

In early March, I learned through Gustave that Loulou and his friend

Léon would pay us a second visit. It had been three anxious weeks since the first, and I could hardly wait for Léon's decision. We met again in the Bois de Ronce where Charles and Christian had provisioned another well-camouflaged shed. Again, I had guards in place for the duration of the meeting.

As soon as we were settled in with hot ersatz beverages to warm us up, Léon told me he had located the three groups he needed. One would operate in the Antwerp area, Marcel's group would operate at the French border, and mine on the east side of Belgium, along the German border. Léon would supervise everything for London. A staff would be in place in Brussels. Marcel Franckson, Sr., Dad, and others would be part of it. Léon's role would be to coordinate the local efforts with the Special Force Mission London office and supply us with armaments and sabotage materials. We would be the saboteurs of the Secret Army, each group working with support from the local branch of the Secret Army as needed. At liberation, we would be incorporated into its national organization. Until then, we would maintain contact and be independent, but under direct Allied control.

We would have assigned tasks to perform at given moments and for that reason it was imperative that we be available and prepared. Léon insisted that from now on, all those selected would have to abandon their other involvements in resistance activities. We would be supplied by air with special materials and would train ourselves for certain tasks which only we would be able to perform. For these reasons we should avoid contact with the enemy. We would be well provided for to accomplish our tasks and defend ourselves, but could only use our weapons for defense during assigned actions. Never should we use our arms for offensive actions. Léon could not emphasize these points enough. To free us from material needs, London would include in the drop a serious amount of money. Thus ended our morning's talks. After a short break for lunch, we resumed.

First, our armament. Léon suggested a package with our group's strength in mind: two bazookas, two Bren guns, twenty Sten guns, five Browning .45s, forty grenades, and an ample supply of ammunition for the weapons.

Second, sabotage materials, including a generous surplus for what we might achieve over and above our assigned tasks, as opportunities presented themselves. The primary task for my group was to sabotage the main Paris to Berlin telephone cable, which crossed our area. The reason, Léon told us, was to force the Germans to broadcast their communications over the airwaves on D-day and later. The Allies possessed the German code and it was imperative for them to learn about troop movements during the first critical days of the landing. Our second important task was destruction of two rail centers, Gouvy and Trois-Ponts, to cripple German communications further and disrupt their supply lines from the rear. Plans for these two railroad centers would reach us from Brussels. It was imperative that we keep the Germans on the alert and force them to maintain heavy security forces at the rear. Léon indicated that during the landing and the liberation offensive we might be asked to act on some unforeseen objectives. Means had been secured to maintain rapid communication between us and Special Forces by radio and couriers. To allow us to prepare for these specific actions, he had compiled a list of the materials he believed necessary to complete them and submitted the list to me for scrutiny, awaiting comments and questions. He indicated that a multilanguage manual would accompany the material. All operations were explained in detail.

Going through the list, I was astounded by the sophisticated armaments to be sent. I had many questions and received clear answers from the man who had been trained and had practical experience with all the materials. He went on to explain how the supplies, packed in steel containers of different but modular sizes, would reach us by air drop. The last but most important point we had now to discuss was the nature and location of a drop point. That would be the morrow's topic, for night had come. Enjoying a leisurely meal in our small hidden shed before retiring to our hay beds, we talked about his and my experiences. I tried to obtain more information about the debarkation, only to find, of course, that it was the war's best-guarded secret as to date and place. All Léon would say was that it would be during the coming summer on the Atlantic coast of France, with probable secondary assaults designed to confuse the enemy.

The next day would be busy, locating and visiting possible drop-zone sites. With this in mind, we lay down and rested while my men kept a not-too-distant vigil. Our excitement had abated slightly now that our curiosity had been quelled, and we slept well. For my part, I was rested in the morning, although I wondered how it had been possible for I had spent the whole night dreaming of blowing up trains, blowing them to Kingdom come.

Our second day began with a breakfast of bread and butter and beverage that the Germans insisted on calling coffee; we had long forgotten what coffee was. For years we had been drinking this ersatz brew of chicory and roasted cereals. But for today, our thoughts were enough to perk us up as we began considering locations for dropping our arms and materials. London organized all secret drop fields by code names. For ease of memorization they were categorized according to countries. The Belgian fields had tree names. We adopted *le sapin*, the fir tree. Now, where was our very own ever-green to be located? What were the criteria? Léon explained them to us: four or five clear acres located in and surrounded by woods, away from roads—if possible on a high plateau, distant from population centers. We were to avoid the Vielsalm and the Rencheux barracks, and the Fraiture marshes. Léon also suggested that the drop be some distance from our established camp. So we looked in the vicinity where Marcel had been in 1942, south of Grandmenil. The Forge à la Plez area seemed best. The Sadzot family, for-mer members of Marcel's group who were engaged in a lumber and sawmill business there, would know a good place. We decided to visit them. It would be a full day's walk to the mill. The mill was an isolated facility at the intersec-tion of two little-traveled country roads, rarely used by the enemy. It was situated near the center of the Bois du Pays, a forest nearly six miles by three miles. Traveling on foot, the four of us—Léon, Christian, Loulou, and myself—reached the vicinity of the sawmill, fifteen miles distant, around five that afternoon. Christian was sent to reconnoiter while we waited at the forest edge.

All was clear. Léon Sadzot, his father, and one sister were at the house. The steam-powered mill, noisy with activity, would soon close for the day. Léon Sadzot returned with Christian to greet us. We would spend the night in a barn close to the house and have all evening to talk. In the morning we would depart early, before the mill opened, and visit two sites Sadzot had in mind. Then we would retrace our steps and be back in the Bois de Ronce before dark.

We had a pleasant dinner and retired early to the hay. In the morning, a substantial breakfast of eggs and bacon fueled us for the day. Léon's sister and the maid had prepared a sack lunch for us. The two Léons, Loulou, Christian, and I departed to look at the sites north of the mill. Léon Joye found both suitable, but had to make a choice. We noted the exact geo-graphic coordinates and bade Léon Sadzot good-bye. Returning to camp in the Bois de Ronce we could evaluate the merits of both and make our choice. We had located the perfect "fir" where, we hoped, our material would soon arrive. Léon said it was already too late in the month for a moonless night and he doubted we could expect such a quick drop. He thought it would probably be delayed twenty-eight days until the next dark night. All de-pended on London and we should be ready for either possibility. Léon asked me to select a short message that would alert us to the drop. I chose: "Le sapin est l'arbre préféré des enfants" (the fir tree is the children's favorite tree). That short sentence in the evening news from London would tell us

Papa Sadzot in the courtyard of his farm at Forges à la Plez, spring, 1945. Christian Mannie *(right)*, in British uniform, is serving with British forces in a light tank re-connaissance unit after liberation.

that the plane would arrive that very night. We were to be on location and in force, moving quickly and prepared to remove and conceal containers and eradicate all traces of parachutes.

We decided to move our camp temporarily to the Forge à la Plez area and prepare the site. Léon had told us what was to be done. Near each corner of the field we needed to dig a hole five feet deep to contain a candle lit only at the moment we heard the sound of the plane's engines. The lighted holes would act as beacons—easily spotted from the air on a dark night, yet invisible from the ground except at extremely short range. Nearby, in the woods and at different locations, we would need a series of holes three feet by seven and four feet deep to conceal the containers. These holes should be covered by old tarps and branches, with dirt spread over the top and pine needles and more branches dispersed over the area so that all would look absolutely natural. The excess dirt would have to be removed from the site. All would be ready for quick action. Containers would be numbered. Number one would be small and could be carried away by one man. It would contain the packing list for each container, money, pistols, and ammunition. It was while retracing our steps to camp, passing near Dochamps, Chabrenez, Tailles, and Pisserote that Léon provided these details. By then, all had been explained, all plans set, save one last question: would London fund our survival until liberation? We reached agreement on half a million francs (ten thousand dollars in 1944).

Our discussions now complete, Léon would depart in the morning, returning to a location unknown to me, to communicate with England and continue to organize and supervise. The men prepared dinner; we ate leisurely and lay down early. It had been a long day and Léon wanted to be on his way at sunrise. He said he did not need an escort; he would be fine. He knew the area better than we did. At daybreak I traveled a short way with him but we soon separated, each to his own destination.

I was home in time for breakfast and had a long talk with Jan at the shop, telling him the substance of the London envoy's visit and of the necessity to move to another location. I provided him with some sketchy information about what we expected to achieve. He was thrilled by the news and we rejoiced, feeling we had a finger in the pie of liberation. I thanked Jan for having made all this possible for me—the result, we reminisced, of our student friendship, of his final paper that had brought him, through me, to the area that had become the home of his little grindstone workshop. I told him we would be funded by London and that all should be well. Soon I would be financially independent and able to devote all my time and energy to the assigned tasks.

Jan had another reason to be happy. During my short absence, a copy of *Combat,* the most important French underground newspaper, had arrived and in it was the third letter in a series to a German soldier from French existentialist and journalist Albert Camus. In his aggressive letter written from the underground to his German correspondent, Camus asked:

What gives you the right to talk about Europe? We are Europe. We, with Czechoslovakia, Poland, Holland, Belgium, we are Europe. Your letter has overtones of blindness but no intelligence; you are a brainwashed individual caught in stupid propaganda. All that you see in Europe are millions of slaves, forced to feed your machine, feed your soldiers, supply your factories. We see Europe another way, the home of the spirit of twenty centuries, the arena of western man.

You try to kill and divide, to subordinate and control. We try to love and unite. Your thousand-year Reich is not going to last much longer. You have ignited the world; the world has been working on your annihilation (author's translation).

You could not have said it better, French writer, Jan and I agreed. We too could see it coming. We sensed the imminence of oncoming events. Great things were brewing, a different history soon to be written.

The next morning I went to Charles Legros and gave him a list of items to be purchased, if possible: knapsacks, shovels, picks, water bottles. Could he provide all these? On my way back I talked with Gustave Jacques, giving him the latest news. He was pleased to learn that the area would be in the center of the early action.

Then, in the midst of our intense preparations, the unexpected struck. One morning hundreds of B-17 flying fortresses in organized squadrons flew over us toward a German objective. In the afternoon, they flew back much disorganized and at all altitudes. The low-flying ones were smoking, showing signs of difficulties and damage. I was home with Jan watching their progress when, suddenly, we spotted a parachute opening and saw an airman floating down over the Bois de Ronce. It was raining. I rushed toward the area where the man had fallen and soon found him, hurt. He had fallen on a fence post, then sideways, and had sprained his ankle so that he was unable to walk. I helped him to a hiding place in the nearby woods, asking him to stay there and not to make a fire. I would return soon with some means of transportation.

In the lower village I asked to borrow a handcart to get some dead wood along the upper forest road. It was evident that from the village vantage point the fallen man could not have been seen. From home I took some large stretch bandages and my gun. I went back to the woods and helped the man into the cart, but could not push it all the way to the shed. He had to walk the last mile painfully while I helped him as best I could.

I explained to Charles and Christian what had happened and said there was a possibility our contacts would be bringing us other downed airmen. From what this one had told me, he had been the next to the last to jump. Another was farther down. Seven more had jumped before him and one was dead on board. I advised Charles to be on the lookout; others might need our help. Having loaded the handcart with dead wood, I went home, unloaded it, and returned the cart to the owner. All was calm and normal in the village. Good. Nobody had apparently noticed anything.

As we were dining that night, a messenger arrived with an urgent request from Gustave Jacques' niece, Malou Halin, for an immediate visit.

I peddled my bike furiously and covered the eight miles to Vielsalm in half an hour. She was all excited by a new, uniformed "patient" who did not speak a word of French. He had been brought to her clinic through the rear garden door. I went upstairs to meet the man and, sure enough, he was another American, alone and anxious. He rose and I asked him his name and rank. He said, "Austin Dunning, First Lieutenant, U.S. Air Force." I replied, "Henri Bernard, Belgian Underground, ready to help you if you are genuine, ready to kill and bury you if you are not."

I sat across the table from him and took a document out of my pocket, a questionnaire supplied by Loulou and devised by the Allies to end the problem of German infiltration of our escape lines. But I soon realized I had a problem. These downed personnel had been repeatedly told to give only name, rank, and serial number. They had never been told they might be asked questions by escape-line personnel. The man facing me was no exception. The document contained many questions which these men were not willing to answer. I had to explain to him that we were risking our lives to save him, but if he would not cooperate I had only one alternative—to dispose of him. I took out my 7.65 mm Browning and repeated that he had better answer the questionnaire. The argument of my standard issue Belgian 7.65 did it. The questionnaire complete, I explained that it would take a day or two to have London verify his answers. In the meantime, he must wait here and be patient. He had nothing to fear if he was truly a member of the USAF. As soon as I received confirmation, I would return with civilian attire in order to move him to his next location. I insisted he stay in the room at the rear of the building, since the *feldgendarmerie* station was just across the street.

Looking over his answers, I saw that he had correctly named the second lieutenant, Charles O. White, as navigator—that was the name of our guest in the woods. But that was still not proof. The fact that the man had arrived at the end of a 'chute did not exclude the possibility that both of them, as well as others who might eventually drift in from the same plane, were phonies. Only a formal okay from London would make them all bona fide. I explained to Malou the procedure and promised to act without delay. Returning home, I stopped at Gustave's to use his phone to relay the information. I was told to expect an answer the next afternoon. My contact would telephone back to say: Message for H. B., the package is, or is not, genuine. We would act accordingly. In the late afternoon of the next day, a messenger came with a letter from Gustave. The package was genuine. I could return to Malou and take the man out of her custody. When I arrived, Malou had already dressed him in local attire. We left through the rear door under the cover of darkness, zigzagging through a maze of gardens till we reached the country and proceeded toward camp. White and Dunning had a happy reunion. I briefed them about our situation, the dangers involved for us, and the strict obedience to our orders that we expected, for the safety of all.

We discussed the possibility that some of those who had jumped earlier might join us, provided they had been spotted quickly by our friends across the border. However, those former Belgian counties were not large and probably the men who had jumped first would have landed in the German Eiffel territory, in which case they were likely to end the war in prisoner-of-war camps. If no others showed up in the next two or three days, we would have to abandon hope for them in order to save the men who were here. These two would be moved to the other shed and asked to stay there quietly. With all that had to be done to prepare the drop site and the delay this would cause, it would be days before they could be moved to the next safehouse in Liège; we still had to provide White with local civilian attire, then supply them both with forged identities and teach them a few French words.

Explaining our food situation to them, I asked them to be happy with what we could provide and not to expect five- or even three-star dining; and we indicated that there would be nothing to smoke except Shit A and B when available. They had a few Luckies and Camels left and they offered these around. We each accepted one and smoked in their presence. I reiterated the need for quiet and patience.

All visible traces of their American origin had to be eradicated. Except for their military tags to be sewn inside a garment, they would have to abandon it all: rings, watches, insignia, and so forth. That being said, I bade the Americans good night and went home, leaving them under Charles' and Christian's care. The next evening when I went back to the shed, I learned that two others would be on their way to join us as soon as they could be clothed properly. And then we received news of yet another arrival.

The five were Second Lieutenant Charles O. White, First Lieutenant Austin Dunning, Sergeant Donald Brown, and, if memory serves me correctly after all these years, the tail gunner Edward Zabinsky and one of the two waist gunners, Ralph Sack.

I considered the rescue thus far an enormous success. And an enormous amount of work and risk right at the moment I was supposed to keep all my energies for Service Hotton, that being the code name for the organization Léon Joye was forming in occupied Belgium. How could I refuse assistance to these men who practically fell on top of me? Or cast off Loulou and all his efforts when he had just given me such an opportunity to serve? I weighed the pros and cons and decided to go ahead with evacuating these five to Liège, then I would end my commitment to the escape line.

All the personal belongings of our five Americans were collected and buried in a cache in the Bois de Ronce. The only things they kept were their shoes and cotton underwear. For the rest, everything had to go. I understood how it must have been for them to get rid of things like a bracelet from a girl, a graduation ring. But those objects were generally decorated with wings or an eagle and would attract attention.

Among their government-issued possessions, each had a survival kit packed inside a waterproofed plastic box. The contents had been carefully planned and were interesting. There was a map of the area they would fly over, printed on a thin silk or nylon material. There was a compass disguised as a steel button that could be sewn on with the needle and thread provided. There were fish hooks and fishing line, chlorination tablets to purify water, and a rubber pouch to hold the water under treatment. There was a hypodermic with morphine as a painkiller, money of the countries over which they flew, and Benzedrine pills to keep them awake and alert for exhausting journeys. The navigator, White, had jumped with the plane's pocket chronometer, a Hamilton twenty-four-hour precision watch. He had to leave it with us. The uniforms themselves were cut out of green military wool. Pants had standard pockets plus two larger ones on the outside of each thigh. The tunics were short with waistbands and large breast pockets. We were impressed by the cut, the material, and the comfort.

It was a frenetic month, April, with five Americans in the woods and the drop to be prepared for, possibly this month, although Léon had said more likely next. In agreement with Charles and Christian we decided to set up a camp in the Bois du Pays and feverishly began working at preparing the field. The Sadzots took care of feeding us all. Reward for that service would come from London via Loulou as soon as possible. But I knew the Sadzots would provide with or without payment, as they would prove many times over during the next months. As for moving the men to Liège, the Sadzots offered us the use of their 1939 Ford V8 sedan, which they would allow us to "steal." The theft had to be organized to protect them. We would steal the car and hide it in the woods. They would report the theft to the local Belgian gendarmes, who would make certain the inquiry would be closed for lack of proof. Organizing the new camp, providing the necessary papers for the escaping men, digging holes and camouflaging them at the drop field kept our days full and busy. Each evening, religiously, we listened to Radio London. Then, against all hope, the message came: "Message for Henri, the fir tree is the children's favorite tree." The drop would come tonight.

Christian bicycled to Ourvary's and, before midnight, eight men with Belgian army carbines were at our service to secure the perimeter of the field. Ourvary was the code name of one of our men living at home on his farm— a former Ardennais, a sharpshooter. So were the seven men who came with him, but Ourvary was the best, the quickest, the most alert. The three of us had complete confidence in those men, who did not hide their army carbines and had somehow managed to secure plenty of ammunition. Léon Sadzot, the five Americans, and the four of us would take care of the drop proper.

On location the vigil started. One o'clock went by, two o'clock—and then we heard the sound of an approaching plane. The four candles were lighted and set at the bottoms of their holes. The plane circled, disappeared, came back for another pass, and before we knew it four parachutes were visible in the darkness. With four dull thuds, the containers landed. One lay at the edge of the woods, its 'chute entangled in a large tree; three others lay in the clearing. No wind. High clouds. Darkness. We worked silently and rapidly, moving the containers to their caches. Container number one was located and opened. The checklist indicated all was there. I would carry this one to camp. The 'chute was dislodged from the tree and buried, the caches camouflaged. We would come back in daylight to make sure all was well and to eradicate any traces of activity. It was four in the morning before we could leave the field and go back to camp. I kept Ourvary and his seven men another day to watch the camp and, later, to go back to the drop field to check our camouflage and help us to carry some containers with armament back to camp. After a hurried breakfast, we emptied container number one. The money was there, all in ten-thousand-franc notes—fifty big ones! The largest and rarest Belgian denomination, a tremendous mistake. The notes were practically impossible to exchange without a bank and a lot of questions, but more about that later.

Out of the same container came six new .45 Colts with boxes of one hundred cartridges and spare clips, but no holsters. From the general packing list which told us the contents of the different containers, such as arms and sabotage material, we identified the containers with Sten guns, Bren guns, and grenades to be dug up and brought back to camp. Bazookas could wait. Sabotage material could stay there a while. First, ensure our security by being armed and ready to defend ourselves.

Throughout the day, forgetting we had not slept, we worked furiously, digging, carrying, unpacking, cleaning, and familiarizing ourselves with our new tools. Six of us already had pistols and by day's end, facing a cauldron of rich hot stew prepared by Léon's sisters, we looked over our Sten guns and Bren guns. We felt secure. We felt elated. We felt like true freedom fighters ready for action. Ourvary's men went home until our next assignment and we slept well. The weather was with us, dry and mild.

Thanks to Mayor Faisant and Loulou, we now had most of the identity papers we needed and the Americans were slowly familiarizing themselves with these. I had decided to make two trips to Liège, the first with two of the airmen, the second with three.

It was time to steal the car and hide it in an abandoned shed in the woods. I would make the trip with Christian as chauffeur. Marcel had told me that Christian was a superb driver and would never lose his control. I contacted the Liège safehouse. They were ready. The Salvation Army shelter was our destination. I knew how to reach it without delay or detour. We set the date and decided to use the Volontaire du Travail as cover. False work cards were provided for each of us. I wore a Volontaire du Travail uniform. We made shoulder holsters for our pistols and on the appointed day left promptly at 6:00 A.M., driving at the speed limit toward Liège. We arrived at the Salvation Army building and delivered our first load, bade them good-bye and good luck, and after a short lunch were back on the road toward Forge à la Plez. All went smoothly out of the city; the most dangerous part was over.

Or was it? We now were in open country. Several bridges over rivers and rails had to be crossed—favorite places for the German patrols to set up checkpoints. We drove out of Liège following the Ourthe River valley to Comblain, where the Amblève River joins the Ourthe. There was no way we could avoid that main road. Soon after Comblain we turned east out of the valley and traveled through farming country using small county roads. We crossed several tributaries of the Ourthe, flowing west of us. Near Mormont, we had to cross the River Aisne. There on the bridge, hidden from distant view, were two feldgendarmes assisted by two members of the Zwarte Brigade (Black Brigade, a Flemish pro-German organization in black uniforms aping the SS).

They stopped us, shouting, "Papieren!" We produced our orders. They were satisfied with Christian's, but objected to mine. A discussion ensued in German and I argued so much that the feldgendarme lost his cool and hit me with his rifle butt on the left of my face. I spat three molars out onto the bridge. It felt as if my upper jaw were shattered. I do not know how I kept my head while saying to him in his language: "Wait a minute. Let me see the card I gave you." He complied and I continued, "Oh, I see, let me show you this one," and reached inside the pocket of my tunic.

His stupid mistake, thinking I was going for another document. With my

.45, I shot him point-blank, striking him in the middle of the chest. He did a somersault and fell, dead. Christian now had his gun ready to assist. The other feldgendarme ran away carrying his gun, while the two Zwarte Brigade men dropped theirs to run faster. Christian grabbed the two guns, put them in the car, and we sped away south toward Clerheid. My mouth was killing me. I was swallowing blood, and my cheek was turning violet and swelling fast. Suddenly Christian spotted a little dirt track to our left and veered onto it, bouncing wildly as he kept up maximum speed. We were approaching the edge of the Bois du Pays woods.

We were near camp and in familiar terrain. The little track began to descend toward the ford of a swollen stream which we knew. Christian accelerated and managed to get us through to the other side. Soon we reached an abandoned stone pit with an old, decrepit building that provided a place to hide the car. From there, on foot, we reached our hideaway. I wished that I had ice to numb the relentless aching in my face, but had to be satisfied with cold water and aspirin. At least the bleeding had stopped. Probing in the left side of my mouth with my finger, I established that the bone of the upper jaw was indeed broken. There was nothing to be done about it now, however. I had to endure. Amazingly, I managed to rest. The next day I felt much better. But I would have to stay several days in camp: there was no way I could show my ugly bruises, attracting attention. For the next trip we would have to select another route. We could not take the chance of being seen again in those parts.

In the meantime, the plans of one of the railway stations had arrived. I asked Ourvary to come and we discussed the problem of gathering intelligence for the Gouvy train station. To reach the large pumping station two miles away from the main station, we would need to cross the border into German territory. It would take many days of twenty-four-hour surveillance at several points to reconnoiter the possible crossing points. Ourvary already knew there were regular patrols along the line, sometimes with dogs. It was imperative to know where, when, the frequency of the patrols, and how many men were in each. I also needed to know how to enter the pump house noiselessly.

We needed to become familiar with all trains: military, passenger, and freight. Long ore trains came from Lorraine, coke trains from Liège. All had to refuel and take on water. Were the repair shops active at night? Ourvary promised me a report within the week. Others among my men were already digging to locate the Paris-Berlin telephone cable.

Through Gustave, in Salmchâteau, Gustave having been alerted by his son

Loulou, we heard that a young Brussels man was being sent to us at his father's request. The man arrived escorted by Charles. Without one of us to help, the man could never have found our camp, deep in the woods near Sadzot's mill. He arrived in miserable shape after a trip on foot from Salm-château to Forge à la Plez. Twenty cross-country miles had exhausted him. It would take some time to get him fit enough to serve our demanding enterprises. Noel was the son of a conservatory piano professor, an accomplished interpreter of Bach, and a friend of underground friends. Because he had been active in the Brussels underground, Noel was judged to be in jeopardy. His dad was afraid he would not survive there and had sent him to us. I could not guarantee his safety with us either, and so allowed the father to decide. He apparently elected to take the risk, as I received no further reply after sending my report.

We were now ready for our second trip to Liège. I sent Christian to retrieve the car from its hideaway, but this time he could not get it over the creek. He returned to camp announcing that he had left the car stuck in the water. We borrowed a strong manila rope from Sadzot and went to help. First we smoothed down the embankment and then, with all of us pulling and Christian driving, we edged the Ford across the ford and were ready to go. We had studied the map and decided on a totally different itinerary. We would go north and west toward Verviers using small rural roads, merely crossing the large ones that were constantly patrolled, and would reach Liège through the suburb of Chenée, thus entering through the southwest end of town.

Christian and I would be armed. He would drive and I would navigate, with the three Americans riding in the back seat. We were unfamiliar with the country roads north of us and twice faced bridges that had been destroyed as a result of war.

Early in the morning, I spotted a woman out by her stable with two buckets of tepid milk hanging from her yoke. We stopped nearby to ask her if she could direct us toward Chenée. She could. Then, from the back seat, came a southern-drawled "Merci beaucoup." The two milk buckets lay spilled on the yard as we sped away, hoping she would get over her shock and keep her mouth shut.

Crossing the water at Chaudfontaine, we were now driving through a valley to Chenée. There, we noticed a group of Germans aligned in two rows along the sidewalk. In front and standing on the pavement was an officer who could not miss seeing us arrive. He lifted his arm to indicate we should stop. Christian downshifted to first and let the car coast slowly toward him.

As we neared the officer, Christian gunned the engine and ran over him, squashing him like an unfortunate skunk. Ahead lay the level railroad crossing of La Troque, fortunately open. Christian was already in second gear and flooring it to shift into third. All of a sudden all hell broke loose. The car was hit by a hail of bullets. Through the rear view mirror I could see the Germans in the middle of the road shooting at us. Providentially, on the right side of the road, parked partially on the sidewalk, was a disabled trolley bus. We jumped the curb and continued with two wheels on the sidewalk, two on the road. With the bus behind us acting as a shield, we moved on and away to safety, with both the windshield and rear window shattered.

I in the front and the Americans in the rear broke out the remaining shattered glass with our bare hands, restoring visibility for the driver and making the car somewhat less conspicuous looking. Christian never slowed down; quite the opposite. Knowing Liège well, I guided him through narrow little side streets of Seraing toward our objective. When we reached it and were safely inside the Salvation Army garage, we inspected the damage. Twenty-one bullet holes, most of them in the trunk. What an outing! What saved us all was our idea of filling the trunk with tightly packed bundles of birch twigs, which had deflected and stopped the bullets. Only one bullet had made it through and it had passed between two of the Americans then through my sleeve, giving me a superficial burn, before falling on the floor below the dash. Incredibly, we were all safe.

The car had no mechanical damage but could not be driven back without having body and glass work done. In its current shape it was sure to attract attention. We decided to have the windows replaced immediately and the holes patched temporarily. It was the afternoon of the next day before we could depart, after having bade our Americans good-bye. We arrived back in Forge à la Plez without hindrance to find that nervous friends had kept an all-day vigil, wondering what had happened to us. Did we have a tale for them—the old woman's milk buckets, the German target shooting. We were very sorry for the Sadzots, but they had known the risk they took when "lending" us the car. They never complained.

Our knowledge about the Gouvy station was growing. A central fueling point providing both water and coal for the trains, it had an engine repair shop and was on the main line from Lorraine to Liège, the vital link for steel production in Belgium and Lorraine (Liège supplied blast furnace coke, Lorraine delivered iron ore). London's interest was clear, as was ours. We wanted to destroy the station, or at least create enough destruction to disable it for a long time.

We refined our inquiries, sending men for more detailed information, while Charles and I studied our sabotage materials to decide what to use. Our problem was of a technical nature: how much explosive to use, especially for the water tower tank? I submitted the problem to Jan but his university education, like mine, had not covered sabotage and he was about as lost as I. Our technical manual was equally useless. It told us how, but not how much. We decided to play it safe and use ten pounds of plastic explosive which we would lower in a waterproof jacket to the middle of the water tank, located at the end of the station. The tank, supported by a circular brick wall forty feet high, was a boiler-type affair of heavy, riveted steel plates. A permanent steel access ladder was conveniently located so as not to be in view from the station.

As our plans took shape, charges were prepared and materials assembled. Soon we were nearly ready for our first action. The month of May was only days away and the weather was mild and balmy. The woods smelled sweetly of resin as the sap rose. The moon was waning and we hoped to be fully prepared to take advantage of a dark, moonless night. One problem remained to be solved: we did not have a large enough assortment of time pencils, timing devices housed in aluminum tubes and used to detonate a charge. We had two varieties: short, which allowed a five-minute fuse and long, providing a two-hour fuse. I had hoped that all our charges would explode simultaneously, although we needed one hour to enter the station, distribute the explosives, and exit to safety. There was only one solution— use the long time pencils and activate them in advance while still on the approach march. It was risky business. At the bottom end of the pencil was a charge of mercury fulminate that would explode when the spring-loaded steel rod triggered and hit it. The rod was held back by a steel wire. Around the steel wire was a glass ampoule filled with diluted sulfuric acid. When the top part of the pencil was crushed, so was the glass ampoule, and the acid would get to work at the speed dictated by its concentration. In time, the steel wire would corrode and snap, releasing the plunger. Carrying preactivated devices was dangerous, but could not be avoided. As leader I would carry them and activate them along the way. That decided, we were ready.

CHAPTER 8

▼

Only the Beginning of the End

"It is not the end; it is only
the beginning of the end."
—Winston Churchill, BBC speech

Quite apart from the general lifting of spirits that spring means, we were
relieved to see it. The snow was gone and we had managed not to be discovered. For those of us living in the woods, snow was a real security problem,
as was smoke. Fires in the shelters could only be lighted at night and even
then only to do the cooking. During the day, we reheated our meals on an
alcohol burner. Alcohol was rare, and it was Charles who supplied it from
the Liège black market.

Officially spring, 1944, had arrived with all its promise of rebirth and there
was nothing the Nazis could do about it. They had not yet invented a way to
deprive us of the pleasure of our seasons. The greening woods were a patch-
work of tender shoots and young evergreen buds. Yet even this blessed season had its dark side. It was a period of sudden rains and they drenched us.
Walking among the evergreens meant misery. Touching the branches, our
trousers collected water which ran down our legs and collected in our shoes.
Our feet were forever soaked. Still, I marveled at our extraordinary power
to adapt. We were four illegals from the city living in harsh conditions in an
environment unfamiliar to us and until the very end, we never had a cold,
never felt sick. Was it the air quality or our adrenaline which protected us?
Yet illness, though inconvenient, was not usually fatal. We faced greater dangers than illness. One or all of us might get hurt or wounded. It would be
prudent to have emergency remedies and first aid at hand. Contact had to
be established with a doctor and a nurse. When I presented this suggestion
to Gustave Jacques, he too thought it a good idea. He supplied just the right
contact—his niece Malou Halin, a licensed nurse and a very distant relative
of mine, who had hidden the American bombardier, Austin Dunning. The

problem with using Malou was that her clinic was located so close to the Vielsalm feldgendarmerie. Gustave urged me to be especially careful.

Meetings with Malou were always a pleasure. Her mother and younger brother who lived with her joined our companionable conversations. Malou promised to prepare an emergency kit and to contact a Dr. Bodson (no relation) and obtain the necessary prescriptions for a few basic drugs and analgesics. When they were ready, she would take an afternoon off and carry the kit to Salmchâteau where we would meet again at Gustave's house. I asked her if she knew Lucienne and Charles Legros, and told her how I had enrolled Charles as a supplier in my group and how he had received, through London, a personal message that proved my official connection. Perhaps she could use the story to persuade Dr. Bodson to help us further. We needed someone willing to come to the woods to take care of our injured should it become necessary. A few days later we met again and she assured me of her support. Dr. Bodson had declined, but suggested a younger colleague who had accepted and was known to be able and efficient. That being resolved, I began searching for a partisan priest. Most of the men in my group were Catholic. Only Christian and I were raised freethinkers and would do without religious counsel. Mayor Faisant put me in contact with a young priest who agreed to serve on an "on call" basis.

By April's end, we had our material and armament assembled, we had secured health and religious care, our intelligence gathering for the action at Gouvy was nearly complete, and the telephone cable had been located. Sixteen special charges had been installed and we would soon be ready to put this communication trunk out of action on very short notice.

On April 29, Ourvary brought back the final details of the information I needed to put the Gouvy plan into action. We had only to decide on the sabotage date. A moonless night would be best. May 5 was near and promised the best possible conditions.

For men on foot, carrying all their supplies, Forge à la Plez was too distant from Gouvy to serve as a base camp, twenty-six kilometers or sixteen miles as the crow flies. Also there were two main roads to cross and villages to be avoided along the way. So we decided to conduct the operation from a location nearer by, the Bois de Ronce north of Gouvy, and we made arrangements for a place to be prepared and provisioned there.

On the morning of May 2 we left Forge à la Plez carrying our material and armament. We traveled east, intending to cross the La Roche highway under the protection of darkness. On May 3, after a night's bivouac in the

Bois de Saint Jean Chanoine, we resumed travel and crossed the road to Houffalize so as to pass north of Montleban and Baclain. We were now at our temporary camp just four miles from Gouvy. The weather had been unusually cooperative and only a little rain had been encountered. We had two days to rest and prepare ourselves and to go over the project once again, minute by minute, detail by detail.

The rail track at Gouvy was oriented northwest to southeast, with the passenger station located on the northeast side, close to the town. Gouvy's main street fronted the track along the northeastern end. Fifty yards beyond the northern section of track was the newly redrawn German border. Our plan called for four demolition engineers accompanied by four armed guards to protect them once inside the station, and four local men, working in two groups of two each, who would cut holes in the chain link fences erected along the northeast and southwest sides of the station. These would be our entrance and emergency exit points. The locals would act as additional guards during the first and most dangerous phase of the operation, when two of us must enter the station, cross the yard and exit to the northeast, then cross fifty yards of open ground and enter German territory to sabotage the pump house. Each of the saboteurs was provided with a good army knapsack in which to carry his goodies: bakelite boxes with magnets and explosives, individually packaged plastic charges for special objectives. These were prepacked in our sacks in such a way that we had orderly access to them as needed. Our itinerary through the station was precisely timed. One slot was made longer than necessary in case we encountered a delay at the border. Only Charles and I would cross into Germany to the water pumps, guarded by the local men. The rest would wait outside the fence for our return. Altogether we carried nine charges, four of which were quite substantial. These were for the pumps, main signal cabin, and water tower. The other five we carried in hope of finding unexpected but valuable other targets.

Thanks to Charles Legros, our knapsacks were good ones of World War I vintage and we had separate canvas bags to carry the timing pencils, detonating cord and, most dangerous of all, the detonators, some preset on our way to the action site. We had not experimented with our armament before this because of the necessity to conserve ammunition and the absence of a noiseless shooting range. We had to trust in what we had received, though according to Leon Joye, the material had been field tested over and over again. The same was also true for our sabotage material. We could not afford practice. Regarding our inexperience, this first action would be decisive on many counts. It would test our material, the quality of our intelligence gathering, and, although we hoped not, our guns. I, for one, knew mine worked as I had learned on the bridge where I had left some teeth.

While the men rested and waited for the dark of the moon in the Bois de Ronce, I visited Jan. We discussed the radio news, the situation on the Russian front slowly moving west now, the Germans losing ground. We talked about Italy. The Allies were in a full offensive around Monte Cassino and a Polish division was distinguishing itself there. The battle for Rome, located between Monte Cassino and Anzio, was raging and as yet undecided. London was silent about plans for France. I told Jan I would see him soon again and asked if in the meantime, he could help me to change the ten-thousand-franc bank notes. I needed one thousands and hundreds badly. Would he talk to Mayor Faisant discreetly to see what could be done? I left him with two of the notes.

The others, which I showed him, were in the drawer on my bedroom nightstand hidden inside a large sharpening stone which Jacques had made and given me. This was Gustave's trick which he had perfected in World War I to move messages and intelligence around. He had manufactured the special stones himself from the stones he was producing commercially by cutting a production stone in half lengthwise and then hollowing out both halves. Shellac was applied after the message was placed inside, to glue both halves back together. Gentle heat from a stove would reopen the cache and gain access to its contents. Gustave had made two for me; an average size for letters and messages, a larger one for money. This was my safe. Jan promised to do what he could. He wished me luck, determinedly avoiding questions as to my destination.

I returned to my men in the woods on the afternoon of May 5. The weather, still with us, was mild and dry. Perfect. The men were excited, confident.

A meeting with our safety group had been set for 10:00 P.M. By then the night would be pitch black. We had determined that we needed two hours to reach our rendezvous point. By departing two and a half hours before our meeting we hoped to enjoy a prudent safety margin. At seven-thirty we were on our way.

We were eight in the group: Charles, Christian, Noel, and I, the permanent woods residents, and Ourvary and three of his best men who had joined us that afternoon. They would be our defense once inside the station. Two carried Bren guns, two carried pistols and Sten guns. We all had grenades.

The woodsmen were the saboteurs and carried all the charges and associated equipment, and were armed only with pistols and grenades to insure maximum freedom of movement while performing our tasks.

We left camp walking in a single file, two of Ourvary's armed men at the front, two at the rear. Ourvary led his men, I mine. We had been walking for quite a while through the dense pines when Noel ran up to my side to show me a furry little animal he thought cute. When I realized what it was, out came my .45! I ordered him to put the creature on the ground. He obeyed and a wild boar piglet trotted away. My fear was that the sow would come looking for her missing piglet.

Most Americans are not familiar with the European wild boar. It may easily weigh six hundred pounds and is a fierce fighter given to charges full of fury. A boar may attack and counterattack ferociously, using its tusks to lacerate its prey with great efficiency. This incident, later funny, was the only one on our way to Gouvy.

We arrived in good time at our hiding place for our prearranged meeting. Our four local guards were already in place at the station fence. At precisely 10:00 P.M., Charles and I passed through the fence, moving toward the pumping station. We crossed the switchyard using railroad cars as cover. We traveled light. Charles carried only two charges while I carried the detonators, time pencils, a crowbar, and a small pair of chain link cutters. The crossing went well. No undue attention had been aroused. It was calm. We reached the fence along the northeastern edge of the switchyard and found our other two locals. A hole had already been cut in the fence. Passing through the yard to the other side, we entered the border zone. The two men who had been posted at the second fence now joined us. They reconnoitered the border, letting two German guards pass. Then we penetrated into Germany. Ahead of us lay five hundred yards to cross to reach the pumps. The terrain was lightly wooded, just enough to provide cover.

We proceeded quickly, knowing we had only twenty-five minutes to plant the charges and recross the border before the return of the enemy patrol. At the pump house, we cut a hole in the chain link fence surrounding it and forced the padlock with the crowbar. Minutes passed. We fitted the charges, inserted the detonators and pencils, and made it back to the border before the guards returned. It had gone well. We were slightly ahead of schedule. Happily the sentries patrolled without dogs, but for that we had also been prepared, just in case. Our trail had been generously sprinkled with pepper acquired by Charles Legros at a price higher than that of gold. We recrossed the yard and regrouped. The local men who had remained behind covering our backs departed for home. So far all was going according to plan.

Ten twenty-seven. In three minutes we would move toward our main objectives.

We passed the fence moving in single file, walking at a measured pace, and then broke off into smaller groups. Ourvary's men covering us, we proceeded through the yard. I was to place the charges, Charles the detonators and time pencils. Christian and Noel carried the charges and passed them as needed. I carried the two four-pound charges.

Arriving near the main elevated signal station under the cover of an ore train that had just arrived, we fitted the signal house with one of the four-pound plastic souvenirs. Then we slipped into the vast forge and machine shop which was, as hoped, totally dark and silent. Having left the night air that smelled so good and fresh, we entered another world, a world that reminded me of hell, a place smelling of sulphur and spent coal and heavy steam engine oil. Noel handed me a magnetic charge which I applied to a giant lathe, then three more which I attached to the three locomotives sitting in the dark, their fronts open for repairs. Next we fitted the large welding unit with one of our extra charges. Once that charge ignited, the huge gas cylinders of oxygen and acetylene would become bombs in themselves. We exited through the far end of the building and moved on. There lay other unexpected prey, two more locomotives awaiting repair. They would soon be beyond repair. Moving cautiously through the night, we approached the turntable. Around its central shaft I fitted another four-pounder and moved on. Charles trailed behind in the shadows, fitting time pencils and detonators. Another train entered the station, a coke train from Liège in need of water. All this new activity was excellent. It made noise and kept the railroad personnel busy and the German guards interested elsewhere, standing at a distance. Behind the steel barrier of trains, we proceeded toward our final objective: the water tower.

Exchanging knapsacks with Christian, I now carried the ten-pounder wrapped in waterproof material. We climbed the cold steel ladder, passing above the forty-foot brick wall supporting the tank to reach the top, where we lay as flat as possible on our stomachs. The manhole near the center was uncovered. We would not need the crowbar. Nearby lay the cover, a good place to attach the rope to suspend the charge midway in the water. Charles fitted the detonator cord and I lowered and secured our gift. Then Charles fitted the detonator cord with a timing pencil. We were now ready to return to terra firma and get the hell out of there.

Once down, we moved again as eight shadows through the darkness, walking along the rails, passing the last fence, crossing the road, and disappearing onto the wooded hillside. In the woods, we climbed until we reached a place offering us a panoramic view of the station and the yard below. We wanted front-row seats to watch the fireworks. Only the red velvet curtains were missing for our premiere performance, a free show without rehearsal and sponsored by London. We waited for midnight and the show to begin. It was eleven fifty-seven.

The distant pump house went first in a flash of white light and a roaring explosion, the sound of which took three seconds to reach us. The station came alive. Lights were turned on all over the switchyard, Germans running toward the explosion site. Then another series of explosions erupted from the opposite end of the yard. Small explosions, probably in the shop. These were followed by two very large ones, the signal cabin and the turntable, both afire. A huge ball of yellow light flashed into the night sky as the oxy-acetylene welding outfit exploded. Guttural shouts and orders rang through the night while we waited for the grand finale, the water tower.

With the loudest explosion of all, it burst into a pale yellow mist which hung eerily over the station, the water, blown into vapor, diffracting and reflecting the blast of the ten-pound explosive. At seven minutes past midnight, as indicated on the precious chronometer left to us by the American airman, it was all over.

What a start to a wonderful day. I was happy and elated with our success, as proud of our work and my men as I could possibly be, and very aware of the first class job of intelligence gathering they had done.

No one spoke until I broke silence and congratulated everyone for the achievement. We had not fired a shot or wasted a cartridge. The enemy would never believe such an operation could have been carried out by a local group. The nature of the explosives ensured that. An inquiry would no doubt be made, but it would only prove the use of foreign materials.

Silently we moved back into the Bois de Ronce and to camp, each man quiet within his own thoughts, Ourvary leading us home through the relative safety of the woods. This time we recrossed the fences traveling lighter because of what we had left behind. It was just past two in the morning when, back at the shed, we settled down to a warm meal.

By custom we assembled in a circle to eat. I could see the joy on every face and I asked my men of their feelings. I felt the need to release the tensions that had been with us these last days of organizing, preparing, and executing our task.

We shared in the pride at having served, the joy at having inflicted a serious blow to the enemy, and the satisfaction at seeing our own all safe. Our worst mishap had been a tear in a pair of pants while barbed-wire hopping.

Noel then made a remark that left me dumbfounded and doubting his brain functions. He had counted the fences we had crossed along the way and they numbered twenty-three. Here I had been thinking of the gods' vengeance, of a just return for our sufferings, and he had been counting fences! War! I wondered how many more denials of their absolute power, such as our evening of sabotage, would be needed to demonstrate to the Germans that they could not sustain control over us. How many of us would still have to offer our lives before the Germans gave it up? Or would they ever? As the conversation again turned general, I reminded the men to keep it low.

From a cache no one claimed to know about someone produced a full bottle of *pequet,* a locally made grain alcohol, a kind of Dutch Schiedam or vodka. Well earned. The eight of us passed the eighty proof from mouth to mouth until it was all drained out. Ourvary had a half-pound of dark Semois fine-cut tobacco and we each rolled a cigarette or two. After a short while, I assigned the sentry duty in two-hour shifts and joined Charles for the first shift, feeling that I could not sleep. My adrenaline still ran high.

The next morning Charles and I returned to the station to evaluate the damage. From a high vantage point and using the binoculars we obtained a good survey. The shop was almost totally destroyed, a long wall collapsed and the roof all but gone. The water tower had disappeared. Its supporting brick wall was pulverized to ground level and we could see only traces of the steel tank. It had blown to pieces. I certainly misjudged the charge there; five pounds would have been sufficient.

Around noon, on our way back, Charles and I parted. He would go back to camp and prepare for his return to Forge a la Plez, while I would go to Honvelez and talk with Jan. Through Mayor Faisant Jan had been successful in changing the two big notes. The mayor had put him in touch with a cattle merchant who instructed him to go to Vielsalm and contact a Mr. Lambert, a notary and an official who could easily take large notes to the bank and exchange them. In the future, the cattleman could be counted on. Another problem solved. Jan had heard, as had everybody in Honvelez and Bovigny, about the Gouvy destruction. I told him we had been responsible.

Next I went to visit Gustave Jacques in Salmchàteau. The Trois-Ponts station was our next target and I needed intelligence contacts there, which I knew Gustave could provide. Then I returned to camp at Forge a la Plez

Gouvy sabotage—what was left of the water tower, a pulverized circular mass of bricks, some remnants of the steel tank.

from where I contacted the Secret Army fifth zone in Erezée. Trois-Ponts was much too far away for the Bovigny men who were not familiar with that area. It was better and wiser to use locals who knew the details of the land. I needed to enlist the support of the Secret Army. They could supply men from their organization with enough firepower to ensure our protection, while the locals, as in Gouvy, would provide security for my group of specialists.

I then went to Vielsalm to talk with Charles Legros as we needed supplies. And as it was late in the afternoon, Lucienne Legros asked me to stay for dinner and I accepted.

CHAPTER 9

▼

Tragedy

On my way back from Vielsalm I made a brief stop at Gustave's house. I was told the Vielsalm feldgendarmes had been in Honvelez looking for me and had taken Jan to Vielsalm, according to a message received from one of our security men in the village. I was quick to decide to go immediately to the Bois de Ronce camp and from there send a message to Mayor Faisant. Honvelez was now no place for me.

I had to speak with Fernande, Jan's wife, as soon as possible to find out exactly what had happened. Fernande, now alone, could not possibly leave her home because of her children, two little girls aged three and one.

Mayor Faisant did not take long to appear, but could tell me nothing that I did not already know. I asked him to set an appointment with Fernande at a place she could reach easily, and to provide care for the children during her absence. On the third day after Jan's arrest, I received word to meet Fernande at eight in the evening at a friendly house on the western outskirts of the village of Bovigny. The good people of that house were related to Mayor Faisant's wife. I had met them once before. I arrived first and soon was followed by Fernande. We were left alone in the parlor and she told me through her tears what had happened.

The head feldgendarme and one of his men had come to their house after dinner, about eight, asking if there was a certain Henri Bernard living with them. Jan had replied, yes, Bernard was his foreman, but was visiting in Vielsalm that night. The German army police had briefly searched my bedroom. They found only the pair of German navy binoculars and confiscated those; nothing else was of interest to them. They insisted that Jan should accompany them. He would be free to return as soon as I showed up.

We sat in silence for many minutes until Fernande spoke.

"Do not go near the police station. Is it not enough that Jan has been taken away? He has done nothing, he will be back. You are eluding the Werbestelle. Stay in hiding and stay away from our house for now."

She handed me the large coticule sharpening stone I had asked to be brought from my nightstand drawer. Did she have any idea of the value of the stone? I asked her to stay in contact, using Mayor Faisant's good offices. I would be close by and within immediate reach should she learn more. I advised her to ask the mayor to inquire after Jan's fate at the Vielsalm feldgendarmerie.

Two days passed. I was alone in the woods. The others were in the Bois du Pays perfecting work on the cable, while I worked on the Trois-Ponts project. Jan's smile would not leave me. In the evening of the second day, Mayor Faisant appeared with the latest news. Before he began to speak, I knew by his countenance that it was to be hard news. Jan was dead.

The feldgendarmerie had told him Jan had died of a diabetic coma. His death was natural and certified by a Belgian doctor. I was suspicious. Jan was diabetic, surely, but in good shape, and he took care to keep his sugar level under control. He took his medication regularly. What had the Germans done to him? What did they know about him? About me?

The mayor suggested that Fernande and her children move back to her family in Louvain. She could not stay alone, isolated and without support in Honvelez. I totally agreed and gave the mayor a large amount of cash to cover Fernande's needs for the next few months. Inwardly, I was crushed. I felt guilty. Accountable. At fault for having dragged Jan into this. It was he who had offered me his hospitality and support. He had asked me not to involve him, yet he had provided me with the means of entering the gestapo building as a Chamebel "foreman" in Brussels after the airplane attack. And yet . . . and yet . . . and yet . . . Contradiction upon contradiction assaulted my mind.

The mayor, sensing the battle that raged within my conscience, tried to calm me. Finally, urging me to caution, he offered me his continuing support, although he felt that for the months to come I should stay away from Bovigny. Contact should be maintained through one of the local members of my group. Henri Bernard should officially move out of Honvelez. After all, Jan's business was now closed and Henri had no employment. He offered to provide me with a new identity. I would become Jules Louis Marechal from Jemeppe sur Meuse, a Liège suburb. Henri Bernard would no longer collect his food ration coupons and would eventually be found guilty of illegally changing his residence without permission and not reregistering with the authorities. Should the Germans question the mayor, he would not know of my whereabouts. At the end of our meeting, he asked me if I had heard of the destruction at the Gouvy station. Evidently several Germans had died and it would be days before traffic could be restored. I said I had heard about it and that it looked like the work of foreign agents to me. I gave Mayor Faisant the name of a contact who could reach me should the need arise. This same man would contact him should I need his services. On that note, we grieved a silent moment together, shook hands, and he departed. I packed my knapsack and left the shed.

A long night's walk lay ahead of me to reach my men in the Bois du Pays. The weather had cooled and the sky had clouded over. A faint rising moon was surrounded by a halo and blurred by the dampness. I walked as one lost. Later a cold drizzle came down. It suited my mood. I stopped several times. I felt drained of my usual energy, exhausted; not tired, but weak; not sick, but chilled from the inside. Then came the anger, the wrath and desire to avenge, and a need to weep alone in the woods, surrounded by the silent darkness.

I do not remember how long I stayed sitting on the damp ground under a tree mourning my lost friend, but I remember the mood in which I reached my men in the early morning. I was determined to continue the fight to the end, with a vigor annealed in my crucible of rage and loss.

I reached the camp as the men were having breakfast. Soon, they would leave to work along the cable. Today they were burying the wiring needed to activate the charges from a distance. They could not help but notice that something was wrong. I told them of Jan's fate and of my feelings. I told them of our long friendship, how we had met, and what we had done to-gether—how Jan had become my friend and how he had come to live here-abouts. I told them of his health and I told them of what I had done for Fernande and the kids, but I could not finish without telling them that this tragedy, among the many others that we had witnessed, only reinforced my conviction to fight and to act with even more determination, relentlessly, for this war to end in victory over this barbaric menace. The more ruthless our efforts, the more quickly our goal would be achieved. We should not give the Germans a moment's respite. I gave my fellow patriots a pep talk they did not need. It was I who needed it.

Only later, in June, did we learn the true cause of Jan's death. This we heard from his cellmate in the Arlon jail. Upon Jan's arrival at Liège, his jailers had checked his small suitcase, which of necessity had been packed in a hurry. They found his insulin and syringe. They told him they would return his insulin to him after he had answered their questions successfully, which Jan did not do. They deprived him of his medication. Still, he revealed nothing about us. They continued to deprive him until he went into a coma. Then they gave him just enough to bring him around and submitted him to questioning, again without success. He was returned to his cell and left without help. He collapsed into a second coma. Again they gave him just enough insulin to question him a third time. No questions were answered. He was returned to his cell. Exhausted, he fell asleep, succumbing in this coma. This time he was beyond their questions. He was dead.

CHAPTER 10

▼

In Grief and Wrath

After Jan's death, I thought often of what he had done, not so much for me but for all of us, and of his love of freedom. I reflected on my life, my upbringing, my education. I evaluated, reevaluated, and evaluated again. I tried to make judgments assessing and identifying myself. My upbringing had provided a generous view of people. I tried to accept them as they were, without prejudice toward them. I made an effort to understand the world and people's different viewpoints. I loved nature and respected its inscrutable complexity with a sense of wonder. Dogma I rejected, and yet I understood why so many people could not live with the question marks of life and turned to religion.

During this second world war in Europe, I witnessed a great change in people's attitudes. Our petty political differences nearly disappeared, save only for the communists, who blindly continued to follow Moscow's dictates. But another, more liberal attitude permeated Europe, crossing borders as the nations held in captivity by the Nazis were forced temporarily to set aside their differences and unite in their desire to regain their common freedom. Occupied Europe comprised many countries, each one different and yet all subject to the same rules of oppression—rules that were not just physical but, more importantly, that attempted to force us into a way of thinking. Rules based on force and prejudice and cultivated ignorance. The same reasons that earlier had caused me to reject communism now steeled me to reject and fight fascism. I longed for freedom and I hated Nazi ideals. I had no prejudice. They had nothing else.

Although I had been raised to hate guns and reject the use of violence, when I faced those issues now, I came to the conclusion that freedom was of priceless value and well worth fighting for. This cruel war would not be won by pacifists. This was not Gandhi's war. The beast of Nazism preaching domination and superiority had to be annihilated. German violence demanded our own. The harder they hit, the more determined we became to be a part of their destruction. Jan's arrest and death did more than anything else to unleash my energies and provide me with the will to abandon restraint.

While we realized that all Germans were not Nazis—many had been forced to serve—there was no longer time for individual evaluations. We were resolved to act for the destruction of Nazi Germany and would do so with clear conscience. We would fight anything and anyone in German uniform or working under their command.

That was our state of mind as May, 1944, drew to an end. Gouvy had been a success, Trois-Ponts was prepared, and the cable ready for destruction. The weather changed. We now had rain, but that did not slow us. My contacts with the Secret Army were established; we had arrived at an arrangement and I was in contact with the head of their underground in Baclain.

In the woods, not far from the village of Baclain, was a Secret Army camp where some ten illegals lived. The camp also housed seven Russians, all former prisoners of the Germans. They had been forced to work in the Belgian coal mines and after their escape had enrolled with the Secret Army. Their leader had been a political commissar in the Red Army and spoke good German. Through him I could communicate with his contingent. The camp possessed some armament which my group could augment to create a potentially dangerous force. By joining forces, we could execute the Trois-Ponts sabotage. The date of the action was set for June 2. We decided to move to Baclain two days prior to the Trois-Ponts action and have an extensive briefing and get-acquainted session.

Every evening we listened eagerly to London—the personal messages, the news—always hoping to hear the coded message that would announce D-day, for which we could hardly wait. D-day! The anticipated landing of Allied Forces. The arrival of the mighty force it took so long to assemble and prepare in Britain. Léon Joye had told me a secret coded message that would alert us and had urged me to pass it on to one or two trusted men in the group, in case something should happen to me in the meantime. Jan had been in on the secret; so was Charles.

Then, while preparing this second action, a totally unexpected event suddenly changed all our plans. A rain-drenched courier appeared at our camp to alert us that several truckloads of Germans had arrived at Bovigny, accompanied by three loaded horse trailers. Among the arriving Germans were some foreign-speaking soldiers wearing armbands emblazoned with the letters R.O.A. From news that had filtered into the Belgian underground from France, we had learned who they were and they indeed signaled real trouble. They were former Cossack prisoners of the Germans who had decided to serve the enemy. The letters R.O.A. on their armbands stood for *Ruskaya Oslobodanskaya Arme*—the Russian Liberation Army. They were here to comb the woods, searching out resistance camps.

Immediate action had to be taken to protect ourselves as well as others. Was Baclain's Secret Army informed? I was assured they were. Our next step was to insure the safety of our supplies and materials. A tightening of security and a call to general alert was issued to all the sentinels in the villages in our sector. Our communication system had been elaborately organized and was functioning well, as was underscored by the message we had just received. We were now on full alert and extreme vigilance was enforced while our system of communication was put to further tests.

I gave orders that the next alert was to be delivered that night to the Sadzots, in distant Forge à la Plez. My men busied themselves burying the material and supplies that we would not use immediately. Two men would be equipped with the Brens, the others would carry Stens, a .45 automatic pistol, and four grenades each. We dismantled the camp, carefully erasing all traces of our occupation. By now we were well trained to that task; we had been doing it weekly for months. Those inexperienced with such subterfuge may not realize how difficult it is to live in the woods without leaving traces of your occupancy or your passage. To an experienced tracker, the slightest broken branch or part of a shoe print in the mud, even a bent blade of grass, soon led to other signs and eventually to a camp. But we had trained ourselves well and were confident in our abilities.

Our tasks completed, we evacuated the Honvelez area and moved toward Forge a la Plez, putting a good distance between the abandoned camp and the German search party. We moved in and out of areas, evading the R.O.A. and the Germans.

The Sadzot family to whom I had sent a message was one of our best contacts. The sawmill was isolated and operated by the family during the construction seasons. Then the mill was closed for winter and all would return to Grandmenil. To reach them we had to cover approximately thirty miles through the woods avoiding villages, two main highways, and numerous country roads. Most crucial of all, we had to avoid the marshy and treacherous area south of La Baraque de Fraiture.

We took with us all the food we had. There were springs and brooks along

Bodson demonstrating the Bren gun to his men in the woods of the Bois de Ronce, 1944.

the way to provide fresh water. As we neared the villages of Pisserote, Tailles, and Dochamp, I sent a scout to each. They reported that all was clear, calm and normal. Our contacts were alerted to our new situation and asked to report that night or early next morning to the Sadzot sawmill at Forge a la Plez.

As we passed through the forest, the rain continued in fine, steady drops— the kind of rain shower in Belgium that you expect to last—and we were already soaked.

It was late when we finally arrived at the mill and Christian and I went to see if we could meet with Léon Sadzot. His father said that Léon had gone to Grandmenil, but should be back soon. The father, already alerted to the danger, was very alarmed for our safety as well as for those in the Baclain camp, who did not have our mobility. The camp was built to be permanent and could hardly be dismantled without leaving substantial traces. The elder Sadzot promised us a hot meal as soon as possible. He would have it brought to us at what we called the south pasture, a pasture surrounded by woods about a quarter of a mile south of the mill. He advised us to wait there until morning and then come back for any new information that had reached them during the night. To indicate danger, he would put a wood-hauling cart in the courtyard, warning us not to approach the house.

We went to the pasture and waited for the hot meal that never reached us. We kept a close vigil. Those not on sentry duty rested on the wet ground, huddled one against the other trying to stay warm. Morning brought no sign of the rain letting up. We waited until 8:00 A.M. before hiking toward the mill, Charles moving a little ahead of us as scout. As we neared the mill, he reported the all clear. There was no wood cart in the courtyard as he approached the house. Léon was back. The news was not good. Germans and Cossacks were also in Grandmenil, Samrée, and La Baraque de Fraiture. We also knew they were in Vielsalm, where they were quartered in the former Belgian barracks. So far they had not reappeared in Bovigny. Had they spent the night in the woods? Possibly. We decided to move to the largest area of unbroken woods in the region, the Bois de Saint Jean Chanoine and Cédrogne, south of Baraque de Fraiture. We had good contacts in Samrée, Tailles, and Pisserote, and would be free to move within a large area, encountering a minimum of roads, save only the main highway between Liège and Bastogne, which passed by La Baraque. We gave Léon our contact points and he provided us with enough food to last us two days. He apologized for the nonarrival of our meal the evening before; he had returned late and his father had not wanted to leave his sister alone.

We resumed our game of hide and seek. That night we slept near Pisserote. The rain still did not stop, and I offered the following proposal: could we risk going back the next day to the Bois de Ronce to recover the two steel drums full of good woolen American airmen's uniforms? They would be better than the cotton drill outfits we were wearing, drier and warmer even when soaking wet. I did not have to say more; a majority was in favor. So it was decided to contact Constant Lomry from the village of Courtil and learn of the enemy's current movements. Christian volunteered for the mission. When he returned, he had good news and hot chocolate! Thank you, dear Constant, and your wife, for warming us when we were so cold.

Bovigny was clear. The Germans had moved their trackers and horses toward Houffalize and La Baraque. Charles believed that the Germans would not actually go there, but would turn north along the way, stopping somewhere between Houffalize and La Baraque. Asked why, he answered that they would probably search the wooded area around "Le Sapin," as we now called the area of our secret drop zone, looking for our drop site. I agreed with his judgment. In fact, I thought from the beginning that this chase had been provoked by the drop, only three weeks before. They had failed to reach us on the night the plane came in and they needed time to accumulate enough information to locate the area of the drop. The Gouvy action must have led them to believe in an enemy presence. Only now were they beginning their search.

Our next logical move would be to change location as soon as possible. I opted for the Bois de Cédrogne, which extends along both sides of the Baraque-Houffalize road and is adjacent on the east to the Bois de Saint Jean Chanoine. It would put us under the protection of good intelligence sources that we had in Samrée and Tailles and would not be far from Forge à la Plez. So it was decided. We would raid our clothes cache and come back as soon as possible, staying in the southern zone of the woods which we figured the Germans had already searched.

In the valley of Ronce, west of Honvelez, we helped ourselves to the beautiful, warm, olive green wool U. S. Air Force uniforms. At that point our only items of equipment that were not U. S. issue were our berets, dear to paratroopers, commandos, and the underground. What the hell! We were as good as dead—if not worse than dead—if caught anyway, so why not travel in comfort?

Still it rained without any signs of abating. The only things we left in the clothing cache were the personal objects belonging to the airmen and other items nonessential to us. From the sealed emergency boxes issued to the airmen before each raid, I took the tubes of Benzedrine. They would help us to sustain ourselves during a prolonged effort to escape.

We then departed for the well-hidden valley of Martin Moulin, avoiding open spaces and the hamlet of Lomre.

We were well, but tired. Noel complained about his feet. We all could have done so, I am sure, but avoided the subject. The following morning we decided to go to Samrée and purchase some food. To our surprise, it was offered to us all prepared! We were treated to a delicious, hot, thick stew with substantial amounts of meat. Food shortages in World War II in the United States never approached the extremes experienced in Europe, although we in the underground did have it somewhat better than those who lived in the cities. Most of our friends were farmers who managed to hide

Engineers of Group E *(from left):* Christian Mannie, Charles de Greef, Noel Maes, and Bodson. All are dressed in American airmen's uniforms.

part of their harvest from the enemy, so that they lived far better than their city cousins. Even so, we often had very unbalanced meals—butter without bread, bread without butter, sugar and nothing to sweeten—but at least we had *something* to eat. This home-cooked stew, provided by the Laloux family, was a complete meal and the meat was not wild pig. We had come to dislike the taste of wild pig, having snared the leathery, gamey creature fairly often while living off the forest bounty the past five months.

By the morning, news arrived confirming Charles' assessment of the Germans' intent. They and their R.O.A. were in Bihain and we wished them good riddance there. We considered the direction of our next move in order to put even more distance between them and us. I suggested we abandon the area of Honvelez where we had spent so much time, because I felt it was no longer safe to remain there. The problem was our supplies. Although they were safely cached for now, they could only be reached under cover of night. Our decision was reached democratically by vote. There was one abstention: Noel complained that it would mean a lot of trips, walking under heavy loads, to move the supplies. I made a mental note to make sure he would be a part of all the missions of resupply from the caches; at least he would build good legs and stronger feet.

We moved to the area of the hamlet of Sadzot and Grandmenil for the rest of our days in the woods and were glad we did. The Sadzot family were nearby and of great help. The Germans and their Russian helpers, having not discovered a thing in our former camp area, now combed the woods west of the highway. They discovered nothing there either. It took them a week to find nothing. Then they abandoned their search. We were glad to see them go. We were near total exhaustion. The Benzedrine had helped us to sustain the nervous as well as the physical energy required when you are the prey, but we had reached our limits and needed rest.

Then the rain stopped. After seven continuous days and nights of alternating downpour and drizzle, it stopped. Our green uniforms served well in providing warmth, comfort, and, for once, enough pockets. But best of all, at journey's end, at the sawmill, there was a bath with hot water right out of the wood-fired boiler, and real soap, made of lye and animal fat by the Sadzot sisters. I still do not understand, even today, how we endured that week without so much as a cold or sore throat. Perhaps we were young and fit, or perhaps we just had no time for illness.

In any event, it was now time to return our attention to our delayed plans for the Trois-Ponts action. The sabotage needed to be rescheduled and contact with Baclain's Secret Army reestablished. The Germans appeared to be on the alert. More than ever, we needed to exert great caution. From the Sadzot region, I sent a messenger to Baclain. I needed to know if their area was still secure and if they were ready for our joint action.

Meanwhile (and usually we paid little attention to them any more), the flying fortresses flew over us each morning on their way to German objectives in well-organized formations. In the afternoons, a disorganized bunch flew back. Many planes were crippled, many flew low. One day, however, a plane did attract our attention. One of its engines was dead and another on the same wing was smoking. Léon Sadzot was with us at the time and remarked on it too. It seemed as if the plane was slowly losing altitude and would crash even before it reached our location. As we watched, the big plane moved steadily down and then disappeared from sight. It must have crashed near the Martin Moulin brook, observed Léon.

The Martin Moulin brook flows through a valley between the two big forests of Saint Jean Chanoine and Cédrogne, toward Baclain. The decision to investigate was quick and unanimous; even Léon urged us to allow him to accompany us in search of the machine. We departed immediately. It was still early in the afternoon and we had time before nightfall to reach the crash area and with luck, to find the plane. Following the previous week's unlucky events, we hoped chance would favor us this time. Late that afternoon, we found the plane. It had landed on a wooded ridge west of the Martin Moulin watercourse, well before the little road from Chabrenez to Wibrin.

The B-17 had landed in an area reforested perhaps fifteen years before. The trees were still young and broke without doing much damage to the plane, leaving it structurally sound. This was the first time we had seen a B-17 at close range. We were enormously impressed by the size of the machine. Compared to the DC-3 with which we were familiar, it was Herculean.

A close examination revealed no gas leaks and we moved to investigate the inside. We entered through an open side door. There was no one inside. The crew must have bailed out and by now were probably in German hands. Charles came forth with an idea that at first seemed crazy to me—to take the machine guns! But on second thought, I became inclined to agree with his thinking. Closer examination, however, revealed that the task was beyond our capabilities, except possibly for the upper turret guns. The other turrets' guns were installed in such cramped quarters that to remove them would necessitate both time and tools, neither of which we had.

We expected a German search party to arrive soon and acted quickly and carefully. The only tools we had on hand were a short crowbar and a pair of pliers. While Charles worked frantically at loosening the upper turret, others mounted guard and I looked for ways to create a gas leak. Charles succeeded in freeing the total assembly of a turntable on which a double-barreled .45 caliber machine gun was mounted. The total weight of our prize, we later learned, was above 120 pounds. My attempts to achieve what the Germans had not done, to develop a gas leak in the wing tanks, had thus far proved futile. I called for help to lower the gun assemblies, first from the turret to the wing and then from the wing to the ground. We also recovered over three thousand rounds of ammunition, although we left much more on board. The ammunition and the turret guns we moved a good mile away from the crash site and hid them under some evergreen branches. Returning to the plane and using a crowbar, I finally managed to break a hydraulic conduit and a gas line in an engine compartment. A bit of paper and a match would now achieve our final goal.

At that moment, Christian spotted people approaching from the west of us. Germans? Patriots? We did not stay to ask. We set the plane ablaze and traveled north at first, then changed our direction east to recross the Chabrenez-Wibrin road. Once on the road, we discovered a German truck parked and unguarded. The rear door was lowered, six coffins leaning neatly against it. For American bodies? Not even a sentry. The Germans were at the crash site nearly a mile away. It was absolutely quiet.

What an occasion for another match! I snapped the gas line from the tank and let the gas soak into the ground. Soon the truck and the coffins nourished a roaring fire. To the west we could see the glow of the burning plane and we could hear the muffled explosions of the ammunition left on board. We retreated in a hurry toward Forge à la Plez, thinking about the Germans' reaction when they discovered their truck. They would have to go back on foot, providing them with time to create the good explanations they would need upon their return. Then the dark of night enveloped us, protecting us for the last six or seven miles we had to go before reaching camp. Léon Sadzot was excited and justly proud of having accurately predicted the location of the plane. He invited us to a late snack at the mill house.

The next day, after a good night's rest, we received news from Baclain. All was clear there. They were happy to know we were safe and they were ready to assist. On June 5, in the morning, we sent another message telling them we were coming soon. Our messenger would also guide them to the machine gun, which we offered them for camp protection. Most of us would join them directly. Charles and Christian would spend a night in the Bois de Ronce excavating a cache in which we had stored all our materials for the Trois-Ponts project. Then they would rejoin us. Or so we thought.

June 5, 1944, 7:00 P.M. On our portable battery-operated radio, we listened to the news: *Ici Londres. Messages personnels: Le moulin se cache sous les frondaisons en fleurs.*

"Here is London. Personal messages: The mill is hidden behind the flowering trees."

We could not believe it. The message announcing D-day. This was it, our friends were coming! With this new invasion of Europe, the end of the nightmare was in sight. The final struggle would begin tomorrow after more than four years of Nazi rule. Only yesterday, the fall of Rome, now this!

I had to keep my head straight. We had a task to accomplish immediately, a task already prepared, the sabotage of the Paris-Berlin telephone cable. Our orders were to keep it out of commission for a week. That would be easy. The sabotage devices were already in place along the cable. Trois-Ponts would have to wait. From the rainy days of the recent chase, the weather had turned dry and sunny; summer was close on. Our spirits were high and our desire to achieve had no limits.

Two saboteurs, two guards, and two reserves were all I needed for the cable. In the early morning of June 6 I sent Christian to call Ourvary and three armed men. Charles I sent to Baclain to explain the new delay. They would be told of the landing and would understand. Noel and I went to the cable site and activated the first thermite charge by touching our hidden wires to a twelve-volt battery. We had no doubt that the German telephone repair specialists would appear in a very few hours. We retreated and kept watch. Noel dozed while I stood guard, thinking, dreaming. A J. S. Bach cantata composed for a religious occasion played over and over in my head. The title was so fitting: "Exultate, Jubilate!" Then another title came to my mind, "Ich habe Genug" (I have enough). I had had enough. Let's finish it. Let us be free again. Let us end the German dream of a thousand years of conquest and domination. My mind switched to Beethoven and the chorale of the ninth symphony. I thought about this renowned and humane German, this giant of music with his great love of mankind.

I thought about Schiller's words used in the great chorale of Beethoven's ninth, the famous "Ode to Joy." No, all was not lost, there was hope, the hope that had sustained us for these last four cruel years. There was hope even for Germany. But first we had to suppress this Nazi poison; annihilate their forces and crush their doctrine under our feet. The light we had seen however dimly ahead was now clearly visible. Continued, relentless action was needed now to precipitate the downfall. Thus I dreamed and watched as Noel slept. I woke him when it was his turn to take the watch and I slept.

Around 8:00 A.M. the sky filled with the usual roar of the flying fortresses passing overhead as two Germans appeared in the distance. Each carried a shovel and a rifle. They approached the cable and began to dig. We watched a little longer to make certain no others appeared. Then we went for a bite of breakfast. Once fed, we returned to our watch. The two Germans were still busy digging along the cable, trying to locate the trouble. We would have to watch them for a long time and at a safe distance without arousing their suspicion. We needed to know how long it would take them to make the repairs. Then, and only then, would we ignite the next charge so that they would have to start all over again. With care on our part the task would be easy, but boring.

As long as the cable was inoperative, the Germans' Paris headquarters had to transmit all messages by radio, scrambling and encoding them, which was time-consuming. As early as 1940, the English had received from Poland a captured "Enigma" machine. They had been at work on the German codes, keeping apace with the German modifications in their cipher system. The Allies were thus able, on radio messages only, to read and act accordingly, knowing German plans in advance. Our action forced the Germans to provide the Allies with the information they needed to conduct D-day operations.

Besides the D-day message, there was another that for reasons of security, only Charles and I understood. It would, in due time, alert us and direct us to heavy sabotage action just before the Allies were approaching our area.

"Message for little Berthe" would alert us for sabotage over all of Belgium. "Message for Cincinnati" would mean for us to limit our action to the Belgian province of Luxembourg, where we were. The general public often wondered about the messages that preceded the news. They were our orders from Allied headquarters and the link the Germans were never able to cut. They were our messages of war and hope. They were the keys to our actions.

June 7, 1944—news of the Allied landing in Normandy was on the airwaves. Little else was said. London was careful not to feed the enemy any useful information.

Christian returned with Ourvary and his three men who had been working on the cable. They had been watching the telephone linemen, activating the charges when needed. The Germans continued working diligently, although it must have been apparent to them that this was not an accident, but the result of a modern and sophisticated sabotage device; a device which completely melted the underground cable in a one-foot section, short-circuiting all pairs of copper wires. I kept track of the repairs in progress by frequently returning to the men. The linemen labored all night and all the next day without respite. As they talked, I could sometimes hear what they were saying, except when they spoke from the depths of their trench.

Charles was not expected to return from showing the Baclain men where the captured machine gun was hidden until the following day. As all was going easily and well, we took the time to catch up on much-needed rest. Following the events of the past few days, we were still in arrears on sleep. What would happen next was a mystery, but we determined to be rested and ready.

It took the Germans three days to locate and repair the melted wires. A half-mile away, Ourvary activated the second charge. When the Germans tested their repair work and found nothing worked, their German became louder. I could now easily hear their conversations and the messages they sent. They were deliciously angry as they waited for the electrical resistance tests to be completed, measurements which would indicate the approximate distance of the new break. They were angry, tired, and frustrated, and began using the eight-letter words required for effective cursing in their cumbersome language. They called for assistance as I feared they might. More Germans, more possibilities for trouble. We tightened our security and called in four more men. The two German technicians, I felt certain, were experiencing a growing sense of insecurity and a growing sense of hostility surrounding them.

During the fourth day, as the two original linemen dug around the second break, two more technicians arrived, accompanied by four soldiers. The latter were immediately given shovels to help with the digging. Trenching along, it took them another day to discover the damaged spot and to begin their repairs. One of our patrols discovered the vehicle that this new group had arrived in, a kind of army Volkswagen, which they had left parked in a firebreak near by. My men wanted to put it to the torch, but I vetoed the idea on the basis that it would spur the enemy to send more soldiers to the area and possibly some violent reaction which we wanted to avoid. We had only one job to do. Léon Joye had been very firm on that point when he briefed us. We were engineers, not soldiers. We should not unnecessarily provoke the enemy, but try to remain in the background, do our jobs, and only defend ourselves if attacked.

It took two days and part of a night for the second set of repairs to be completed. We activated the third charge. London had asked for the telephone service to be interrupted for one week; we gave them ten days and still had enough charges installed to provide more interruptions if needed.

Meanwhile, information was pouring in to us from different sources. Through Gustave Jacques we had a copy of a report from a friendly station master who monitored the rail traffic between Gouvy and Trois-Ponts. This I read with great interest. It provided me not only with dates and times, but also with the nature of the transport. In addition to the usual coke and iron ore trains, there were also troop and gasoline convoys, which offered promising targets for later. I sent a message to Gustave for the station master, asking him to continue watching and taking notes. We would use his services later, but for now we focused on our current task. Among the other news, we learned that the original Germans barracked at Rencheux near Vielsalm had departed only to be replaced by older, more experienced troops and that the area was now being very actively patrolled. They were evidently aware of a hostile presence.

We also were aware of a hostile presence of another kind: traitors. Some camps had been raided at night, all patriots killed. These traitors would not hesitate to lead the Germans to us. We had learned a long time before to minimize the risk by changing camp every week and posting sentries every night.

We also noticed that the food situation in our area was worsening by the day. There was practically nothing to be obtained even with food coupons. Farms were searched, but farmers had learned a few tricks and continued to share their meager supplies with us. Dad, with whom I was in frequent though indirect contact, reported that the situation in town was very serious. Many people were hungry, although morale remained high because of the recent news.

At the completion of our assigned tasks on the cable disruption, it seemed appropriate to turn our attention again to the Trois-Ponts station. Again we made arrangements to meet the Baclain group. Ourvary and his three men went home and awaited our next call, leaving four of us to go to Baclain. We arrived there on the June 14. It was a tiring march because of the heavy loads we carried, all the explosives and material for the sabotage, plus an extra load of armament for the Baclain people who would protect us. Their camp leader, Joseph Istasse, showed us the B-17 machine gun. They had mounted the piece on a wooden sled, giving it mobility. That evening we spent getting acquainted. I spoke in German with the Russian commissar and learned that all of his men had fought at the front and had seen a lot of action, unlike the Baclain men who had never been in a combat situation. Logically, I selected the Russians to be our bodyguards and gave the Belgians perimeter duties. A full briefing would follow the next morning, while the afternoon would be devoted to packing and relaxing before the meal. Departure for Trois-Ponts was set for 8:00 P.M. We knew it would be an arduous trip, twelve miles to cover across country, some of it over difficult terrain. We would travel along the crest of the hills on the west side of the Salm River, enjoying little moonlight but dry, mild weather.

CHAPTER 11

Baclain under Fire—
and a Revenge

The evening before the final briefing, we slept well on crude, straw-lined bunks. The next morning, in both French and German for the benefit of the commissar, I described the Trois-Ponts station, outlined our objectives and the order of destruction, and guided each man through the action from place of entry to place of exit. As this was the first action for the Baclain men, I emphasized and reemphasized the need for strict and exact observance of the plan and the timing. We finished with a question-and-answer period, after which I felt confidence in the plan and the men. These new comrades-in-arms knew of our big success at Gouvy and trusted us. Lunch was announced and quietly eaten. Then each man went about his own activities. Charles and I conducted a second session with the Russians. We wanted to make absolutely sure that they were familiar with the use of the Bren guns, the Sten guns, and the grenades. To my surprise, they knew all they needed to know about the Mills grenades. They had used them at their front. Whether they were imported from the United States or made in Russian factories, I do not know.

The Baclain Secret Army camp, situated three miles from the village of Baclain, lay on the sloping side of a valley, concealed under the branches of an old pine forest which grew partially down the valley. Beyond that was a barbed-wire fence and beyond that a meadow that continued down the slope to the creek. Our camp was about 150 feet above the upper edge of the meadow. Above our camp to the west, the woods led up to a narrow plateau over which the Langlir road was built. Across the creek, on the opposite side of the valley, another meadow sloped up to a narrow strip of woods huddled against a high, vertical cliff.

Late that afternoon, we were alerted to the sound of a small German reconnaissance plane flying over the camp. It circled several times and on the last pass dropped a red flare directly over us. Alarmed, camp leader Joseph Istasse and one of his men left immediately for the village to see what they could find out. Were German patrols operating in the area? We had to know. In his absence, I took command and sent my people into the forest surrounding and above the camp and to the edge of the meadow. I feared that the Germans would quietly try to surround us and attack at night. After a while my men returned, empty-handed. All was quiet. They had seen no sign of the enemy.

Suddenly, a hail of bullets rained about us, coming from the narrow strip of woods which hugged the cliff across the valley. Bullets from four German machine guns peppered the forest camp. I shouted to the commissar to get his men to the double-barreled turret gun and fire at the top of the cliff. In seconds the cliff was alive: *tumptumptump, tumptumptump,* a tracer, a piercer, an explosive; a tracer, a piercer, an explosive. Momentarily, the German guns fell silent, their operators surprised at our firepower, but then quickly resumed firing. As the protective rocks behind them splintered and showered in the air, blown apart by our barrage, the German guns fell silent a second time, and we scrambled for cover behind large trees, safe for the moment.

At the same time, a company of their infantry emerged from their narrow strip of woods and entered the meadow. The rhythmic *tumptumptump* of our machine gun filled the air, punctuated by our Bren guns firing in short, well-aimed bursts. The Germans moved quickly, losing men as they came, but still they came. Some were already across the creek, among them an officer, Luger in hand. Joseph Istasse's camp dog leapt at him, on the attack. The dog reached the officer, passed him, then turned and attacked him from behind, attaching itself to the seat of his quarry's pants. The man, impeded in his progress and slowed by this new appendage, was shot.

I put Christian in charge of the defense and Charles and I made our way to the sheds to booby-trap them with the charges intended for the Trois-Ponts raid. Arming the charges with thirty-minute timing pencils took only a few minutes, but by the time we returned, the enemy's fire had slowed considerably and it was time for us to evacuate. Shouting orders in both French and German, I broke the men into three groups: one to go south, one north, and one to go up the hill with me. Our rendezvous point would be the very small hamlet of Pisserotte. Two of the Russians, with one Bren gun, and Charles with another were to remain to slow the Germans down.

But the Germans retreated, retracing their steps down the hill and leaving at least ten dead and twenty wounded littering the field.

Our own retreat was more successful. We managed to take all our arms and ammunition with us. The Russians even dragged off the heavy machine gun in their retreat to the north through the woods. The only real thing of value left behind were twenty bicycles, and they were wired to five pounds of plastic explosive.

We progressed slowly through the woods, fanning out, ducking behind trees at first. Later as we gained distance from the meadow, we moved more easily, but with extreme caution, always certain that Germans lay in wait, just ahead; adrenaline and tension surged in the silence. Halfway up the hill we heard the roar of an explosion as our first charge went off, followed by others. We hoped that Germans were in the camp and enjoying the reception we had organized. We also hoped the explosions would shake the confidence of any Germans still waiting for us above.

We reached the Langlir road without encountering any enemy. The road looked clear and we walked silently through the woods following the road until we were above the Lomre fork. The darkness was complete now and still we had heard no more shots, meaning, we hoped, that the other groups had not been attacked. Around 2:00 A.M. we were all reunited safely at Pisserotte. I could not believe the Germans' stupidity. They had had us in the nest and had chosen the most dangerous approach without bothering to close our obvious escape route. I realized that our firepower surprised them, but still their attack was poorly organized. I could have done better and my infantry training was zero.

The Russians dragged the sled two or three miles, camouflaged it well, and held firm in their intention to retrieve the toy that had saved our lives.

After a brief discussion with the Baclain people, we decided to abandon the Trois-Ponts plan for now and to return to our area, while they established a new camp. The Russians agreed. So we bade them farewell and good luck and returned to Forge à la Plez.

The German account of the attack at Baclain appeared on June 22 in the daily *La Legia,* a German-controlled newspaper published in Liège. In an article entitled "Banditry," several actions were described involving bandits and terrorist repression by the German services. The article highly praised the Germans for capturing arms and material. The paragraph dealing with Baclain translated as follows: "The same day in the Montleban area, a German patrol had been attacked by gunfire. The area had been immediately surrounded and cleaṇed. There, they found 1,000 pounds of dynamite, 20 pistols, several carbines, one automatic pistol, thousands of munitions rounds, three radio transmitters and other material, such as false certificates. The camp, composed of three sheds and several tents, had been discovered and destroyed."

I am letting you be the judge of the Propaganda Abteilung's ability to lie. What is remarkable is that in the article from which I translated this, only a small part concerns our episode. It also reported seven other actions in the Liège and Ardennes area, indicating the intensity of the underground activity and the inability of the Germans to maintain control over the conquered territories. It demonstrated the problems they were facing, the problems we were creating.

When we returned to Léon Sadzot's farm, an urgent message from London awaited us. London wanted help in locating a train loaded with aviation gasoline. I immediately sent all available hands with messages to all known patriots asking them to be on the alert for any information that might be pertinent. Gustave Jacques was asked to talk with his station master friend and indeed he proved able to give us the information we needed. Through the Secret Army's Zone Five, Sector Four transmitter, we communicated the coordinates of the train's location to London. RAF bombers came that same night, only to find an empty track. The train had moved, but we found it again. Another game of hide and seek? This proved too much for me and I decided to try something on my own. If possible, my group would destroy this precious cargo. Perhaps this was the occasion to try our bazooka. In the area where the train was reported, the rails meander through the valley bottoms and the land offers many wooded hillside areas, good cover for an action of this kind. Through the station master, with whom we now decided to work hand in hand, we learned the latest news: our quarry was slowly moving toward Liège, just south of Trois-Ponts. The Germans waited in a high degree of preparedness along all tracks and stations. For some months all locomotives had had a German armed guard on board accompanying engineers and coal tenders. The station master indicated that among all of the possibilities, one of the best would be to force another train to collide with the twenty-car gasoline train.

Eight of us moved into a wooded area not far from the rail line and close to our friend's station. We had with us a bazooka and rockets. We were ready for an opportunity and armed with patience.

We didn't have long to wait. The station master, monitoring the train, let us know that the gasoline had been parked for the day in a tunnel north of

La Gleize. He said this was an ideal place for sabotage. He described in a long note the way it could be done at a minimum of risk and his proposal was so well thought out that I decided to follow his advice. He also sent us three official railroad smog signals that we should have at hand. Smog signals are flat, round, sheet-metal devices filled with a special explosive that detonates under the pressure of the locomotive's wheels, creating both noise and fumes. In fog, they replace the otherwise visible signals. One smog signal means extreme caution; two in a row means prepare to stop; three means emergency stop.

We intended to take advantage of a heavy ore train traveling toward Liège. I sent Christian and one other man to the south entrance of the tunnel with the mission of blowing up the left rail on the right-side track twenty minutes before the ore train was due there. Nobody would use the track in the interim. My men would probably have to get rid of a sentry—only one, we hoped—to achieve their task. But, they said later, it had been easy; he never knew what had hit him from behind. They did not fire a shot, did not alert anybody. They placed one pound of plastic against the rail with a time pencil to explode in due course. Then they hurried up the valley side and hid in the woods at a place where they could watch the tunnel entrance.

From our location, between Salmchâteau and Vielsalm, four of us approached the track under the protection of two others who stayed above, armed and ready to assist.

Ten minutes before the iron ore train arrived, we attached three smog signals at sixty-foot intervals and waited, hidden several hundred yards down the track, the distance the station master had said it would take for the heavy train to stop. It was now 10:20 P.M. The air was calm, the weather dry, the night dark.

Waiting, I thought of Jan. This was the Salm River valley's deepest and most enclosed part, an area where violent and powerful contractions of the earth's crust had created what in geology is called an area of intense metamorphism. We were in the very center of Jan's study area for his final dissertation; in hills that have been and still are drilled and excavated for slate and coticule honing stones. There was scarcely a hollow we had not entered and sampled together. If anything should happen to me or my friends tonight, I thought, if we had to run for protection, I knew where to go and the *Boche* would never find us. *Dear friend Jan, I wish you could see us; participate in our action. I know you would agree. . . .* My thoughts were interrupted by the noise of the approaching train.

Charles and I were on one side of the track, Ourvary and Noel on the other. The train passed over the signals with three loud detonations. The engineer applied the brakes and we saw sparks fly from the brake shoes all along the convoy as the locomotive came to a screeching halt almost in front of us. Ourvary shot the German guard dead, a bullet in the head. The engineer and his assistant were surprised but understood very well what we wanted. I told them, in a mixture of French and Walloon, to build steam and let the train go all alone down the track toward oblivion. As the engineer adjusted several valves and levers, his assistant climbed down. The engineer opened the brakes, pushed the lever forward admitting steam, and jumped down with his lunchbox. Both faded into the darkness with large grins on their faces, lunchboxes swinging at their sides. The train gained speed as it passed us. It would roar through Vielsalm, Grand Halleux, and Trois-Ponts and then reach the tunnel entrance. For us, it was all over. We quickly climbed back into the woods with our guards and returned to camp. Christian and his partner would join us later and report how it had gone at the tunnel. It would be a long vigil for us at camp. Christian would have a very long way to walk back from the tunnel, ten miles as the crow flies, probably fifteen walking to avoid villages and roads. Happily, there would be no large watercourses to cross and only one main road, connecting Baraque to Liège.

When these men finally reached us the next morning, having walked most of the night, they were elated.

The train had arrived with the screaming thunder of full speed, the rails and the wheels spitting fire from the friction of the curves. It disappeared into the tunnel. The earth shook. From inside the mountain, a muffled explosion was heard and an enormous black cloud appeared at the tunnel entrance. The air filled with the odor of gasoline, an expulsion of smoke, and the sound of great suction as the tunnel replenished itself with air, then another muffled explosion and more black smoke, and so it went all night and all day and was still going on when they left. Later we learned of the fate of the citizens of La Gleize: a week at forced labor.

As the fire subsided, the cleaning crew faced a difficult task: remove the entangled remains of two trains, reforged in hell's heat. No large crane could be used inside the tunnel, only small ones; long hours of torch work and the removal of some seventeen hundred tons of iron ore, twenty-two cars at eighty tons each. All La Gleize men aged fifteen to sixty were given wheelbarrows and shovels and were a part of two human conveyor belts emptying the tunnel of ore and dropping it in the valley, one piece at a time. Remnants of cars were dragged out. It took two weeks to restore the traffic. This was one of our best efforts and achieved several objectives: the disruption of rail traffic for two weeks—no ore to Liège, Lorraine deprived of coke; two locomotives and lots of rolling stock destroyed; and, best of all, the elusive gasoline train had been blown up. It certainly was worth a message to England. Thank you, our friendly station master. I will not, even now, tell who you are. It will be our little secret, forever, for one never knows. So ended the month of June, 1944.

La Legia did not publish even a paragraph about this licking. No, the Germans only printed lies. The truth to them was offensive.

In Normandy, the Allies had reached Cherbourg and found the harbor, the pride of the French navy's Atlantic fleet, destroyed and in a shambles. It could not be used. The advance was slow. Germans brought to bay acted like animals fighting for their lives. The tables had been turned; they were dying stupidly for the cause of domination. The Americans, French, and British offered their lives for freedom. So did the men from the different undergrounds in France and behind the lines. We were trying our best to help shorten the ordeal.

In France, fighting groups were mobilized and armed in areas to be liberated. All these activities were coordinated by Allied headquarters in London. For specialized units, like Service Hotton, the responsibility of coordinating fell to Special Force Mission.

Not knowing when or where the invasion would take place and totally divided about the Allies' intentions, especially the British deception tactics, the Germans had wisely kept two heavy tank units in rear reserve. One such panzer division was in Belgium, east of Antwerp. The outfit waited, living in tents along the track on which their tanks sat loaded on railcars, armed and at the ready. It was essential to the Allies to delay as long as possible these men and machines from reaching the beach landing zone. The bridgehead would necessarily be weak for a few days while men and materials were offloaded. On June 6, finally knowing where the landing had taken place, though still uncertain if this was the real one or a diversion, German HQ gave orders for the panzers to move. (The Pas de Calais north of Normandy was still, in some German minds, the real invasion site.) Marcel Franckson's group was charged with delaying the panzer trains crossing the French border and forcing them to detour. Having built strong intelligence in the border area, they were able to keep track of train locations and sabotage the rails, forcing the trains to ever more detours.

He and his men successfully kept the German tanks in Belgium for four days. When the tanks finally did enter France, they would only face French engineers doing the same job. They were so delayed that they had minimal impact on the Allied forces.

The summer of 1944 replayed the weather of the summer of 1914. Belgians are accustomed to having rainy summers in one out of every two—rarely three—years. The Germans had chosen to invade us in 1914 and had had a dry summer in their favor. This time we had the advantage of dry and beautiful weather, which certainly facilitated our tasks.

Feeling insecure, attacked from the Atlantic, harassed from inside, the zealous Germans redoubled their efforts to clean us out. They used all the possibilities at hand. They took advantage of traitors as informants who would lead Germans at night into the woods, to our camps. The Germans would then surround the freedom fighters and mercilessly machine-gun them to death. It happened many times in France, in Holland, in Belgium. It happened at Graide at the Secret Army camp near us. The attack we broke out of at Baclain had been the exception. To avenge some of our friends who died under machine-gun fire in their sleep, and to induce fear in traitorous minds, we had to act. And we did, brutally.

When my group was asked to act against traitors, I thought it was just. It had to be done. But I also thought of the war's end, of the need to protect ourselves from the courts that later would ask us to account for our actions against Belgian civilians. Generally, orders for killing were protected by a military chain of command. Such a case happened to us. An order came to execute a man convicted of being a gestapo informer. My group was selected to liquidate him. Somebody had to pull the trigger. After discussing the order with the men, I suggested we draw straws to designate the executioner.

The shortest straw fell to the hands of one of the youngest in my group. He was a fervent Catholic and reeled at the idea of having to take a human life. He simply would not do it. I tried the best of my persuasive talk but to no avail. I called upon the services of our priest. He joined us in the woods, said mass for us, and then took our young warrior for a walk into the deep forest. An hour later they were back and his persuaded parishioner was eager to act. A week later, with the help of others, the gestapo informer was found and shot.

Shortly thereafter, Mayor Faisant contacted me with a similar case. He had proof that a young man of nineteen had, under the cover of night, guided the Germans through the woods to a camp where they had killed a group of Secret Army men. He wanted us to execute the lad and his mother, who was the real informant. The father and two other sons were away fighting the

Russians as members of the infamous Légion Wallonie, a creation of the traitor Degrelle. I trusted Mayor Faisant, an official, but he was no man of law nor was he in the chain of military command. Yet I wanted to act and do so quickly to eliminate the danger. I had to explain to the mayor that I would only act after having received from him a written and signed report that I would transmit to the Secret Army staff for recommendation. He provided one, and it was not long before we received an official go-ahead. Still I was not totally at ease. I wished to obtain proof of my own before acting.

After surrounding the house, a substantial Ardennes stone structure with outbuildings located on a triangular piece of land at the intersection of three rural roads, Charles and I entered the building and confronted the two. They first denied the charges. We applied a little coercive persuasion and soon they were at the table writing a confession of their crime. When the document was dated and signed, we tied the two to chairs and spread a gallon of gasoline on the floor. A small explosive charge and a time pencil were left behind. The bodies were incinerated in the building. When I last returned to the village in 1954, some wall remnants were still standing, untouched. No one would touch such a piece of despoiled ground. The villagers were thankful for our action. The signed confession was given to Mayor Faisant and he, after liberation, transmitted the document to the judicial authorities, who closed the file.

Every evening I faithfully listened to the London news in case a coded message should be broadcast. When I was not available, another was in charge of taking note of the personal messages. Some only I understood; some Charles knew about. It was essential to stay in contact. The Normandy area news was scant, but the campaign seemed to be progressing to the Allies' advantage against a stubborn German defense. While they moved slowly, too slowly for our liking, the Allies never lost any gained territory.

We stayed quietly in the woods when inactive, confident that our contacts in every village around would bring us fast warning if needed. Nevertheless, there was always the possibility of infiltration; we were living in treacherous times. So we were alert and never slept without sentries. As was our habit, we moved camp every week or so, so as to not leave too many signs of our presence. By experience we preferred areas where the trees were still young, fifteen to twenty years old. These offered the best cover as their branches sloped to the ground. We cut a few low branches away all around the camp in a hundred-foot radius so that, lying on the ground, we could see people arrive without ourselves being seen. Two Brens were permanently stationed at the ready.

One night I remember being rudely awakened from my sleep by Charles who whispered to me, "Henri, wake up, somebody is coming." I jumped from under my lean-to, attached my belt, put on my shoes, and grabbed my Sten gun. I toured the short camp perimeter and stopped near Christian, lying on the ground with a Bren. He was looking at me with a finger to his lips, indicating silence. I listened intently. There was the unmistakable sound of someone approaching a few steps at a time, carefully. Each breaking of a twig was followed by silence, then the steps resumed. We were very tense, the four of us. Our nerves were raw. Whoever was approaching was certainly taking his time. Charles had the second Bren ready. Noel awakened, too, and was ready with Sten, pistol, and grenades. The night was slightly breezy but there was no wind at our level, at the base of the trees. The direction of the approaching stranger or strangers was now certain. Whoever was approaching ascended the slope from a distant meadow fenced from the woods below. Then, all of a sudden, Christian muffled a laugh while looking at the end of his Bren gun. A young calf was quietly licking the muzzle of his weapon. All of that for a calf that had found a weak spot in the fence and a way to the greener grass on the other side. I decided to relieve Christian and took his tour of duty, knowing I could not have gone back to sleep after that. I was fully awake with torrents of adrenaline flowing through my system.

The next morning Léon Sadzot came and surprised us with a beautiful piece of meat. He had butchered a cow, illegally, the previous night. He also had with him a large, and still warm, crusty loaf of whole-wheat bread—and a message from our station master, who asked to see me to discuss the possibility of another sabotage.

I immediately sent him a reply suggesting a meeting at his best convenience; he should give me at least a day's notice. Why not at the provincial insane asylum in Lierneux? The director, a Dr. Mathien, was the youngest son of one of my father's dearest friends. I knew that I was always welcome there, and the place was easy to reach for both of us. Besides it was a haven of calm. Nazis hated the insane and avoided the place. It was such a large locked compound that one could be there and never be found should the place be searched.

Two days later, another message arrived from our friend on the rail track: Lierneux asylum was OK, 2:00 P.M., two days hence. From Forge à la Plez, by foot, it was five or six miles, with only two roads to cross, but there were many bare spots to negotiate and many fences to climb over. It would be better to travel by night. I sent a message to Dr. Mathien announcing my visit with a guest, and another message to Ourvary telling him of a possible action soon—to keep his men on the alert, ready to come on short notice.

I spent a lazy day in anticipation, enjoying a beautiful summer day. That night we were invited to dinner at the mill house. Léon's sister and the maid had prepared a feast. Steaks, french fries, salad fresh from the garden. After dinner, Léon's father came back into the kitchen with a bottle of *pecquet*. Only cigars and coffee were missing.

How marvelous were those friends, risking their lives to help us in any possible way, taking time to entertain us, to feed us, to lend us their car. They went as far as teaching me how to milk a cow, so that I could milk her at night in the pasture below our camp. She was a calm, gentle beast, living like us in the woods, but confined to a hidden, fenced pasture. Charles became a good milker too. We all enjoyed the fresh lukewarm milk.

The following night I departed for Lierneux, accompanied only by my .45 and planning to return the next night. I wore an old cap and a light old coat to camouflage my American wool outfit. The trip to Lierneux would have been pleasurable had it not begun to pour with rain around 3:00 A.M. Since I had only a few miles to cover, I had delayed my departure until well after midnight. I arrived at the Lierneux asylum in the very early morning, drenched and dripping puddles on the anteroom floor.

Dr. Mathien was glad to see me and extended his most cordial hospitality. While my cap and coat were sent to the laundry to be dried, we breakfasted together, one of those breakfasts rarely eaten in wartime, an Ardennes early meal with eggs and bacon, bread and butter, a breakfast that stuck to your ribs—served with the inevitable ersatz coffee.

As we talked, he told me that the home of his youth, in Cointes near Liège, was half demolished. The bombardiers had attacked the bridge, the station, and the track going toward Brussels. Bombs had fallen parallel to the track but six hundred yards to one side, demolishing houses and killing people. These things had happened everywhere. We regretted it, but there was nothing to do about it; such were the risks of war. Those able to make an omelette without breaking any eggs had still to come forth. Happily for the Mathien family, the house had been empty.

While talking with Dr. Mathien I realized that he knew many of my men but was totally unaware of their underground activities. He was surprised at the intensity of our actions, surprised at what we could achieve. He had heard about Gouvy and the tunnel. I told him the Secret Army had done it and I didn't feel like a liar since we were part of it, their engineers. My learned friend had his duties to attend to and he left me in his study with a couch and good reading. Needless to say, I fell asleep and he had to wake me for a pleasant lunch with his wife and the children.

When the station master arrived, we retired to the study for our meeting. What the man had in mind was nothing less than the destruction of a troop train. He said German troops were traveling more and more frequently through his station—trains loaded with troops, mostly reserves of older soldiers taking the places of younger ones in Belgium, often moved through at night. One train every other day was the average.

He had thought of a plan: use the train to detonate charges which we would install under the central arch of a high bridge crossing the Amblève River between La Gleize and Stoumont. I asked details about the bridge, its exact location, the track design in the area before the bridge, the height of the bridge above the water. It was a three-arched brick structure, with the rail level more than a hundred feet above the river. Its location was a good distance away from the road, close to a little village atop the hillside. I told him it would be a very difficult job and I would need to inspect the site after having received the plans of the structure, without which I could not estimate the charges that would be needed. Probably the amount would seriously deplete our small stock. Besides, the execution would be very delicate. I really could not give him any answer before I had studied the problem, although in principle it had attracted my fancy.

I could foresee the charges being triggered by smog signals and a detonating cord. Everything could be prepared and wired in advance. The last connection should be wired only after we had received a signal telling us an appropriate train was on its way, at night. There was too much traffic and surveillance for it to be done in daylight. I wanted to be absolutely certain that I was not going to spend precious plastic on an ore train, and that the bridge's central arch would be blown apart so as to destroy both tracks, blocking the traffic for a long time.

How to organize safe and rapid communications between us on the site and him was another problem we discussed. There too he had ready answers: a telephone connection with the nearby village and a courier from there to us, ten minutes tops. It was well thought out and could certainly work. I was impressed. The man was talking business. What about the life of the engineer and the coal handler? No problem there, I was told. German crews operated all troop trains. He told me we would have twenty minutes before the train reached the bridge. The telephone would take only a minute to alert a man he trusted in the village of Cheneux. He in turn would need ten

minutes to reach us. We would have enough time to attach the final connection and install the smog signals. My conclusions were positive. I told him it
would take ten days to obtain the drawings, a few days more to study the
site. In two weeks I would give him a final answer through our usual channel,
Gustave Jacques.

By late afternoon, Dr. Mathien was talking with Dad to request the construction drawings, using a private coded language I had given him. Dad and
I routinely communicated thus. The drawing number was made of latitude
and longitude coordinates. Dad would contact Marcel Franckson, Sr., at the
S.N.C.F.B. (the national Belgian railroad company) who would have them
sent to Gustave. In less than a week the drawings and specifications were at
hand and Charles and I inspected the site in daylight. In the early evening
we looked at more details. We found a good place for a temporary bivouac, in
a wood close to both the bridge and Cheneux. The work would be extremely
difficult and risky, but I was certain we could do it.

It would be an acrobatic feat. The positioning of two twenty-pound
charges under the arch would necessitate using hundreds of feet of thick
manila rope. Hundreds of feet of detonating cord also had to be installed
and camouflaged under the ballast stones. All had to be engineered in such
a way that it could stay on location without being spotted and without endangering other rail traffic. It should be possible to activate the trap in a matter
of minutes with a smog signal trigger. As I saw it, our greatest risk was of a
German rail inspector noticing the presence of a rope, a wire, anything out
of the ordinary. Our camouflage job had to be perfect. We might have to
wait two or more days before a suitable target would come by. Until then,
we were in constant danger of being discovered. It would take forty pounds
of plastic, half of our remaining stock, but it was worth risking.

Christian and Noel were sent to the Bois de Ronce to retrieve the explosives while I organized the Forge à la Plez camp, using men from Ourvary's
subgroup, and the delightful Sadzot sisters. They would dye the ropes brick-
red using aniline dyes, which I would later deliver. We were able to secure
the tinctures and the ropes without much difficulty and by the time Christian
and Noel returned, we were set to act.

Traveling in the quiet of night, through the woods as much as possible, we
reached the village of Cheneux. Passing around it, we continued to the Bois
de Rahier where we would establish our temporary camp. By first light, the
bridge had a fascinating beauty, its three graceful arches reminiscent of an
ancient Roman aqueduct.

While the others searched the nearby woods to make sure we were alone,

Marcel Franckson, Sr. (alias Nestor), engineer.

Noel and I set up camp. By early afternoon we were enjoying our place in the warm July sun. By evening we were rested and ready to begin. Altogether, we were ten. It was a moonless night and we had much to accomplish.

Our task was complicated by the very real possibility that we would not be alone on the bridge, that trains might also be using it, that we might have to evacuate quickly, camouflaging our intent as best we could manage. Trains traveling north represented little difficulty. We could hear the puffing of the hard-working engine as it climbed the steep grade to the bridge. But those traveling south toward Liège were another matter. Running downhill, their engines were nearly silent, and any sound was dampened by the muffling effect of the curved tunnel emerging from the hillside to the north, about a half-mile above us.

Also in the woods above us were Ourvary and his best marksmen to protect us. We who were to plant the explosives had decided to work unarmed. The acrobatics of the task ahead rendered weapons useless, perhaps even dangerous: a dropped weapon, a clatter on the stones, a shot? Too risky.

At a nod from me our point man began his steep descent over the embankment to the river bed below. The rest of us peered into the darkness one last time, searching for anything unusual. Soon, a whistled bird call came from below and we began to walk out of the woods and onto the bridge. The men with the ropes led, men with charges following. We passed along the dirt- and ballast-filled rail bed warily to near the middle of the central arch. There we located the water drainage holes in the parapet walls on either side of the track. There were two to a side, at track level, spaced four feet apart. A hundred feet below us, the Amblève River wound its quiet way through the mountains. Four men were assigned to the drainage holes, one to each hole, while the fifth man stood apart, listening for the sounds of approaching trains.

I began by lowering a length of manila rope through the portal along the southbound track to our man in the river below, while Charles, my counterpart along the northbound track, dropped a lighter cord. Below, they were tied together, and with little effort, Noel returned the length of manila rope to the north side of the bridge. This he passed to his partner, who lowered it through his opening to the river. The process was repeated, returning the rope to my partner on our side of the bridge. When the ends were securely tied, we had effectively created two parallel slings, hanging snugly under the central arch. These we would use to "rock" two twenty-pound babies directly under the north- and southbound tracks, but first our task was to get them there. This Charles and I would do. We each fashioned a double loop at the end of a rope, large enough to receive our legs and act as a seat. We knotted our harnesses. Sitting in these, each carrying a length of clothesline and twenty pounds of explosives wrapped in red-dyed cloth, we were ready to be lowered over the sides.

When I was at eye level with the arch, I whistled and my descent abruptly stopped. Above, the others wound the rope through the drain and over the railing, securing it with a knot. Should a train come by, we were prepared to dangle precariously, though securely tied, over what in the darkness appeared to be a bottomless abyss.

Steadying myself against the cool brick with one hand and extending my other arm with a length of rope in my hand, I edged my way to the manila cable farthest from me. I maneuvered the rope over the cable. When I had the end of the rope securely back in my hand, I swung back. Putting the other end over the cable directly in front of me, I pulled the rope taut and tied the two ends securely. Then I had to remove the explosives from my jacket and hold and tie them in place using my hands, my teeth, and the dangling ends of the clothesline. With some difficulty, it was accomplished. I double-checked my handiwork. Good.

For the next phase, I slid the rope until the bomb hung directly between the cables and, pushing off a bit, grabbed the far cable again. Hanging, like the bomb, between the cables, and using my feet against the clotheslines, I inched the bomb further under the arch until it hung beneath the tracks. My body swung away and my hands reached again for the security of the bricks. I whistled softly. The safety rope was untied and I was pulled slowly up to the track bed, feeding out detonator cord as I rose. Back on the bridge, we all nodded approvingly at our luck. No train had passed. In the remaining darkness of the night, we worked quickly at completing our task. No train yet meant every minute brought one closer.

Running the detonator cords several hundred feet along the tracks toward the tunnel, we marked their ends with small stone cairns. Then, back-tracking, we covered the cords with ballast stones.

One final examination of the site: did anything suggest the existence of that which we had hidden? Satisfied, we headed silently toward camp. Part one completed, a hot meal and the easing of the tension lay ahead.

Over dinner we set the night watch and relived the hanging of the bombs until our conversation turned to part two. How long before a troop train? Was our camouflaging good enough to escape detection? Would it be a large troop train? Would the two charges destroy the bridge, would it work, was it worthwhile?

We decide to recheck the work at first light. Then, if necessary, we could return tomorrow night and make our corrections. On that, we retired for the night.

From our vantage point on the hillside the next morning, all seemed well hidden and in order. The day progressed watching trains pass up and down the tracks and counting cars. The end of day brought no troop trains, no sign of the courier from Cheneux, and night descending on the calm and beautiful Amblève valley. Through the night we waited, smog signals close at hand.

Day two came and passed slowly. Late in the afternoon a troop train did pass, machine guns mounted on flat cars, manned and ready. The enemy was evidently feeling the need to traverse the occupied territory armed and on the alert, but still there was no Cheneux courier.

About 11:00 P.M., as we stared at the stars rising in the night sky, our courier appeared panting his one-word message, "Victory." Rapidly, we moved through our predetermined plan. Christian and I fastened a smog signal to the detonating cords, while Noel and Charles set three smog signals on the northbound track down the line, to warn future trains to stop. We had no desire to take civilian lives.

Ten minutes later our quarry came speeding out of the tunnel and onto the tracks on its way to Liège and to hell. As it reached halfway across the first arch, a deafening roar rent the air and the central arch fell away. There was no possibility of stopping or even slowing the train in time. First the engine disappeared into the void, pulling cars in behind it. Then came the roar of the exploding engine as it hit the river bed, and the sound of the cars as they piled onto the growing wreckage. As the cars fell into space, the older, third-class cars, made of pine boards bolted onto steel chassis, broke into pieces. Each piece was a thorn, a dagger, stabbing our enemy. Then followed deafening, oppressive silence.

Recovering from our fascination at the grim scene before us, we retreated quickly to the safety of the woods and camp. The explosions would have wakened the countryside for miles around.

In the days that followed, we learned the measure of our success. The next day, the river ran red with blood from dawn to dusk. The train had carried six hundred soldiers. There were no survivors. A crew began rebridging the gap immediately, but it would be fully ten days before traffic resumed. We were well satisfied.

A hard revenge it was for the attack at Baclain, for the suffering and the misery, for the disruption of peoples' lives and the suppression of their souls. For all the violence. For Jan.

CHAPTER 12

▼

Verviers

Our gruesome action depriving the Third Reich of some of its warriors at a moment when it could have used more was at the end of July. The Normandy front was in flux, Aromanche retaken.

While the summer was glorious and not too hot, the food situation was at its worst in four years. The bread could hardly be called bread any more. The only thing it still had left in common with that staple, that basic element of our diet, was the outside shape of the loaf. The size had decreased, but the weight had not. When you tried to slice it, it stuck to the knife and glued itself back together behind the passing blade. Separating slice from loaf was a problem generating sticky threads. The stuff made a mush in one's mouth, was heavy on the stomach, and offered no sustenance. Meat was all but absent, potatoes rare and expensive. Happily it was summer and produce was available. People seemed to sense an approaching end to the nightmare and they endured.

The Germans were more and more active: more controls, more arrests for more and more futile reasons. Mom and Dad managed to spend a few days out of the city, in Erezée with Mr. and Mrs. Franckson, Sr., and I was able to see them there in a clearing in the woods. How thin they all were. We did not push our luck. Our meeting was brief. Mr. Franckson told me there was a possibility that my group would be asked to sabotage a major railroad tunnel between Liège and Germany, the Verviers tunnel. It was being discussed in high places, but nothing had yet been decided. The London agents in charge of Hotton—there were three altogether, not just Léon, as I had thought— were in hiding or under arrest; their circumstances were unclear and were being investigated.

Mr. Franckson asked my reaction to the prospect of blowing up the tunnel. I had to answer honestly that I was not optimistic. The Germans were on their toes. We had only five pounds of plastic left and for a tunnel we would need much, much more. I was certain that the enemy was going to care very much about one of the remaining rare escape routes *toward* Germany. All such rail routes will be heavily guarded. Was there any way we could yet receive more explosive? Was there any stock elsewhere? Another parachute drop seemed too risky to us. More to the point, I did not see how I could move my group to such a distant location and especially not to the populated Verviers area. Would it be possible to put us in contact with the Verviers Secret Army? One or two of us could possibly go there and coordinate the engineering work, but a strong and well-equipped security force would also be needed.

I asked him if there was news of my friend, Marcel, Jr. Mr. Franckson told me that his son had been very active, mostly in the Chimay area. His group had had a severe confrontation with the enemy and, unhappily, had some casualties and wounded. But Marcel himself was safe and was as hopeful as we that the end was near. Although we realized that playing those last cards was the most dangerous part of this game, we seemed at last to be gaining the upper hand. Together we would beat these Germans. Our meeting thus ended on an optimistic note. Dad told me that on the roadside embankment between Erezée and Soy was a stretch of ripe wild strawberries. They were going there to pick the delicious little fruits, and on that mouth-watering note, we parted.

Back in the group, we suffered from a temporary lack of activity. This problem had arisen before, but not to this degree. We were restless after the numerous actions of July. Waiting was hard on us and inactivity brought its own problems. Although I had always counseled abstinence to our fighters, they were young and in good physical shape, which did not favor abstinence or celibacy. I had a special problem with Noel. He was hard to control, and, I must agree, Léon's sisters were healthy and very good-looking girls. Noel invented any pretext to go down to the mill house. One evening Léon and his sisters brought us a pot of hot stew. As we ate and chatted, I noticed that Noel had disappeared with the younger girl. I did not like it; nobody liked it. Charles and I left Christian with Léon and the other girl, trying to locate the young buck and his friend. They were not far off and we brought them back. Later I had to ask Léon not to bring his sisters with him any more, explaining how hard such charming visits were on our systems.

It was a situation that could not be ignored, since it could lead to security trouble. If I let discipline slacken by one ounce, we might soon face a ton of problems. One thing could bring another. An ill-considered word in a young girl's ear might bring disaster. Not that I had the least doubt about Léon's sisters, but they were the spark that could ignite desire and I could foresee one of us sneaking off toward a village in search of adventure. This could bring Germans. It seemed harsh, but this was the price of safety for all of us, so I preached to my men.

One evening, after sunset, as we were going down to the mill house for a meal offered by the Sadzots, it was raining and we proceeded slowly to avoid touching the dripping branches. Because of the rain, I had tucked my glasses into a breast pocket. Visibility was hampered by the rain as well as by the vapor ascending from the warm, wet ground. We emerged from the woods perhaps a little too confident about the isolation of the place. We had moved some thirty yards into an open meadow sloping toward the mill when a shot was fired and a bullet hissed past us. Then several more. We raced back up under cover as fast as we could. As I dove head first into the pines, a dead twig hit my right eye, my only good one. I twisted my head sideways but was badly wounded and in agony. The other men had to help me back through the woods to camp. I was nearly blinded and any effort to use my eye brought intense pain. I ended up closing both eyes and being guided.

The first thing to do once in camp was to cover both eyes; one would not be enough—it is well-known how they interact. I took some strong painkilling pills and asked for a sentry at the edge of the woods and a reconnaissance mission to the mill. I stayed alone, the pain slowly subsiding. But the medication was so strong that my mind was cloudy. Charles soon reported that a company of Germans was around the mill. They had an army kitchen smoking and several trucks parked about. Everything seemed calm; there were no signs of aggression. There was no sign of any investigation either. Possibly they thought one sentry had simply been seeing things and gotten trigger happy. Nonetheless, I ordered a guard of one-hour watches to be maintained through the night.

The night passed uneventfully and by early morning, the Germans had left toward Dochamp. I called for a volunteer for a mission to Léon to arrange for medical help. Charles went, but did not get far before meeting Léon already on his way to us. He admitted it had been a freakish affair. The German trucks had been on his property before he even knew they were approaching. There had been no way to warn us, as the family were all inside the house preparing for dinner. Happily, said he, the table had not yet been set for nine instead of the usual four. Léon asked for details about my eye, and Charles explained about the shooting. I told Léon I was afraid my wound was serious and I would need the help of an ophthalmologist or risk infection. Léon, always ready to help, rushed home and called their doctor, who recommended two specialists, one in Hotton, one in Laroche. He then arranged for transportation. I would travel in a horse-drawn cart, hidden in a nook among bags of bran. When Léon gave me a choice between the two physicians I did not hesitate to select the one in Hotton for reasons that had nothing to do with medical expertise. Laroche was a place favored by the Germans, a busy summer vacation spot on the Ourthe River, certainly not the best place for us to visit. Hotton was a sleepy little town offering no particular interest to the enemy.

The twelve-mile trip to Hotton went well enough, although to me, being rattled about in the dark, it seemed endless. We entered the rear courtyard of the doctor's house, where Léon unloaded the "bran." The clinic was already darkened when the doctor removed my blindfold. I had suffered a serious laceration of the conjunctiva and also a deep and dirty gash on the cornea. Thank God, said he, the lens was intact. He told me he would have to give me local anesthesia in order to clean all the debris the twig had left in the wound, and said it was essential for me to stay in a dark room for at least eight or ten days. I would need to have an ointment put into my eye twice daily and must keep it covered with a sterile pad. He would have liked to keep me at the clinic, but did not think it would be safe for me or him. I answered that we would manage to create our own dark room in the woods.

Be certain, he added, to watch for complications. He gave me an ample stock of medicine and pads. A physician should look at my eye in a week. I told him we had access to one who would visit us in camp. After having cleaned and dressed my eye he asked me to relax while he wrote to our physician, explaining what to expect and what to do. He could foresee two complications that might force me to come back to his office, though he hoped it would not be necessary. So did I. The good doctor refused to be compensated for his services and wished me the best of luck, telling me I had been extremely fortunate not to have damaged the anterior chamber. Provided no infection developed, I should recover fully. I thanked him for his attentive care and was returned to my niche in the cart. In the afternoon I was back in camp and all hands went to work building a small shelter with a frame of pine branches. The walls and ceiling were made so thick that the dwelling was pitch black inside. There was a low tunnel entrance with two doors made of thick pieces of old tarpaulin which totally blocked out the light during entry and exit, allowing my friends to take care of my needs without exposing me to light. All things considered, it was lucky this accident happened when the group was inactive. The men now had something to do, and that was excellent.

The first days in my dark cell passed very slowly. I was in pain and under sedation, although I kept my appetite and could sleep. The pain slowly subsided, perhaps aided by good news. It looked as though the Germans' initial eager resistance to the Allied invasion was crumbling in France as Laval fell on August 6. I put Charles in charge. Léon came every evening and comforted me with his good humor and stories. He always brought us a few cookies baked at the mill. Ourvary (Charles Derouck), Constant Lomry, and Mayor Faisant came to visit. After a week, Christian delivered a message to our doctor, who came soon after. He read the note from the ophthalmologist and examined my eye. He was pleased. The healing had progressed fast and without any sign of complications. He suggested that I keep the wounded eye protected for a few more days; although I could now expose the other eye to shaded light, I would still have to avoid direct sunlight. That certainly was a great improvement. At least I now had a blurred picture of the world around me through my imperfect left eye. On August 9 Le Mans fell and masses of German troops were taken prisoner with all their matériel. My friends prepared a new camp. We had stayed at the same location longer than usual and it was time we move and obliterate the traces of our presence at this place.

We then received a message from the Secret Army to be ready for further sabotage of the telephone cable. I interpreted that as a good omen, meaning the imminence of another important action in France. On August 15 the order came to decommission the cable for one week. This for us was a pleasure. All was ready and easily activated. We waited for news. Two days later London gave us the answer: the Allies had started a second front in the south of France with a landing at Saint Tropez. No particular message was directed to us on the BBC and no other request came from the Secret Army. Simultaneously with the landing at Saint Tropez, London announced the fall of Falaise, Chartres, and Dreux. On August 23, General George S. Patton's men of the U.S. 3rd Army crossed the River Seine near Mantes. And then, on August 24, General Leclerc's troops of the 2nd French Armored Division entered Paris! The Germans were still in some parts of the town, but the underground was fighting them hard. On August 25 London announced that Paris was entirely liberated. Our turn would certainly come soon now. The month closed with another important French town being liberated from the Germans: Amiens. The liberation armies were pushing north toward us.

Then came another urgent message to our group. Proceed to Verviers and investigate the possibility of destroying the tunnel. I had already given Marcel Franckson, Sr., my opinion about problems there—something new must have happened. I was told that contacts had been established with the local Secret Army and that a safehouse would be provided for Charles and me. Immediately I sent a courier to our drop man, Gustave Jacques. When he returned, he carried a large manila envelope containing a long note from Dad, the building plans for the tunnel, and maps of the area. I carefully studied the plans, but could not see any obvious spot to place the explosives. In the note, I was told to contact an architect in Verviers named Carlos Thirion. He would take us to our safehouse and establish contact with the local Secret Army. The most difficult part was left to us—to reach our destination when all roads were intensively watched.

Civilian rail traffic had been suspended and nearly everyone stayed home. The distance to cover, in a straight line between Forge à la Plez and Verviers, was nearly thirty miles. From the sparsely populated area where we were, our route would of necessity cross densely populated zones. The Amblève River would have to be crossed, and it was a mighty river. The bridges were all guarded. We would have to ford it. The areas around Stavelot and Spa were German nests to be avoided. It is difficult for an American unfamiliar with western Europe to realize the density of the Belgian population and the difficulty we had trying to travel undetected through the maze of roads, villages, and towns. The only way for us to reach Verviers was by a circuitous route avoiding population concentrations and German checkpoints. It would increase the distance considerably, also taking us across high country that would slow our progress. We had by now learned that safety had its price.

Not completely trusting my own judgment as there would be stretches with which I was quite unfamiliar, I asked advice from both Léon and Ourvary. Finally we agreed on a path that would cover nearly forty miles of mostly wooded terrain and cross the Amblève between Stavelot and Trois-Ponts. Next we would cross an extended marshy area northwest of Stavelot. We could see no other way, if we were to avoid the heavily patrolled roads to Spa and Liège. Bypassing Spa to the south, we would go due east toward the woods of the high plateau of the Fagnes and later turn north toward the Gileppe dam. From there our way was downhill to Verviers, which we would enter from the east. Along our way, I thought, why not sabotage the power line that brought 250,000 volts to Liège from the Butgenbach and Robertville dams? That would keep the Germans on their toes and harass them a little. It would sustain their fear and insecurity as they awaited the approaching armies of liberation.

Once before, while surveying the area for the Trois-Ponts sabotage, we had spotted an ideal place to work on the power line, along an old road from Stavelot to Francorchamps. There the power line crossed the Eau Rouge valley in an unusually long span supported on either side by heavy steel-legged pylons. On the Stavelot side, the power line made a slight bend, causing the tension to be higher on one pylon leg. A little charge at the base of one leg should be enough to cause the pylon to bend and the cable's weight might do the rest, provoking the entire span to collapse. Charles and I could easily do that on our way. Thanks to the extraordinary efficiency of the plastic explosive, a pound should suffice. A thirty-minute time pencil would give us plenty of time to take cover and witness the results. Charles agreed we should do it. In our absence, Christian would be in charge.

Messages were sent to our Brussels headquarters predicting our arrival in Verviers around September 6. We would have to travel by night most of the time. Rare were the areas we could proceed through in full daylight. Thanks to Léon, we had two safehouses along the way, a sawmill around Somagne south of Stavelot and another outside the village of Creppe. The man from Somagne would help us ford the Amblève River. We had no time to lose.

Early on September 2, carrying our .45s in breast holsters and a lunchbox each, we departed dressed in farmers' clothes, looking like locals going about their daily business. The clothes were provided by Ourvary and his men. I carried a detonator and a time pencil in my pockets, Charles a pound of plastic. Traveling through the woods we knew so well by now, we reached the Salm valley near Rochelinval at sunset. We waited for darkness before crossing the railroad, the river, and the road. It was night as we knocked at the door of the first safehouse, the Somagne sawmill. We ate there and rested before resuming our trip to the Amblève River and, with a slight detour, to the foot of the pylon. A young man from the mill accompanied us across the Amblève and then left us alone. It was one-thirty in the morning by the time we had applied the charge and retreated to the edge of the woods. When our charge exploded, we witnessed the longest and the most magnificent fireworks display I ever saw, with an aura of green light as the copper wires short-circuited to create the spectacle. After some twenty long seconds the wires melted and parted. With the line broken, we hoped the other pylons would collapse on both sides of the ruptured section, but we could wait no longer. It was time for us to enter the woods and proceed toward Creppe.

The second leg of our trip went smoothly as we traveled on firm, dry ground, until we crossed the two little rural roads south of Exbomont and Moulin du Ruy, where we entered dangerous territory. We knew we had to be very careful, not because of enemy patrols but because of a natural enemy that could swallow us alive. We were in bog country. Traveling through unfamiliar peat bogs was dangerous, if not fatal. In summer, old holes where people had harvested peat were hidden under the thin new growth of sphagnum. One could easily drown in the brown acidic water filling these overgrown holes. Léon had cautioned us to stay as close as possible to the elevated road bed, but to be ready to jump into the bog if necessary to avoid being seen. With slow and cautious movement we edged toward a turn in the road that would indicate we were again on firm ground. There the sparse forest petered out and we continued across high plateau meadows. Quietly we detoured around a sleeping village, crossing meadows and jumping fences. Our safehouse was farther north. Finally we recognized the low-lying stone farmhouse that Léon had described. The farmer, who lived with his wife and a young girl, was quick to open his door and his wife wasted no time in serving us a substantial breakfast of browned potatoes and eggs. We were then provided with a soft hiding place in the top of a hay loft. Having expended a good deal of physical and nervous energy, we slept like angels, not even dreaming of last night's green flashes.

Waking up when the day was nearly over, we heard our host down in the stable. We waited until he gave us the signal to come down from our warm and cozy niche. Again the family provided a simple but nourishing meal, which would sustain us well during the next long night. While we were eating, the mistress was busy buttering large slices of farm bread made out of coarsely crushed local wheat, wheat that never saw the mill, wheat that would never reach the Russian front. It was homegrown, home-crushed, and home-baked well away from German supervision. Once night had fallen, we departed, thanking our hosts for their hospitality.

To stay safely under forest cover, we had to retrace part of our previous night's route. Soon we passed the busy road to Spa, traveling in an easterly direction toward Germany. In fact, we would soon be close to the realigned border and patrols would be frequent. We hoped to reach Jalhay and possibly farther north before daylight. We walked steadily at a brisk pace and were able to reach the woods above Gileppe dam before daylight. It was perfect timing. We could now relax comfortably on a thick mattress of pine needles, effortlessly assembled. The weather remained dry during the trip and our clothes were relatively clean. This was important, as we would soon enter Verviers and needed to look inconspicuous as we approached Carlos Thirion's dwelling. Around midday we resumed our walk toward the suburb of Stembert and entered the town. It was September 5.

Events in the outside world had moved quickly while we had been on our way. In Somagne we heard with immense joy of the liberation of Brussels by a British guard division and on the same broadcast mixed news about Antwerp. The good news was Antwerp's liberation with the harbor intact and available to the Allied forces. The British Eleventh Armored Division had made a dash for the city while the underground had been in the harbor preventing the Germans from destroying it. It had been a beautiful and well-coordinated action. The bad news was that German flying bombs, the infamous V-1s, had begun landing in the city. For months to come, Antwerp would be under the fire of V-1s coming from Holland, which was still under German control.

In Creppe we learned that Charleroi and Mons had fallen to Allied hands. Clearly the Germans were being routed from western Europe and the Allies were in hot pursuit.

Entering Verviers would not, surprisingly, present any problem. The Germans paid us no attention. It seemed they now had only one objective—to get out and take with them all they could. Heavy German traffic was everywhere, and there was a noticeable absence of checkpoints. Clearly the situation had changed in the past few days. The Germans knew they had been beaten out of most of France and Belgium and were hoping only to be able to get home. At this point, they couldn't have cared less about two young civilian workers entering town. Still we were wary. Charles and I talked about how vividly we remembered the arrogant faces of the Germans in Brussels and elsewhere a few years before, when they had been the conquerors, the victors, the rulers; we the slaves, the losers, the servants. Now that they were retreating before the American, French, and British forces, their attitude changed from arrogance to insecurity. Of course, in Verviers, we were not looking at fighting troops, only occupying forces, men in their forties for the most part, very busy loading and moving out. Their propaganda machine could no longer support the false notion of victory. Paris had been retaken, Brussels liberated. Tanks were advancing rapidly on Germany. They had to evacuate. They must have received orders to retreat to Germany with whatever loot they could, but that would not begin to replace all that had been destroyed in Allied bombardments. The prospects ahead of them were certainly gloomy and so were their faces. Perhaps they were also afraid of armed civilian rebellion, as had happened in Paris and other areas. Insecurity for them—what a change!

Still taking in this pleasurable scene, we rang the bell at 14 Rue Tranchée in Verviers, Thirion's home. After entering, we quickly discussed the situation. He had contact established with the local Secret Army command. They were waiting for us and eager to meet. I told Thirion that there was no point in meeting them before we had surveyed the tunnel site and investigated the situation further. He directed us to a safehouse ideally located for that purpose, on the Rue de Bruxelles, bordering the rail yard and offering an unobstructed view of the tunnel's west entrance. We told him it was an excellent location and praised his efforts. We were now ready to meet our hosts and get to work. He guided us to the house where we rang the bell only after he was already on his way home. We had a card of introduction from him that we presented to the two middle-aged ladies who came to greet us. It was understood that we would see the architect again the next afternoon, by which time we would be ready to meet with the Secret Army.

It was early afternoon when we entered the house of the Ransonnets and were warmly welcomed by people eager to help and to please. Had our fame as old warriors preceded us?

We were shown to quarters on the second floor, a large bedroom with a balcony and panoramic view of the yard and tunnel's west entrance. They apologized for having only one queen-size bed for the two of us. For us, a bed of any size was an almost forgotten luxury! Not to mention the adjacent bathroom. It mattered not that warm water would have to be brought up from the downstairs kitchen and could only be heated around seven when there might be some gas available. For now, would we have some lunch? While we were eating, the ladies marveled at the fact that we had walked all the way from distant Erezée. We did not think much of it, but they considered it impressive.

We asked many questions. In recent days, the activity in the yard had been intense, train after train loading and departing for Germany. An endless convoy of trucks had entered the yard to transfer their contents onto waiting trains. The Germans had been very harsh in their control of civilians until a week before. Now that was over. They ignored the civilians. The yard was the only well-guarded place in town. The feldgendarmerie was closed and various German offices emptied and evacuated. Only the old Kommandantur continued to show some activity. We asked about the gestapo. It too was gone. We decided to risk a tour of town in the afternoon. Before leaving the house, we went back upstairs and again surveyed the yard. It was full of troops actively working at loading, their guns stacked nearby. Around three, Charles and I went out to investigate. The yard entrance was heavily guarded, but there was no trace of machine guns. No trace of civilian labor, either. In town, except for speeding German lorries, all was calm. Smiles on the Belgian faces indicated that people were aware of the apparently close liberation. German offices around the theater were empty, some doors standing open. As the ladies had told us, only the Kommandantur seemed still to be operating. Only there had we seen armed sentries.

At 6:30 we were back, well in time to hear the radio confirm what we had heard second-hand in days past. I listened to the news while Charles enjoyed a bath upstairs. Lyon, on the Rhône River in southeastern France, had been liberated, the good work of forces that had landed at Saint Tropez two weeks earlier. No news of further military advance in Belgium or the north of France. No personal messages for us either, nothing that would force us to return to base immediately. After a meal necessarily simple and frugal, we returned to the balcony and surveyed the yard of loaded trains getting ready to move east. At sunset the activity decreased and then stopped altogether. Curfew and blackout. We went early to bed, but were rudely awakened around 1:00 A.M. by rifle shots. From the balcony, we peered and listened. German guards were shooting at shadows in the yard. Civilians were trying to empty some loaded cars. Belgians were risking their lives—for what? Probably they were just plain looters. The rest of the night passed calmly.

Superbly rested, we faced our second day in town. We inspected the perimeter of the yard, where loading went on unabated. We found a large hole in the fence, probably the opening that had given access to the night's invaders. On the ground nearby lay an abandoned sewing machine, one leg broken. While walking, we arrived at the conclusion that short of an entire, well-equipped infantry platoon, the yard was off limits for sabotage. Reaching the tunnel access was unrealistic without a strong force. Then we considered the engineering aspects. The tunnel, lined in solid, bricked limestone without niches, would require three to four hundred pounds of the best explosives if we were to achieve any lasting results. With this information, we were ready for the afternoon meeting.

After a Spartan meal, we were on our way to Thirion's residence. There we met with two Secret Army representatives, an infantry captain and a major in the engineers. First we asked the questions: where was the explosive and how much was available? How many armed, experienced men could they assemble for the task? The answers were so pathetic that we wondered why they had asked us here. Explosives? None. Men? Twenty at most with army carbines and a few munitions rounds, no modern, parachuted-in equipment. Most serious was the aspect of harsh German reprisals against the town. There would be no way to hide from the enemy that the attack was by locals. They *would* retaliate.

Agreeing with us that the task seemed impossible and that headquarters should be informed of our common decision, the Secret Army men planned to send a message to Zone Five, Sector Four that we were returning to base; estimated return, September 9. Inside I was boiling mad and frustrated, amazed that this could happen. Charles and I returned to the ladies demoralized. It was incredible that we had been asked to risk our lives to reach conclusions we had already predicted in Erezée with the Hotton staff representatives, Marcel Franckson, Sr., and my dad. Nothing of what we had asked had been done, no explosives provided, no attack force assembled. This confirmed my lack of confidence in professional army men. Things would only change when generals would again lead their men to the front, risking their lives as they used to do in the Middle Ages.

That evening, news filtered through about the situation in Liège. The Germans were still there and apparently shooting a large number of their prisoners, while others were being evacuated to Germany. Saint Leonard jail was said to be empty. For our second evening with the ladies, we helped them dye old bedsheets in black, yellow, and red, the colors of our national flag, as they prepared for liberation. We were unable to finish our task as the gas had been cut off a little earlier than usual. Aiming to depart in the early morning and retrace our steps toward Forge à la Plez, we were early to bed and so early up.

The next morning, the ladies prepared the best breakfast they could and packed our lunchboxes with food for the day. How could we thank them enough for all they had done, depriving themselves of food so hard to come by? We promised to stay in touch and were on our way to Gileppe and Creppe. On our way we passed the power line we had sabotaged. The pylons lay on the ground as far as we could see! We spied a few Germans speeding along the roads, but there was no trace of roadblocks or controls. By now they certainly knew more about their situation than we did and cared little about us. They cared only about themselves. We were making good time and stopped only briefly at our safehouses in Creppe and Somagne. We continued with a growing sense of security.

The last night of our return trip found us on the high plateau around Rochelinval. We decided to stop for a short rest. Although the weather was clear and dry, we were cold sleeping on a mattress of pine needles. We hoped the winter would not be too harsh and that coal would become available before fierce cold came. For that to happen we needed a quick and total liberation of our country. In the wee hours of the morning the air grew even crisper and we decided to warm ourselves by traveling at a brisk pace. Late that night we were back in camp, having taken but two days and a few hours to cover the distance. We reported our findings to our friends and listened to a résumé of the latest news.

Again the news was mixed. Besançon had been liberated on the eighth, but on the same day, flying bombs arrived over London. Most important to us, the radio had just announced the liberation of Liège. Allied troops were now only fifty kilometers (thirty miles) from us. We were conscious now of being in the middle of the Ardennes, a natural forest fortress where the nature of the terrain might well slow the advance and favor the German retreat. There were no visible enemy troop movements to report in our area. The units in the Vielsalm barracks were reported still there and the feldgendarmerie still operating in town. The telephone cable sabotage had gone smoothly for ten days and the operation was now over. All sixteen charges had been used; our stock was totally depleted.

Then came a message from Sector Four, Zone Five of the Secret Army: be ready to move for the final assault against the Germans. I had to contact them urgently to learn about the assembly point. The head of Sector Four, in Erezée, asked if I could be at the safehouse there early in the morning. The next morning, Charles and I departed for Erezée only three miles distant. We were meeting the Sector Four head, a man I knew only as Hoss. I had learned from OMBR headquarters in Brussels that we had been officially reassigned to the Secret Army as their engineers.

At the safehouse we did not have to wait long for Hoss to appear. His face was radiant. The news must be good! He was actively preparing for the last confrontation with our oppressor. He confirmed that he anticipated the order to assemble at any moment and that six hundred to eight hundred men would show up in the woods near Petites-Tailles at La Baraque de Fraiture, at the intersection of two important highways controlling movements in the area, the La Roche-to-Vielsalm road and the Liège-to-Bastogne road. The elevation was above two thousand feet. It was clear why the Allies wanted this point to be occupied, secured, and defended.

The problem was that the Secret Army had little armament to speak of. One important difference between Service Hotton and the Secret Army was that we had been armed and supplied before D-day; they would receive Allied weapons only at the moment of liberation. Hoss told us we would have to wait a few hours for a drop nearby after the rendezvous time, which was yet unknown. He was counting on us, with the little we had, to ensure the security at the drop. It was essential for us to come early and bring all that we had. He was particularly interested in our two bazookas, should German armor show up. I insisted that what I had belonged to us and that I intended to keep command of my men as a trained and cohesive group who had already been under fire. Some of my men, and I named them, had armaments of their own. These would keep their guns and serve under my orders. That made clear, he gave me twenty-two small triangles of cloth printed with the image of a lion in our three national colors: black, yellow, and red. There was one for each of us. This was the Secret Army badge (in my opinion, a futile attempt to persuade the Germans that we were protected by the Geneva convention; they never had respected it). Hoss said that to complete the uniform, khaki overalls would be distributed at the rendezvous point.

It was nearly afternoon when we got back to camp. Now it was urgent for us to make one last trip to the Ronce valley and empty our remaining caches, bringing all matériel and ammunition to Forge à la Plez. The four of us could not accomplish that task in one trip. There was too much weight, especially the bazooka ammo, still packed in wooden boxes.

Christian volunteered to go to Ourvary and ask him to join us, bringing five of his men. The others would receive messages to be ready to assemble on short notice. I was excited. We were going to see the end of the long fight. We were confident. For most of the local Secret Army men, it would be an adventure. Only a few had been in the border regiments that had seen hard fighting in May, 1940. These were the accomplished soldiers. On September 10, London, during the usual 7:00 P.M. broadcast, announced the fall of Luxembourg city to the south of us. The next day along with Ourvary and his men, we listened again and learned that the Americans had liberated the mustard city of Dijon. The following day, facing the disinterred boxes from Bois de Ronce, we learned of the liberation of Le Havre.

The situation in Belgium was still very confusing. We knew that Brussels, Liège, Antwerp, Charleroi, and Mons had been liberated, but what about the coast? The north toward Holland? Though Brussels radio was back on the air, it was under Allied orders to keep tight-lipped about some areas of our territory. When would we hear the message I had memorized months ago: Message for Cincinnati? It was clear that the message for general sabotage in Belgium—Message for Berthe—had never been issued. As much as one can organize, there are always unpredictable events and the best-laid plans often have to be abandoned. Was sabotage any longer necessary? Perhaps this explained London's silence.

As a matter of fact, we were not only ready but anxious to raise hell behind enemy lines. We did not have much matériel left but still could shoot bazooka shells at passing trains and disrupt telecommunications.

I was anxious to begin. The pacifist in me had changed progressively into an active saboteur, and from saboteur to an armed and determined terrorist. I had truly become the man the German gestapo searched for in 1943 after our action at the Brussels post office. I had become an armed terrorist. Was now the time to go a step further, to take up the final task, to be the cold killer, the hunter, the liberator?

CHAPTER 13

▼

Foxes and Hounds

Dad, when corresponding with me, always signed his messages "Bietme." Bietme was the name of a mischievous fellow out of old Walloon children's stories, a character who encouraged children to commit all kinds of pranks and tricks. Innocent, but appropriate vis-à-vis the enemy. We had devised a set of code words that would be judged totally harmless if read by the censors. I signed my messages "Henri." Loulou Jacques was Mr. Cousin, his father Gustave was Mr. Cousin, Sr. "Grindstones" referred to explosives, "the engineer" was Marcel Franckson, Sr., and so on. No real names were ever used, no locations ever divulged.

On Tuesday, August 28, 1944, Bietme wrote to me, "The engineer is very ill." The next day, "The engineer cannot be found nor his secretary." These messages both arrived while Charles and I were en route to Verviers. They would have disturbed me greatly had I been in camp to receive them. In Verviers I received a telegram that did not make sense without the earlier messages: "Engineer's health better. . . ."

Later, while in Verviers, I received a note in which Dad told me he had been talking with the engineer, who "has to take great care of his health." Clearly, Mr. Franckson was in trouble, certainly in hiding. The Germans, near the very end, seemed to have identified some of the staff of our service. Léon Joye had recently disappeared while in Brussels—we hoped into hiding. This news came by way of Gustave Jacques as we awaited the general assembly at Petites-Tailles. Gustave told me how concerned Loulou had been carrying the weight of the latest news that our liaison officer to the Special Forces, an active staff member and friend of our family, was in hiding or had been arrested. Terrible premonitions shadowed my mind as I pro-

Fernand Bodson (alias Bietme), architect.

ceeded with the preparations for battle, though I kept these thoughts to myself, not wanting to add to my men's concerns.

As summer slipped away, the aromas of fall began to tinge the humid evening air. With Charles' agreement, I decided to train four men in the use of
bazookas. It would be our only defense against armor should we need it.
Charles, already familiar with this incredibly simple, light-weight rocket
launcher, trained the others. Ourvary and two of his best marksmen completed the group. All three were former border regiment soldiers who had
seen a lot of action in 1940. We had to exclude practice with live ammunition
as we had a limited supply of rockets and could not make any noise. The
total strength of our fighting group ready to join the Secret Army forces was
twenty-two, plus thirteen noncombatants recruited to provide information,
supplies, and medical care. Our armament was from the Le Sapin drop plus
a few Belgian army carbines which some of our local men had managed
to conceal.

On September 14 came the message to assemble at Petites-Tailles. We were to be there the following afternoon. It was less than ten miles away and we planned to leave Forge à la Plez at noon. We sent messages to all our men still at home to join us at Forge at noon, at the latest. Most, eager to participate, came early. We had one airman's uniform left over and gave it to the one it fit best. Each combatant was asked to sew the triangular tricolored badge to the top of his right sleeve. Arms and ammunition were shared out. Charles and Ourvary received their bazookas and the two carriers they had trained were assigned the rocket supply. Christian received one of the two Brens, while the other was given to a former border regiment machine gunner. We, the five who had spent time in the woods, had our Sten guns and our .45 automatics in homemade boarskin belt holsters. We all had two grenades each. The remaining Stens were given to the men without carbines.

When I finally assembled the group for departure it was a group for which I had all reasons to be proud. Well trained, well armed, all in good shape, and carrying extra equipment in backpacks. We left Forge à la Plez punctually at noon and traveled east through Freineux, to just south of Odeigne where we would cross the La Roche highway. Scouts were sent ahead to spot for Germans, but none were seen. To tell the truth, we were no longer overly concerned. Isolated soldiers would be eliminated; small groups would be engaged. An encounter with a large group was unlikely. We crossed the road without hindrance and proceeded through the woods toward Chabrenez to cross our second highway, the Bastogne road. Soon we were at the rendezvous point south of Petites-Tailles, a large private residence well hidden a half-mile into the forest. The trees were old and tall, their branches starting at eight to fifteen feet above ground, allowing us to walk freely under the dark cover. Nothing was visible from the highway, where younger trees with branches low to the ground bordered the road, creating a natural blind. When we arrived, Hoss was already there with at least a hundred men. As armament they had only a few carbines and shotguns. The impression we made on the men was evident. We were recognized as a small force of seasoned fighters and our modern equipment was looked upon with envy.

Hoss told us he had posted sentries and asked us to stay with him at the ready in case Germans showed up and made an attempt to attack. These were critical hours, the hours of waiting for the large arms drop. Hoss told me there were to be two drops, one at ten that night, the second at ten the next morning. The first would consist of men and equipment, the second of arms only. The night drop would take place in a meadow south of Petites-Tailles and just north of our present location; the morning drop would be in a large area of meadows near the village of Fraiture, north of the road to Vielsalm.

In a building adjacent to the mansion, cooks were already busy preparing a hot meal for the evening. Men were now arriving in large numbers, mostly from the west and north where the population was denser. Their average age was around twenty-five. The older ones were nearly all former soldiers, the younger ones just farm boys, but we all had in common our willingness to engage the enemy and our determination to fight for liberation. By seven, when we were called for hot soup, the group had swelled to more than six hundred men.

Hoss and his staff asked my group to participate in the defense of the two drop zones. At nine that evening we were in position in two main groups, one close to the highway, the other near Petites-Tailles protecting the field from a possible enemy approach from Bihain or Vielsalm. The beacons were in place and ready to be lit. The sky was clear except for a few high clouds.

At precisely 10:00 P.M. we heard the noise of approaching airplanes, big ones, two of them. Right on target, the bays opened. From the first plane came seventeen white parachutes, from the second four sets of four large orange parachutes. Soon we could distinguish the men hanging from the white 'chutes and dark crates dangling below the orange ones. Uniformed men landed safely and the crates hit the dry ground with loud thuds. One landed so close to me that I instinctively jumped aside, just missing being flattened by a jeep! We had just received seventeen Canadian skydivers and their matériel. In a matter of a few minutes, all parachutes were rolled and moved out. The leader of these men wore the two silver bars of a lieutenant. His face, I thought, looked familiar. The way he looked at me seemed to confirm my thoughts. But he avoided me and was all business as he ordered his men to action. Quickly the platforms were emptied, and in a matter of minutes, jeeps rolled away from them, fueled and equipped with fore and aft double .45 machine guns. Each vehicle also had a powerful searchlight and a three-inch-thick transparent plastic bullet shield. There were jerry cans of gasoline, boxes of ammunition, boxes of field rations.

When they were nearly finished, the lieutenant called me aside. Under cover, he shook my hand, calling me by my real name. He turned out to be an old high-school friend who had later been a student in another department of my university and who had been in England since May, 1940. He had been trained there by Special Forces and had learned a new trade: parachuting into enemy-occupied countries to help the underground fight the last battles. After the area where they had been dropped had been secured, he and his men would fly back to England and be assigned another jump. He told me he had already accomplished four missions in France but this was his first in Belgium. His group were all members of the Belgian forces in Great Britain. When I asked him why the Canadian uniform, he told me and asked me please to keep it strictly to myself: it was an attempt to fool the Germans in case of capture. As Belgians fighting out of Britain, they were often denied the protection of the Geneva convention by the Germans. So we both had direct connections with Special Forces, both knew Léon Joye, and both had fighting experience. He suggested he ask Hoss if we could work with him. I could not have agreed more and we went to see the chief to discuss the matter.

As we joined Hoss, he relayed some frightening information: one of his patrols had just reported the presence of four light German tanks, well camouflaged and all together in a pack on a little logging road not far from there. How long had they been there? For what purpose? Perhaps German intelligence had been informed of the Secret Army's rendezvous. Did they know of the next drop that would bring arms to all of us? The "Canadian" lieutenant told Hoss that the tanks should be attacked at once and destroyed. He suggested we use the men of Service Hotton who had the bazookas and rockets. Together we could do the job.

The action was organized without a minute being lost. We would approach the site guided by the patrol that had spotted the tanks and proceed from there. There were no other possibilities except to use the bazookas. Neither the Secret Army nor the Canadians had anything to attack armor. The lieutenant, looking at the map, suggested that sentries should be located in Chabrenez, at La Baraque and along the road toward Houffalize. Should any tanks escape our attack it was important to know their whereabouts and direction of travel. We were ready now to attack the lair. Five of us from Hotton joined the Canadians and climbed into jeeps carrying our bazookas and rockets—Charles, Ourvary, the two other former border soldiers, and I. I took a seat beside the lieutenant in the lead jeep with the Secret Army patrol man, our guide.

The lieutenant insisted that we not approach in our vehicles, but only use them to get closer faster. From a safe distance, we would proceed on foot and in absolute silence, reconnoiter the place, and then plan our attack. We left camp driving south on the highway until we turned left toward the village of Tailles. We stopped about a half-mile from the village where the road forked, leading to the logging road where the tanks had been sighted. We parked the jeeps and left them for the Canadians to camouflage. They would remain there, watching the road for any tanks attempting to escape. The Canadians were well trained for a woods patrol of this kind, as were we. Moving silently, we were not long in finding the place. We surrounded it, observed it, and regrouped at a distance to establish our strategy.

The tanks, four mid-sized units, were wedged together, heavily covered with fir branches, in a clump of trees close to the logging road. The lieutenant suggested a plan that had to be executed well and rapidly since we had only two bazookas and there were four tanks. The tanks must be hit at their weakest point—that is, in the rear plate at the height of the upper track. Without doubt the rockets would penetrate and explode, killing the occupants instantly. There was every chance that the ammunition stored inside would also explode. The men with the bazookas should know of this possibility and prepare for it by assuming a firm shooting position, legs spread, one in front, the other behind, so as to be able to resist the shock wave that would otherwise knock them down. Those with the bazookas should keep calm, firing at each of the tanks in rapid succession. At the same time we would use our Brens to shoot bursts of bullets aimed at the sight windows of the tanks' machine gunners. This would not damage the tanks, but would hamper the gunners' ability to aim bursts at us. The optimum range for the bazookas was fifty to sixty feet. Again: "Be prepared for the blast when the tank explodes! Do not lose your cool. Move quickly to your next target." We were set.

The lieutenant and I took the Brens and positioned ourselves flat on the ground, each aided by a man who would pass the clips and be ready to change barrels should one jam. Charles and Ourvary knelt in front of us beside their helpers carrying rockets. At the signal two rockets were off, both hitting their targets. Ourvary's tank exploded, sending him falling backward but unhurt. The lieutenant and I kept up our bursts of fire at the two remaining tanks' gunsights. Charles changed position and fired his second rocket at tank number three, disabling it. Then Ourvary was again up and ready to shoot at number four. In the few seconds of delay, tank four started its engine while furiously machine-gunning in our direction, but without aim. Nevertheless, Ourvary fired another rocket while the machine was turning. His projectile hit its rear obliquely and exploded without effect. Ourvary called for another rocket as he repositioned himself. His rocket carrier stood, moved, and fell to the ground; a machine gun bullet in the forehead had killed him instantly. The tank was fast moving out of shooting range and there was nothing we could do. The action was over. The silence of the night, so violently interrupted for a minute, returned as we contemplated the scene. There was nothing to be done for our friend, the second casualty of my group. First Jan, now him. We abandoned the place, carrying our dead comrade-in-arms, walked back to the jeeps, and returned to camp.

Immediately reporting to Hoss, we learned that the escaped tank had taken the road toward Houffalize. Later we learned that it ran into American forces along the road and was destroyed—more Germans who would never see their *Vaterland* again. From then on, the Canadians and the Hotton men stayed together.

We smokers took advantage of the Benson and Hedges cigarettes our friends had in ample supply. Soon we lay down to rest. Tomorrow our duty would be to protect the new drop area. Hoss sent the Canadians and my group to sleep under the roof of a hay shelter. Although there was ample hay on the ground, and the facilities could be considered luxurious, it was difficult for us to find sleep between the intensity of that day's work and our expectations of the day ahead. Slowly, one after another, we drifted to sleep remembering what Hoss had said: he had enough men to be posted all around our camp. "You have saved many lives already," he had told us, "and merit rest." The night remained calm and the patrols sent out at the break of day came back without any alarming news.

In this atmosphere of confidence, a sunny day rose up around us. We breakfasted and participated in a short staff meeting where the strategy of the day was laid out. The drop would take place in a large meadow located north of the junction of roads coming from Liège and Vielsalm. From this intersection one could only go down. We were at one of the highest points in Belgium. Vielsalm, only ten miles distant, was already seven hundred feet below us. For all we knew, it was still a German infantry nest. Our view was an almost unobstructed panorama of rich meadows dotted with charming villages of buildings made of worked stone. The roofs were of slate from the nearby Salm River valley. The land rolled very gently. These were the old Ardennes mountains that had had the time to erode and acquire the soft contours of great geological age. The hay had been harvested first in June and was in the process of being harvested a second time where the cows had not grazed. The landscape had a unified softness in the gentle slopes, the low-lying stone buildings, and the lush green pastures. It seemed more a place for peace than war.

In order to protect the drop zone it was decided that we and the Canadians would stay along the top of the Vielsalm road, covering the area to the north of us. Small groups of riflemen would take positions along the same road toward Liège and Vielsalm. At nine we were in position with the jeeps parked in between the sparse evergreens alongside the road. They would cover the meadow with eight double-barreled machine guns and our Brens and bazookas. Again we were ready. At precisely 10:00 A.M. the planes arrived, four Lancasters protected by fighters. The drop was well executed and fell where expected. Our men rushed unarmed from under cover toward the 'chutes and containers.

Simultaneously German trucks emerged from out of the woods west of Lierneux, disgorging soldiers along the country road. They were to the north of us. The drop zone lay between us. They were so close that they could retrieve containers. Our guns clattered into action, surprising them. They had not expected such firepower. They had machine guns, but we had the advantage of the first shots and silenced them quickly. Charles and Ourvary aimed their rockets in high arcs, landing them in the midst of the Germans. Christian and I were shooting bursts of Bren bullets at selected enemy groups. We stayed thus engaged for fifteen to twenty minutes, until the Germans withdrew, leaving their dead and wounded. They retreated toward Vielsalm from where they certainly had come.

Deaths were few among the Secret Army men, but casualties were numerous. These were well cared for by doctors at the camp with nurses to assist. Among my immediate group of Canadians and Hotton men, we reported only scratches. The Germans left many of their own on the field and their weapons were collected. What would have happened if the four tanks had gone undetected and had attacked us from the rear as we were engaged with the infantry from below? Our strong line of defense, our four jeeps, would have been their prime targets. It would have meant the deaths of the paratroopers, for certain. Without doubt, the Germans had access to good information. There must have been a leak, a serious break somewhere.

The unarmed Secret Army men who had rushed into the drop zone gave a good fight. Some had the bravery under fire to pry open containers in search of guns and ammo. When their search was successful, they fired at the Germans from close range, killing and wounding many. When not, they crouched unarmed dodging bullets.

By noon that September 16 we were back at Petites-Tailles and relaxing as Secret Army men unpacked, cleaned, and familiarized themselves with carbines, Stens, and the like. We now had several hundred well-armed men instead of a few dozen. In early afternoon we were again alerted, but this time it was the alert we expected—Allied troops preceded by armor. These men were of the U. S. First Army, Seventh Corps, under General J. Lawston. They stopped at La Baraque and their officers talked with ours. They had come straight from Marches through Hotton and Erezée. Others had entered Houffalize. La Roche was not yet secured. They would proceed to Vielsalm and engage any enemy still there. Our job was to patrol a large, well-defined area destroying pockets of enemy resistance. Allied troops would keep to the main roads and towns. Our task was to secure villages, secondary roads, and the sparsely populated areas between.

We began that very afternoon, with my Canadian friends in the lead jeep, manning the front machine gun. No longer obliged to practice without slugs, we made all the noise we needed to and fired bullets at fence posts, practicing. We had been assigned this relatively large area because we had jeeps and the mobility of a motorized unit. We patrolled the back roads, entering the villages of Bihain and Ottré. Then we moved south to Baclain and Montleban. We returned to camp traveling north through the beautiful woods of the Cédrogne forest. We covered the area well and were received in each place with joy bordering on tears. After dinner we resumed patrolling, our mounted searchlights sweeping the horizon in search of Germans. Next we were assigned the area north of the Baraque junction. About four in the morning, we met a single German standing in the middle of the road, rifle lying in front of him, hands raised, fear in his eyes. I no longer had the strength of will to shoot him and he was made prisoner. We took him to join the other few captured by Secret Army patrols. Those who resisted were given no quarter and were left where they fell. Our Hun said he had deserted in Liège and was trying to make his way back to his country. He was exhausted and famished. For us, the night's mission was over.

At camp we found a happy Hoss. He had just received a message from Zone Five. The fight was over in our sector. We could disband and go home. Our friends the parachutists invited us to join them in a celebration. They had come prepared. Johnnie Walker Black Label, chocolates, Benson and Hedges—no more Shit A and B. I could not avoid thinking about the man we had lost two days ago, about Jan, Léon Joye, and Marcel Franckson, Sr., afraid of the bad news that might reach us sooner or later. But for now, we were free of the Germans and it would only be a matter of days before they were totally out of eastern Belgium. It would take a little longer to rid the north of our country of them. Our Canadian friends would return to England to be dropped again where they were needed. We, from Hotton East, could go home. The Ardennes men could walk to their farms, although we from the city needed transportation to Brussels. For all practical purposes, Belgium was liberated.

What had been our cost? Eighteen thousand deaths during the eighteen-

The plaque reads "To Jean and Francois Soetens, who died for freedom: Homage and recognition." François was OMBR chief and was assisted by his brother, Jean.

day campaign of 1940. One hundred and eighty thousand civilian lives lost during the occupation through May of 1945—mainly civilians who had been forced to work in Germany and, ironically, died under the weight of Allied bombs crushing the Axis industrial complex—but also thousands arrested for intelligence, escape lines, and sabotage; most of these died in concentration camps. These figures do not include the deported Belgian Jews, very few of whom came back from the extermination camps in Germany and occupied Poland. The physical destruction in the country was of enormous proportions, resulting from the initial eighteen-day war, our acts of sabotages, and Allied bombing before and during the battles of liberation. All in all, we faced a devastated landscape and a shattered industrial complex. We had no cars, no trucks. Our railroad lines were in a shambles and nearly all our locomotives were in Germany. We had little food and not much more for a long time after. It would take a tremendous effort to put ourselves back to work. Happily, Belgians never feared work and help would come as soon as Antwerp harbor was functioning again.

I cannot close this chapter without telling something of my former OMBR group. Hard hit by the arrest of the chief and his brother, the Soetens, it had bounced back to see the battle for Brussels liberation. They lost many good men. Marcel lost many. There were dear and brave faces missing from my group. The entire Service Hotton lost many, some forty-five out of three hundred fifty. Much too many.

Soon after the war we erected a monument to our fallen comrades and friends. In a simple building in the depths of the Chimay woods stands an altar in the middle of a square base. At each corner, a column supports the dome where the names of our lost friends are engraved. They are remembered there, among the singing birds and the quivering leaves. They are remembered and visited by the few who still remember. I am glad they are honored in that secluded place, a place resembling the place where they fell, the places they knew, the places that had offered them asylum. They did not fight for ribbons or honors; they fought for an ideal so great and so pure it could not be remembered in a busy place. Bound together by friendships, they fought and died for freedom.

For us and for them, it was over. But was it really over?

CHAPTER 14

▼

Debriefing—Special Force

Brussels was a hundred miles away and we needed transportation, not only for us, but also for the military matériel that was still under my authority. As a temporary measure, we went back to the camp we had left just days before with Léon and Ourvary and the others from the Forge à la Plez area. We traveled much lighter. Our rockets had been fired in battle, as had practically all of our ammunition for the Bren guns. We had only a few thousand rounds left for the Stens and fifty grenades that, happily, we never had to use.

On the way to camp, Charles reminded me of a conversation we had had with Carlos Thirion in Verviers in which he had said he knew of a collaborator who, during the war, had baked cookies for the Germans. He knew that the man had an Opel hidden in a rear building at his bakery. It was certainly worth investigating. When we mentioned it to Léon Sadzot, he immediately offered the use of his Ford to go to Verviers. Soon, Charles and I were on the road. Our first stop was Vielsalm, where we contacted the American military authorities. They confirmed, after checking our affiliation with Special Force in Brussels, that there would be no problem obtaining an army requisition should we discover a car in the possession of a collaborator. The army provided us with a pass and allotted us enough gas for the trip.

That same day we arrived in festive Verviers, liberated just two days earlier, and at Mr. Thirion's door. We traveled the roads the army had advised us to take, the main roads through Trois-Ponts, Stavelot, Spa, Pepinster. From the south as we entered, the town was resplendent with flags hung from many houses and often across the streets on cables stretched from house to house. Carlos was, needless to say, happy to see us in good shape and happy to tell us that his town had been liberated practically without a fight. The Germans simply withdrew, covering their rear with some half-hearted skirmishes. Carlos confirmed the car story and offered to join us for a visit to the local American HQ. There, facing a young lieutenant, we told him who we were and showed him the pass delivered in Vielsalm establishing our attachment to Special Force. We were still in our airmen's uniforms with the Secret Army sleeve badge. The officer was most obliging and supportive, suggesting we pay the cookie man a visit with two MPs he would provide. Carlos declined the honor of accompanying us. He preferred to remain in the background.

In the early afternoon, depositing Carlos at his own front door and promising to see him and the Ransonnet ladies later, we proceeded to find our collaborator, accompanied by a jeep and two imposing, white-helmeted military police. We had enough information to locate the man and his car. The man at first denied having a car, but when we told him the make, the color, the model, and where he garaged it, he gave it up. We were well-informed and the MP's indicated to him that resistance was futile. Climbing into their jeep, he directed us to his bakery, where he showed us the vehicle parked on blocks, wheels missing. It was dusty, but apparently in good shape. We forced him to show us where the wheels were, and soon he was reinflating them with a hand pump, after which we mounted them on the vehicle, checked the oil, and found that the battery was dead. I pocketed the keys, and we took the battery with us, promising to return the next morning with requisition papers. Then we followed the MP's back to their headquarters and received our papers and a pass for the local motor pool, where we secured a battery and gas. Last but not least came my next request. Was it possible to obtain food for us and the friends who would shelter us for the night? The young lieutenant was very generous and had our car loaded with all kinds of goodies. He even included a carton of Lucky Strikes and several packages of Camels.

We went back to report to Carlos Thirion and then, with him, went on to visit the Ransonnet ladies on the Rue de Bruxelles. With a lift of pleasure we saw, floating from their windows, the finished flags for which we had helped to dye the material days before. Hundreds were displayed on their street alone. From our car came the boxes and parcels the lieutenant had arranged for us. Soon, in the kitchen, we faced a mountain of canned meat, vegetables, and fruits. There were cookies, cigarettes, chocolate, sugared sweets, pouches of dehydrated fruit juices. There were several freshly baked breads and a large tin of butter! The U. S. rations were new to us and we found them superior to the Canadian. To crown the meal we had dehydrated coffee. Over dinner we told the ladies what had happened in La Baraque

and more. After a shower, we went to sleep in the familiar bed we had slept
in not long ago. The following morning after breakfast, we left to collect the
collaborator's car. After we installed the battery and made several attempts
at starting the car, the engine sparked to life. We lost no time in leaving the
requisition papers with the baker, telling him it probably was the first decent
thing he had done during the war.

At the motor pool the car was checked and we were assured it was in good
shape and that we could take to the road with great hopes of reaching Brussels. Soon we were on our way back to Forge à la Plez. Charles drove the
Ford, I the Opel, now emblazoned with white stars stenciled on doors and
trunk to indicate that it was an American army car. We rejoiced at the luxurious way in which we would travel back to the capital. But first we would
return to the Sadzots' mill house, to our Ardennes friends, for a last meal
together. When we arrived, there was a message waiting for me from Zone
Five of the Secret Army in Liège: "Please stop and contact us as soon as
possible." I wondered what was going on. We spent the early part of the
night loading the car with our belongings. Though they were few, we had to
pack them tightly to be able to carry them all and yet have room for the four
of us.

Around midday on September 21, I visited the Liège Secret Army HQ. I
soon learned that the bodies of those shot at the citadel, an old fort overlooking the Meuse, four days before the Germans' departure had been transferred to a makeshift mortuary at the de Waha High School gym. I was asked
to go there and see whom I recognized. Many were still unidentified. I approached this ordeal with great apprehension. My anxiety was confirmed. I
recognized two bodies. The first I did not know by name, but I knew he had
been a fireman at the station close to the Salvation Army headquarters. He
had supplied me with gas when I went to Liège with the second load of
airmen. The second body I could identify by name. It was Léon Joye. In the
office operated by the Liège Red Cross, I was asked if I would go to Salmchàteau to tell his widow, Laurence. I had known Laurence, born Crasson, since
high school and we had renewed our friendship after her husband became
my boss from overseas. I was close to refusing this painful mission. Then,
thinking about it, I realized I could not refuse. I had to tell her. It would be
much better for her to learn the news from one of her husband's men than
from some unknown official, a stranger. My friends would stay the day in
Liège as guests of the Salvation Army with whom we had had such wonderful
contacts in the past, through our evasion line. I would take the day and accomplish my delicate and very painful mission. Arriving in the village at

nightfall, I went to spend the night with Gustave, who was terribly pained to learn of Léon's fate.

The next morning I walked across the charming village and up the road to La Baraque de Fraiture. Soon I stood in front of Léon's house. It had been months since I had seen Laurence. Just after her husband had parachuted back into Belgium and had contacted me, I had been to see her, and had even delivered messages. But soon it became too risky for me, and Gustave Jacques took over. When I called to her, she came promptly to the door.

With tears in her eyes, tears of joy, she gave me a hug, a close, friendly embrace. Nearly sobbing, she told me she had been informed that I had been killed at Fraiture. I told her I had not even been scratched. Without waiting longer, she asked if I had news of Léon. Yes, I said, but it was not good. I told her how I had learned of Léon's arrest in Brussels nearly four weeks before. Then, preparing her as gently as I could by speaking very slowly, I had to give her the final blow. Léon had been transferred to Liège, where his body had been discovered among those shot by the Germans at the citadel. I had identified his body at the Lycée de Waha gym. Léon had been shot on September 4; he was thirty-one years old. We had to talk about her wishes. She wanted his body brought back to Salmchâteau for burial. I gave her my address in Brussels and asked her to contact me before the burial ceremony so that I could come back to pay her husband my last respects. That same day I was back in Liège with my men and then soon on the road. We did not stop before the four of us were in Brussels. I drove my three friends to their respective homes, and we separated knowing very well we would not see each other again soon. Then I drove to the Rue de l'Ermitage and rang the bell—I no longer had a key. Having left without military status except as a former sergeant in the medics, I was back as a lieutenant in the Secret Army's elite sabotage group, Service Hotton.

Mom and Dad were overjoyed to see me healthy and unhurt. I told them of Léon and asked Dad for news of his friend, Marcel Franckson, Sr. There was none. The last he knew, Marcel had been transferred to Germany. So there was still hope, faint hope, for all of us to hang onto. This waiting for news was one long nightmare for the families of those deported to Germany; days gave way to months of uncertainty and anguish. It was only after the German capitulation that the brutal truth became known. Marcel Franckson had been arrested in Dinant in May, 1944, and had died in the Buchenwald concentration camp; but that was to be a later heartbreak. For now, I went to the car and returned with tins of food and sweets and gave them to Mom. The car, still full of armament, was parked under padlock in the garage next door. I had to find out what to do with the arsenal for which I had no further use. It did not take long. I delivered my cargo to an army barracks the very next morning, receiving a receipt and a note allowing me to keep my .45 as a memento. In the afternoon I was to meet with Special Forces.

Dad had told me I would have to go through their debriefing, a long and thorough process. It was the final part of the procedure he had already gone through himself. For days, at the dinner table, my parents learned about my experiences and I of theirs as we shared our elation—here we were, all together, again at home. Mother had kept, for my return, a jar of the canned tongue which I had prepared in Honvelez in the fall of 1943. We would eat it with this evening's meal when I returned from my first meeting at the Special Force Belgian HQ on the Avenue des Arts.

I dressed in old civvies and took the streetcar. It was good to be back on the cars I had known all my life in this city. Clearly the prewar city atmosphere was returning, but with minor differences. There were fewer civilian cars and many military. The military were friendly and mostly British. Since Brussels was Eisenhower's headquarters in those days, there were also a few American cars. People's faces were open, jovial, alert. Conversations had resumed and the fear of saying the wrong thing was gone. On the sidewalks, people were walking. Freely. Smiling. It was a superb end of summer and start of fall. How good it felt to be home, in my city, with my parents and friends. How pleasant to see the familiar, the streets and boulevards, the known townscape.

Upon reaching my destination I was immediately introduced to Captain M. Simms and then to a Major Malinson. We had a very pleasant meeting in which it soon became clear that they knew a lot about me, what my group had accomplished at their request, and what we had not, like Trois-Ponts. He also knew of what we had done without orders: the gas train, the troop train. Léon Joye had kept them well informed nearly to the end. Our successful attack on the tanks with our bazookas was the crown jewel, which Léon unhappily could not report. After several more questions about actions I might know about or have participated in, my first debriefing ended. Another appointment was set for the next afternoon. Later that evening, over supper, Dad told me I was soon to meet the real Belgian chief of Service Hotton, Alberic Maistriau, head engineer at the Belgian Purfina oil company. I looked forward to that visit.

Several days had passed since I had seen Laurence Joye when she called me to give me the day and time of the funeral service and burial. In two days my group would be all together again, less one. At graveside the army had

Alberic Maistriau, engineer and chief of staff, Service Hotton.

its honor guard, as did we, the Secret Army. Dressed again as for war, we lowered our friend, Léon Joye, to sleep forever in the sweet earth of his adopted village.

When I returned to Brussels, my thoughts moved toward winter. We would need heat and food. Through Special Force we secured coal. But food represented a problem. There was bread worthy of the name, but in short supply; potatoes, fruits, and vegetables were available. There was very little meat, and sugar, tea, and coffee were still totally absent. Due to the lack of sugar, there were no preserves. The liberation of Brest on September 19 had still not yielded the Allies the harbor they so badly needed for the next massive invasion. Antwerp harbor was intact, but still could not be reached from the distant sea until the Allies controlled the south of Holland. Antwerp, like London, was under fire from the V-1 German flying bombs. Some were launched into Liège and a few into Brussels. German guns still controlled the traffic on the upper Schelde estuary. The relatively slow progression of the Allies was now a supply problem. They had only what could be unloaded through temporary harbors in Normandy. Supplies were available, but in Britain. This situation would eventually change as repairs were completed on French ports, but the opening of Antwerp harbor would make an immense and immediate difference.

Some industrious Belgians, practiced in the black market under the Germans, now handled Allied products: cigarettes, gum, liquor, food rations. All were available at exorbitant prices.

Ghent, close to the sea, was liberated on September 22. Soon after, another German nest collapsed when Calais gave up the fight. We eagerly looked toward Antwerp next.

Afternoon by afternoon my debriefing continued. I was asked, among many things, why I had disobeyed the order to abandon our escape line. I had had an opportunity to rescue five Americans. They accepted my answers because they were honest and, more probably, because we had been successful.

During our last session together, they invited me to ask the questions and air my grudges. My biggest was about the money—not that the amount they sent was inadequate, but that it was sent in ten-thousand-franc denominations. They said the point was well taken and that this had been a general complaint, a thing to avoid in the future. My second grudge was the absence of armament accessories, holsters and the like. This could have been a great disadvantage had we been attacked at the moment of the drop. A third grudge: why had it taken so long for them to come to our rescue or even to support our meager efforts? Was it a matter of trust? They explained that so much had had to be done, and there had been so many theaters to be served. Priorities had to be established and often changed. It was only then that I began to comprehend the enormous magnitude and complexity of the task. We had lived thinking of our group only, not perceiving the total picture. The debriefing over, Captain Simms invited me to lunch.

While dining, I asked about the origin of Service Hotton. He told me that the idea of a special sabotage group for the Belgian Secret Army originated in the summer of 1943 and began when a Belgian intelligence officer named Adelin Marissal was parachuted into Belgium. As a result of his mission, a colonel in the Secret Army took charge of the earliest sabotage operations. They blew up a troop train traveling between Brussels and Liège, causing two hundred deaths among the Axis forces. German response was immediate and brutal. Numerous arrests followed. It seemed the colonel was known to the enemy, so the staff was changed and another man known as Mardulier was put in charge, but not for long. He was arrested in November. Facing such hard beginnings and the apparent German penetration of the Secret Army, London, with reason, insisted that the service should be totally reorganized, keeping connections, but being independent.

At that time the name OTHON first appeared. A Major Lempereur was placed in charge. He was arrested early in 1944. At the suggestion of the Belgian intelligence net (code name: Clarence), the name of Alberic Maistriau was put forward. This engineer, who had already gained experience in the field by directing some sabotage that had impressed London, was put in charge. Maistriau, losing no time, determined to select groups having no previous connection to the Secret Army, yet groups that had solid experience. Specialists were sent from London trained by Special Force. These agents were to identify which actions to undertake and to train and supervise insurgents. Among the groups recruited were Marcel Franckson's (code name: Martial), my group (former OMBR member, code name: Henri), a group in Brabant, another in the center of Belgium, and a final group with loose connections to Hotton, as the service was now called. This last group belonged to the Army of Belgian Partisans, the ABP, and operated in the Mons area. The total force of Service Hotton never exceeded 350 men. During its relatively short existence, Hotton suffered severe losses as a result of the danger inherent in our operations. Forty-four were dead or missing, twenty-seven wounded, forty-two prisoners returned alive. It took quite a long time for Simms to tell me this story, but at its conclusion, I understood how Marcel's group had been recruited, one friend to another, to my father, to Léon Joye, to me.

As I pondered the connections, Simms interrupted my thoughts by discreetly inquiring as to my future.

Bleak right now. With our industry in shambles, it would take months to recover. The law allowed me to return to my prewar employer, Van der Heyden, but I had left them voluntarily to join the war profiteer I later robbed for the OMBR. In essence I believed I faced a long period of unemployment, and I had no inkling that a British captain might have any ideas that could help.

As we sipped Drambuie with real coffee (where did it come from?) the time came for us to leave and visit Alberic Maistriau. Once in the car it did not take long to reach the Purfina headquarters building.

Captain Simms and I were led into a large office, where there soon appeared a giant of a man, a red-faced, good-looking, fiftyish giant who seemed to have been carved out of an oak log. What a commanding presence! He went to the captain, pumped his hand, and then shook mine. "Alberic Maistriau," said he. I presented myself. The conversation proceeded in an informal manner as between friends. Maistriau told me how much he knew about my father and through him about me. There was no talk of business. There was no need. I learned that Maistriau had been partly responsible for organizing the preservation of Antwerp harbor. He asked me a question that I was answering as best I could when he lit a cigarette while listening to my answer. He took a long puff, inhaled the smoke, and then my words got stuck in my throat. As he exhaled, smoke came out of both ears! He laughed, we laughed, but I still could not figure the trick.

No trick, Henri, he volunteered, using my Hotton code name. He had directed the work on the tunnel under the Schelde in Antwerp. The work site was under pressure and there was an entry lock chamber to acclimate people to the pressure change. One day he got an urgent call. Water was leaking. He rushed to the work site and to gain time did not observe the rules of pressure change. He broke both of his eardrums, and the rest was a matter of eustachian tubes and muscle control. Now he could startle people, he grinned. It took me a while to recuperate and resume answering his question. After a few more moments of conversation he apologized for having to make this first contact shorter than he wished, but he had pressing business. Captain Simms and I returned to the Avenue des Arts, where Simms asked me to meet with the major, who wanted to put a proposal to me.

Without much preamble the major asked if I would be willing to continue to work for the Allied cause. The war was far from over and they could use my help as well as the services of some of my former underground people. The Supreme Headquarters of Allied Expeditionary Forces, SHAEF, was assembling a force of fifteen former underground leaders for tasks they would be well suited to perform. It would consist of inquiries of a confidential nature. Members of the group would work as independents using all their former contacts, as well as the Belgian authorities and the Allied forces. The pay would be according to rank achieved in the underground. Business expenses, car, and gas would be provided. Was I interested? In principle, I was, but wanted to know more precisely what was involved. Major Malinson told me Captain Simms would brief me on that. Would I give the matter the most urgent attention? I assured him I would.

Back in Simms' office, the captain put a file in front of me and asked me to look at it. He left me alone in front of a bulging file he had just taken out of a padlocked cabinet. I started reading. It was the file on a certain Belgian citizen named De Zitter. It soon appeared that the man had been involved in penetrating escape lines for the enemy and had been responsible for widespread arrests of Dutch, French, and Belgian citizens. But the file was extensive and the afternoon was over. Before leaving, Simms told me that as I read the file, I would discover that De Zitter might have been connected with the arrests of both Marcel Franckson, Sr., and Léon Joye and that the master spy might still be in Belgium working behind the lines. Would I return in the morning to resume my reading? Would I try to make up my mind and give an answer by noon? For the very first time, Captain Simms called me Herman, bidding me a good evening.

On the way home, I considered his proposal. I would have a job while the country slowly recovered and the industrial fabric mended enough to provide employment. Realistically, I should be grateful to them for this opportunity to earn a living, but more than that, I began to become excited by the character of the person I might eventually hunt. A traitor of the first order, a cunning, evil man, a man the British secret service had every reason to believe was still at his dirty work. With growing anticipation, I entered Simms' office the next morning to learn more about De Zitter, the man responsible for hundreds of arrests and deaths. He had infiltrated several escape lines, several underground groups. He had worked with the gestapo and the *Abwehr,* secret military intelligence of the German army. I wanted to find him, to arrest him, to bring him into daylight and to justice. He had

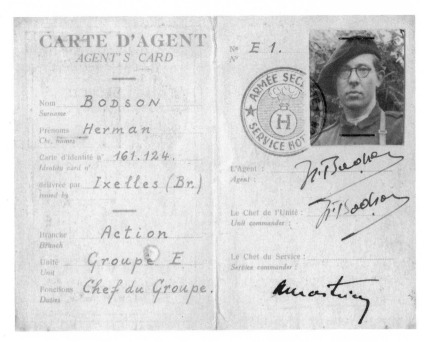

Bodson's postwar identity card as agent in the belgian secret army/hotton.

many answers to give. For that, he had to be captured alive. At lunchtime I gave Simms my answer, an unequivocal yes.

In two days my paperwork was processed and stamped. I would carry a rare pass signed by General Eisenhower, the supreme commander. The pass would give me unrestricted travel privileges, as well as access to army gas and help as I should need it. I was officially attached as a civilian to the security branch of Special Forces. The Opel car became my official, un-marked army car, the white stars erased.

I was underground again, but in a very different capacity. I was under-ground in a free land, as hunter and avenger. I saw nothing wrong with the work. I would face a master war criminal, a cunning individual without con-science, indeed a dangerous man. Was I afraid? Oh yes, but I had resolved that the risks would not deter my efforts.

CHAPTER 15

▼

De Zitter and Others

Reading all day, it took me a good week to absorb the voluminous file. I did not wish to believe that traitors like De Zitter existed. It had been positively established that he worked for the gestapo and Abwehr. He was a man of intelligence who put his abilities to the enemy's purpose. He sold himself body and soul to the enemy. He had a great appetite for food and women. He sold himself to satisfy his hungers. Betrayal was his way. The Germans must have paid him well and realized an excellent return on their investment. De Zitter was a superachiever. From all that had been put together, piece by piece, fragment by fragment, De Zitter's image emerged quite clear and, even if incomplete, fascinating.

To gather all the information he had obtained, leading to all the arrests for which he had been responsible, he must have traveled extensively through Belgium, Holland, and the north of France. If he was feeding the gestapo their arrests, they in turn told him all that they learned during the torture of their prisoners. The man must possess an incredible memory and have a great ability to impersonate, to fool, to induce confidence. I tried hard to analyze his thoughts, penetrate his methods. If he was still working for the Germans, and most of what was in the file pointed to that, then I must figure out what he would look for now that would interest the enemy. There I would find him. It would probably be military information: troop concentrations, depots, logistics. He could also be organizing an enemy fifth column, a German underground in liberated Belgium.

I concentrated on the places he would have to visit to gather valuable information. There was so little to go on, only his past, to construct his present. Through conversations with Captain Simms, I gathered information and precious advice. Then I visited several population record offices where I could trace De Zitter back to his schooldays and establish his family ties. I learned about his parents, where they had lived; his relatives and where they lived; his wife and his only son, now twenty-five. I tried to penetrate his life. I gathered some facts, but soon became lost in a tangle of blind alleys. He was a man of great secrecy and did not leave much behind. There was no recent photograph of him. The best I had available to show people was a composite portrait similar to those the police obtain from victims using professional artists. I visited the house where his wife lived in a Brussels suburb and was soon persuaded he was not, at least now, visiting the place. I learned of some of his lovers, but they were all nearly impossible to locate. One, as it appeared from the file, clearly must live in Liège.

But I was handicapped by the fact that the land had returned to legality as a way of life since liberation. I had to operate according to our laws and work within the system. I had no legal status, was not a sworn officer, had no power of arrest. If I discovered something interesting, I had to report to the authorities and work with them. While the man I was looking for was agile, I was slowed down by the law.

For my own protection, I carried my .45 in a discreet breast holster under my sport jacket. This in itself was illegal. The only thing protecting me was my affiliation with the armed forces, although during the war, our Belgian authorities were lenient and flexible as long as there was no abuse. My friends and I, selected by SHAEF, were counterspies working for the country and the Allied forces. We were not connected in any official way to any agency, although temporarily we had the support of the Belgian legal organizations to whom we reported and with whom we would eventually collaborate—the Belgian police, local and state, the judiciary, and the Allied intelligence branches, both American and British.

What we needed were informants who knew what to look for and what to report. We trained our former friends in the underground to report on the areas where they lived. They would not, unless asked, do anything other than report unusual sightings, rumors, or unknown faces in their area. It would be for us to screen the information and decide if leads were worthy of further investigation or should be abandoned. I traveled frequently between Brussels and the Ardennes, contacting all the former men of Hotton East and telling them specifically what to look for, cautioning them not to neglect other unusual happenings that might justify a search. I circulated the composite De Zitter portrait. My men were instructed how to contact me and Special Force took note of all incoming messages. I kept in touch with them daily, if not more often. I also enlisted the services of friends and acquaintances who had not been part of my former group. From the old OMBR, I recruited others to observe the Brussels area.

Near the end of October, 1944, I was directed by a Brussels contact who had a friend in Liège to a house in that city, one mentioned in the file. A brief inquiry revealed that the house was the center of an unusual amount of traffic, despite the fact that the only occupant was a single woman. One of the frequent visitors fitted De Zitter's description. Was this woman one of De Zitter's lovers? Armed with this tenuous information, I contacted the local district attorney, who in turn obtained from a judge the power to investigate. Strict surveillance was organized. It soon brought enough evidence to justify action. The authorities obtained a search warrant and the house was surrounded by armed official investigators, as well as by members of Hotton and myself. We rang the bell, entered the dwelling, and searched it carefully. Except for the occupant, nothing was found. She was alone.

Taken away for questioning, she was interrogated relentlessly at the D.A.'s office until she finally admitted to a former liaison with the man in the composite portrait, a man she knew only by an unfamiliar name. The man with whom she had associated appeared to be the one we were looking for. We asked if she had a current picture of him and she answered that her companion would never agree to having his picture taken. She refused to admit having seen him recently. Our surveillance reports indicated the opposite. We believed her to be lying. In the wee hours of the morning I decided to move her to British intelligence in Brussels and have the interrogation continued there. She was gagged and handcuffed. In the car her feet were restrained in a most unpleasant manner, so as to make the two-hour trip very uncomfortable. She lay on the rear seat for the duration of the drive. I took the road to Brussels accompanied by an inspector from the Liège D.A.'s office.

We had a most memorable drive to Brussels that dark night. Between Saint Trond and Tirlemont, there was a deluge of such an intensity that I had to slow down considerably. To make matters worse, just before Louvain we nearly collided with a semitrailer parked perpendicular to the road and partially standing in our lane. Americans were loading lumber on it. I saw it only at the very last moment and slammed on the brakes. The hood of the car disappeared under the trailer frame, the windshield touched the trailer bed, and the woman rolled onto the floor and became wedged between the seats. She was badly bruised but otherwise all right. When we arrived in Brussels, we had to await the arrival of the agents who would pursue the interrogation after we briefed them on the results of the Liège session. She was hungry, but we only allowed her water. We wanted to lower her guard.

The Brussels interrogation did not bring much more than we already knew, save one important thing. Out of jealousy, she gave us a Brussels address, a place we already knew, a place where her lover was meeting another woman. This happened to be De Zitter's wife's house and so we knew who her lover was—the man we were after.

The Brussels house was immediately placed under surveillance. We were certain our prisoner knew more than she had told us, but we had no way to make her tell more. We were limited by a return to civility. We could question at length, but use no violence. We were tough, not brutal. When this failed to produce further information, we let her go and she was driven back to Liège. I stayed in daily contact with the Brussels district attorney in charge, following the details of the investigation around the wife's house. A man resembling De Zitter came and went frequently, but he was much younger, probably his son. A woman was seen hanging washing in the rear garden but was never seen using the front door. She seemed to live as a recluse. I wished the search would move faster, but learned patience as I waited, analyzing all the leads.

News trickled in from my Ardennes contacts of strange occurrences that might warrant further investigation. Several times I had received reports of sightings of civilians unknown to the rural people. Also there were reports of low-flying aircraft that could not be identified as American or English. I asked my contacts to be extra vigilant and to take clear notes to be certain they did not forget anything.

One morning I parked my car in the army lot in front of the north railway station in Brussels. The parking covered the whole area of the Place Rogier and had been enclosed, offering only one way in and one way out. The entrance was always guarded by two MPs. Everyone had to show papers to be admitted. While parking in front of a military jeep, I backed up a little too far and touched the legs of a man in an American uniform. He had been standing in front of his vehicle leaning under the raised hood, doing something to the engine. He turned, irate, and yelled, "Donnerwetter!"—a mild German curse. I was out of my car instantly, .45 in hand and calling for assistance, while keeping this man in place, fearful of a bullet until he raised his hands in surrender. Handcuffed, he was led away. Later I learned he was a German in disguise, carrying the papers of an American wounded near the German border. We had been warned that in Belgium there were many Germans in Allied uniforms. Some, like this one, even had an Allied army vehicle. The fifth column was real and hard to detect. I had been lucky. Surprised and caught off guard, he had burst out in his mother tongue.

We hoped for more from the surveillance of De Zitter's Brussels house. A man resembling De Zitter and of about his age had been seen entering. He stayed a few hours and then left. The D. A. and I agreed it was time to increase the surveillance. I alerted several Brussels friends, among them Alberic Maistriau, who had told me he wanted to be in on capturing the man. We decided to storm the house. I was glad to have Alberic in the crew. His massive frame, strength, and weight would do marvels for gaining entry. It was not our intention to act politely and ring the bell. We would enter quickly, violently if necessary. We decided to act at 6:00 P.M., when De Zitter should be in. We waited for the signal from the D.A.'s office. When it came, the house was quietly surrounded by armed officers. Four of us moved to enter. Alberic, gun in hand, forced the door while I covered him. Then the four of us burst inside. Maistriau went to the kitchen and held two people with his nine-millimeter pistol while the rest of the house was stormed from basement to attic. No De Zitter! Wrong information—or the man who had been seen entering earlier must have exited through the rear without being seen.

I inspected the massive oak front door that had yielded to Alberic's lunging shoulder first in a hail of splinters. The police were called, the occupants taken away to be kept under guard while we searched the house. That paid off. In the pantry I found a two-gallon galvanized bucket of unusual weight. Upon closer examination, it revealed a false bottom containing a shortwave radio transmitter of German origin. The two suspects did not know we knew the bucket's secret. As the interrogation continued fruitlessly, we came in and showed them the incriminating object. The De Zitter woman finally admitted to having been visited by her husband. The son, especially at night, was easily confused for his father. He had the same build, stature, and bearing.

My blood boiled. I was glad not to have been left alone with this woman. I have rarely felt such anger. The transmitter was sent to the British and, I'm sure, put to good use. They had on several previous occasions used captured radio equipment to send transmissions that led to interesting results. This, however, was to be as close as I was to get to De Zitter in 1944. In 1946, I would be much closer. A year after the war with Germany had ended, I was on the Brussels Grand Place at six in the morning, in front of city hall. I was there by special invitation to witness the death of a traitor by military firing squad. De Zitter had been found in the British sector of occupied Germany. Brought back to justice, he faced a military tribunal. Most of the others faced only civil courts which, in Belgium, could not give the death penalty. Before facing the Belgian military court, De Zitter confessed everything to the Allies, perhaps hoping for clemency. But he was guilty. Guilty of untold deaths of civilians and freedom fighters, of treason and of espionage. Because of him many were dead. He was executed in front of his home town hall in front of a wall of sandbags. He refused the blindfold as he faced the firing squad. Belgium made examples of only a few. He merited it the most.

From the Ardennes Constant Lomry contacted me several times, always with similar information: airplanes at night, strangers in the area. I knew Constant too well not to believe his reports and moved for two weeks to Salmchâteau as a guest of Gustave Jacques to investigate. I listened to Constant, Ourvary, Léon Sadzot, and Marcel Luchie, an agent who had been active since early in the war and who now worked establishing liaisons for Groups D and E. They all had similar stories. There was strange activity in the area, no doubt, but what?

As the British inched their way north, liberating the last portions of occupied Belgium and fighting in the Schelde estuary, flying bombs reached Antwerp in large numbers causing damage and casualties. Not designed for accuracy, they targeted wide areas. A few reached Brussels. Then Liège was battered, like Antwerp. And, of course, they fell on London. With the approach of winter, a general offensive against Germany seemed remote. The Allies would need time to build stocks of material on the mainland. For that they needed Antwerp.

One morning, after having talked with Constant in the hamlet of Courtil, I was walking toward Bovigny one and a half miles to the north when I passed a wooden hay barn built some thirty yards from the road. I thought I saw a motion from the corner of my eye. I stopped, looked again, and decided to investigate. As I neared the barn, I heard a shot and a bullet whistled past me; it sounded like a nine-millimeter, a shot from a Luger or parabellum. I retreated to the road. By coincidence, an army truck was approaching from Courtil and I stopped the truck, showed my credentials, and asked a young lieutenant for his assistance. I wanted him and his men to circle the barn and search it carefully. It was empty, but in the loft were fresh and visible marks of someone having bedded down there. We conducted a thorough search of the small place, but found nothing more. The shooter must have escaped while I was parleying on the road. I thanked the Americans and they continued on their way to Vielsalm.

In Bovigny I talked, as I intended, with Mayor Faisant and my anxieties were underscored by similar tales. It was time to make a decision. I resolved to go to Liège and talk with army intelligence, the American army's counter-intelligence corps (CIC). Their attitude was of indifference, even disbelief. After all, the war was nearly over, the Germans nearly kaput. They could not possibly mount anything against the mighty armies opposing them. I was only an amateur interfering with American security business. There was nothing I could prove. The shot fired at me in Courtil became simply the bedding place of a vagabond in the hay. Unidentified airplanes in the area, unknown persons passing by? All were dismissed as not very serious, certainly not a CIC concern.

I decided not to argue. I really had no tangible evidence, no proof, no prisoner to bring forth. Instead I went to talk with Captain Simms at headquarters. He was sympathetic but could do nothing. My search had been in the American sector, and I must deal with them. It was in General Omar Bradley's territory. Simms advised me to continue, to pursue my task and try to obtain proof of direct German involvement. He did not have to persuade me to go back. I knew I was right. I knew I was not seeing ghosts. I needed proof with a capital P. I went back to Constant and we organized a permanent watch on Le Sapin, our former drop zone, that splendidly tucked-away meadow in the woods. I organized my men into pairs who would take turns watching twenty-four hours a day. The men were willing. The heavy summer work was over. Winter was at the door and they had time to offer. I insisted on no intervention, just observation. One week passed without anything unusual happening.

November ended with superlative good news: the first Allied ship had entered Antwerp and was unloading. From now on, the traffic would be like a floating conveyor belt bringing supplies from England and the United States. Boats were unloaded as if the German flying bombs were nonexistent. Our dockers were as good as soldiers and hard workers under fire. In less than a week, there were visible changes for the civilians as food was unloaded along with war matériel. Flour, a little meat, and sugar appeared in the stores. But what made me happiest was the arsenal being built and supplied. One U. S. boat arrived loaded with steam locomotives. Coal arrived too, promising less bitter cold in our houses. December brought cooler weather and soon we had freezing nights in the Ardennes. In Brussels, at only three hundred feet in elevation, the temperature was several degrees warmer.

In early December our watching paid off. I finally had something positive to report to the CIC. While Ourvary and another were on duty at Le Sapin, they had witnessed the arrival of two parachutists in civilian attire. They had backpacks and were met by two men. All departed in an easterly direction. This time the CIC listened seriously. They asked me to continue the surveil-

lance and to let them know of any further activity. They would communicate
our findings to the higher echelons.

Constant and I would, like the others, spend a full day a week in the
woods. We built a lean-to to protect ourselves from the frequent cold rains.
By mid-December the weather had cooled further and even Brussels had
freezing nights. In the Ardennes we had freezing days, too. The men on
watch could not build a fire to keep themselves warm. They had to stay quiet
and cold. A fire would have transforn.ed them into targets for the fifth col-
umnists. But the long, cold waits paid off again. On the night of December
16, when Constant and I were on guard, a plane dropped two more men in
civilian attire at about two in the morning. They were received by two others
whom we had not seen arriving. We clearly saw them leaving with backpacks
and some sort of equipment, radio transmitters we thought, since they were
boxy and appeared not to be heavy. As I was the only one armed, confronting
them was impossible. But we had additional proof of the use of our former
drop point. They left without our being able to follow them in the darkness
of night.

We waited a while and then, frozen to the marrow, went back to Constant's
home in Courtil. He made us hot tea that we eagerly drank before going to
bed. We slept late and after a hearty breakfast of fried potatoes and pork, I
departed to report to the nearest intelligence unit. That was in Bastogne,
thirty and some miles distant. On the way I stopped at Montleban to speak
with another of our men, asking if he had spotted anyone or anything unusual. No, nothing new, he said, except those same unknown characters in
the area. I continued on the road through Houffalize and turning south from
there, I entered Bastogne in the early afternoon of December 17.

Militarily the city is one of the most important in the Ardennes, not so
much for its size, but as the junction of no less than seven roads, four of
which are major highways. It is a transportation hub only six miles from the
border of the Hertogdom of Luxembourg. Having located the American military offices there, I asked for the intelligence officer and waited quite a while
in an anteroom full of military personnel entering and leaving the office.
Finally, I was introduced to a young lieutenant who seemed to be very busy
and in a bad mood. I told him what we had witnessed the night before and
what I had earlier reported to Liège. He gave me the impression of being
overly tired and somewhat dull, not unduly cooperative. Although he listened to me, it looked as though what I said to him had passed over his head.
I was frustrated and told him so in my limited English. I also told him that I
was going straight to Liège to tell my story to his superiors. When he said he

would not permit me to do that, I became quite irritated and informed him that I was responsible only to General Eisenhower. I reminded him of my pass. Struck by my snapped answer, his attitude changed visibly. He apologized for having expressed himself so as to provoke a misunderstanding.

Don't get me wrong, he said, I am just concerned for your safety. We were being approached by enemy forces, he continued. The front was breached and heavy armor was approaching. We would have to wait and see how the situation developed. I would need to wait a few hours and come back to see him around six. He would know then if it was safe for me to go. I was flabbergasted and felt as though someone had punched me hard in the stomach. I fought for air. I tried to learn more, but the officer was busy and could tell me little about this very confused situation. I left in my car for the Place du Carré and, finding a café, ordered a hot ersatz coffee.

Then, to pass the time, I walked through the city. The citizens, not knowing that German forces were approaching, looked calm. Business went on as usual. Were it not for the 101st Airborne Division entering town, Bastogne would have been a very peaceful place. The men of the 101st to whom I talked simply told me they were moving toward the border as replacements. I learned later that they had been sent here to defend the town. The gray sky menaced precipitation. With temperatures dropping, this could mean snow. About six, back at headquarters, I learned that the Germans had advanced farther. I was advised to stay for the night and check again in the morning. I did not take up any more precious time. Telephones rang incessantly; the office was abuzz with activity. In case it proved possible to depart in the morning, I drove my car to the motor pool and had the tank filled. Then I secured a room at a local hotel, had dinner, and went to bed. I was tired from the night before and nervous about the day's news. The public was still unaware of this new development and I was certainly not about to disturb the few peaceful hours left in Bastogne. As the Teutons moved back into Belgium, I slept.

In the morning when I came down, the city's atmosphere was radically different. The people now knew and were stupefied. The front had broken and the enemy's armor was returning. The Germans were back! At headquarters the situation became a little clearer; several armored divisions were reinvading Belgium. Plans were drawn to stop them, but the attack had been so sudden, so unexpected, so forceful, that no one could yet predict the outcome.

In retrospect, it is easier to figure out what had happened. The retreating Germans had taken what they could out of France and Belgium. Behind the

Siegfried Line, they stopped and reorganized. The Allies advanced to the border, but with little gas and not much ammunition. They had received only the meager allotments that came through the temporary Normandy harbors and, since September, through Marseilles and Antwerp. All those ports except Antwerp were far away and much gas was expended just to move the goods. In addition, the arrival of winter made things more difficult.

The Allied positions in mid-December were as follows: in the north of Belgium and through Holland the Allied armies faced Germany. The Canadian First Army, the British Second Army, and the American Ninth Army were preparing to force their way into the Ruhr valley after establishing a passage to the Ruhr River. To the south in Luxembourg and in the north of France, Patton's Third Army and the French First Army were readying for a push through the Saar, Rhine, and Mosel valleys. Connecting these combined forces there was practically nothing. The thirty-mile front from Montjoie to Vianden was protected by only two American divisions, the 106th and the Twenty-eighth. German intelligence must have discerned this. They evidently had enough informants and radio operators to convey exactly what the situation was.

We who had been working for SHAEF had witnessed nothing less than the build-up of a fifth column. We had seen their arrival. Only the Americans did not believe us. They felt secure behind the success of their past offensives. The Allies have since been accused of carelessness, of not taking enough precautions. But there is another explanation. It may have been by design that the border was left vulnerable. Perhaps it suited the Allies' purpose to let the Germans mount an attack. Allied general headquarters knew that such a foolish German enterprise would never succeed. This has been stated and published. Eisenhower spoke of "calculated risk." It was true that not even the Allies could simultaneously build an effective attack force and mount a strong defense along all of the borders. There were weak points and they knew it. Even if the Germans did penetrate Belgium again, it would only be for fifty or a hundred miles. With the mechanization and air supremacy the Allies had, they could regain the lost terrain and annihilate many of the remaining good German units. This was the Allied point of view, of which we learned only later.

On the German side, the main objectives seemed to have been to gain time to reorganize the *Vaterland* defenses against the oncoming Allied offensive and to acquire new armament by capturing their opponents' weapons, perhaps even reach Antwerp and the growing arsenal there. It was the desperate hope of the trapped animal.

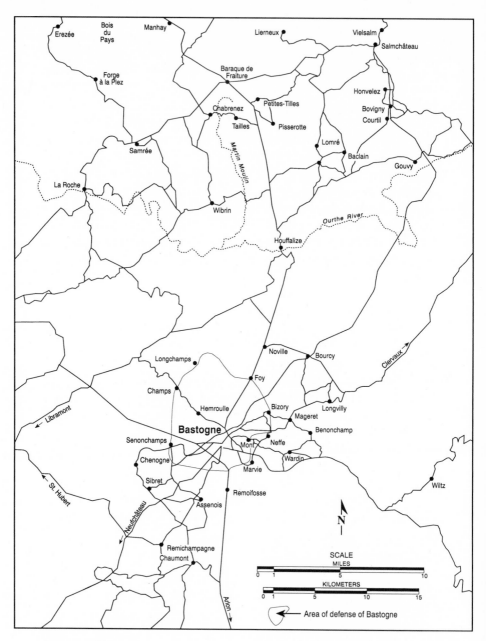

Area around Bastogne

The Germans massed four armies on a fifty-mile front from Montjoie to Vianden. Two flanks, north and south, the Fifteenth and the Seventh armies would hold against Bradley and Patton. Between those two flanks were two motorized attack units, the Sixth SS Armored to rush to the south toward Liège and the Fifth SS Armored to try to cross the Meuse and retake the Namur area.

These were the forces that would attack and reenter Belgium and Luxembourg. These were the forces that would penetrate the greatly extended American divisions along the line. The American Eighth Corps were at rest in Liège and Brussels. It would be for the 106th and the Twenty-eighth divisions to receive the blow of the attack on December 16 at 5:35 in the morning, in the dense fog that covered the high Belgian plateau. And these men, accustomed to a war of forward motion, were now forced into defensive positions and outnumbered fifteen to one. This German counteroffensive became known as the Battle of the Bulge.

CHAPTER 16

▼

Christmas in Bastogne—
December, 1944

Unusually, deep winter set in early and stayed with savage persistence. Temperatures, rarely above freezing, fell frequently to freezing or below, hovering there through damp, overcast days and long, bitter nights. Early in December began the rain, which turned to sleet, which turned to snow, and then, toward the middle of the month, the temperature plunged, and the landscape froze and remained frozen as fierce, intermittent winds blew over the plateau, numbing the skins of both cattle and men.

December, 1944

The medieval Trier gate to the north end of town stands as moot reminder of Bastogne's ancient past. Its massive stone walls, long a symbol of strength, now stand as a beacon of resistance and survival. Close by is the more recent though still old church of Saint Peter. They alone stand impervious to the cold.

A rare fog has settled in, thick, viscous, impenetrable to the eye. It clogs the breath. The Germans, halting their retreat out of France and Belgium to regroup behind the Siegfried Line have turned back upon their attackers and begun an awful war of attrition. The fog, full of phantoms and the muffled sounds of machinery moving through the shadows of war, makes everything seem unreal, illusory.

Saturday, December 16

On the first day of the attack, December 16, we had no idea of the magnitude of the German offensive, of which Bastogne was only one point along the way—one small-town crossroads to be occupied by this new offensive. It was only on the second day that the extent of the battle front began to become known, and along with that, the extent of our real peril.

Germans attacked an entire western front from Montjoie, fifty miles to the northeast, to Echternach/Vianden, forty miles to the southeast, with panzers and infantry. Under the cover of the weather, they appeared to be progressing quickly toward Bastogne and the River Meuse. Soon they would reach the position of the newly arrived 101st Airborne sent to oppose them, but trapped in Bastogne by the overwhelming massiveness of the attack. These defenders had come a hundred miles from Reims in one day, in a column of four hundred trucks and vehicles carrying men, armor, artillery, and supplies, and had departed so quickly that many men, on leave in Paris, were left behind. Others had no armament. Some were dressed in light clothing. Most lacked overshoes, critical in this weather, and at least one asked, "How long will the battle last?"

Monday, December 18
From conversations with the soldiers in town, I learn that the American Thirty-second Glider Battalion has taken a position about three miles to the southeast in the village of Marvie, while Allied tanks are in position along the highway about four miles to the east just above Marenwez. A small regional headquarters at Château Michotte, at the same distance and under the leadership of a Captain Merril, has been forced to retreat out of Wardin two miles east of Marvie. Such is our situation on the evening of December 18 in Bastogne. Thanks to the heroic resistance offered by the Americans at the front and during the well-organized pullback that followed, the Germans have been unable to reach Bastogne before the arrival of Brig. Gen. Anthony McAuliffe's men.

After spending the night before at Le Sapin with Constant Lomry, I have slept easily at the Hotel Lebrun, mostly undisturbed by the sounds of the military and civilian traffic and the distant noise of battle reaching us from the east. Before going to bed last night I talked with a few civilians crossing town, who are from the eastern villages. They have abandoned their farms and animals, fleeing the approaching Germans. They are terrified, cold, and drenched.

I am up early to a miserable morning with misty rain and very low cloud. In the absence of wind, the rain comes straight down. I walk to headquarters, where I learn that the situation has only worsened. I am told it would be foolish to try to leave town, although a civilian tide from the east is passing unabated toward the west. Not picturing myself a fool, I decide to stay and await further developments. I may be of some help. In the meantime I am free to visit the city I know only vaguely from having crossed it occasionally before the war. I familiarize myself with the town and seek out the locations of different army offices. I go around to the old Belgian army barracks occupied by our American friends, the Heintz barracks west of town, where I meet the men of the Tenth Division bivouacked there. Along the way I manage to secure an army oilskin to protect myself from the rainy weather. Happily I have warm winter clothes and very good, waterproofed shoes.

Some small units have already been dispatched to the east while the rest are on full alert. The men are cold, ill clad, and tired. Traveling those hundred miles from Reims in open trucks has not helped. But what matters now is that they are here.

From the eastern front vague bits of information filter through. The 158th Engineers Combat Battalion is ready to fight the Germans at Mageret. They face a platoon of tanks and panzer grenadiers. Colonel Roberts is moving out with three detachments. One, under Colonel Cherry, is the last battalion to take position at Longvilly. Another, under Colonel O'Hara, moves toward Wardin. A third detachment, under Major Desobry, moves toward Noville. The intention is clear: block the roads from the north and northeast to gain time to organize the town's defenses. Many units are entering Bastogne from the south and west. The 705th Tank Destroyer Battalion and two artillery units are expected soon.

From the east, in front of the advancing Germans, isolated survivors of the Twenty-eighth Infantry Division are arriving. These valiant men have received the full blow of the Germans' new offensive. The total force of the city's defenders approaches the eighteen thousand mark. Soon we will all have to confront the German march.

As midday approaches under an overcast sky and a meager forty-two degrees, the fog thickens into an ongoing drizzle. By noon, the Germans are nearing Bourcy and on their way to Noville, north of Bastogne on the Liège highway. The sounds of battle intensify. Artillery duels are clearly audible to the northeast. Near three o'clock in the afternoon the first German shell lands in town and explodes near the Sainte Thérèse Chapel. At four, Colonel Roberts with the combat command of the Tenth Division has crossed Neufchâteau and entered Bastogne from the southeast.

Again the fog thickens. The night promises permeating darkness—a perfect night for Germans to advance to battle positions undetected. We are nervous and preparing for the worst.

At the Hotel Lebrun life goes on, at least on the surface. The café does a brisk business, although it is said that the town's population has dwindled by half. Animated conversations exchange rumor and fact. The owner tells me the basement has already been prepared for a shelter. He shows me the way to it in case of shelling. It is spacious, but not very safe. The ceiling is made of heavy beams with an oak floor above. Should the stone building collapse, I doubt the floor would carry the load. I say nothing to him, but I would feel safer outside, taking the risk in the open.

By the end of the day I have decided to stay in town and help as best I can, and I ask some army medics from the 101st to introduce me to an army doctor. They oblige as soon as they learn I am a trained medic. Meeting a young doctor, I offer my services, hoping they will not much be needed. My qualifications and the fact that I speak French make me a good recruit and a possible liaison with the locals. The doctor points out where he will open a first aid post the following morning, a café nearly facing the Sainte Thérèse Chapel, and he offers me food and shelter there. He is short of help and I am welcome. Promising to return early in the morning, I go back to the hotel and lie on the bed a long time, unable to sleep. Hearing the roar of distant guns, I wonder what the next day or days might bring. It is a crapshoot. Only one thing is certain: the Huns will attack in force and the fight will be terrible. For now, though, the night has returned to relative calm, and I succumb to sleep.

Tuesday, December 19
This morning the air seems cooler than yesterday. The military traffic, intense throughout the night, continues. For the most part, all the civilians who wished to leave have done so. Those left now are determined to stay. We are determined. The 101st Airborne, since late yesterday, have been taking positions around the city as more men arrive in town. I awake promptly at seven and have breakfast at the hotel. The night has been calm to the east. Unbelievably, the fog is even denser than yesterday. One wonders how any military activity can take place under such conditions. Visibility is less than ten yards. Making matters worse, the bone-chilling, misty rain continues. I arrive at the first aid post to disquieting news. General Norman G. Cota from the "Keystone" Division, Twenty-eighth Infantry, has moved his HQ out of Wiltz to ten miles to the west of Sibret, four miles south of Bastogne. Will the Germans push to the south of town and cut the Arlon road?

The doctor tells me that the Forty-second Field Hospital, operating in an old château in upper Wiltz, has departed under such German pressure that they have left behind twenty-six men in too serious a condition to be moved.

The news is also bad from the north. At six this morning, advancing elements of the Second Panzers were at Bourcy and to the west, blocking the Liège road at Noville. Taking advantage of the night, German soldiers infiltrated the twenty-house village of Neffe which had been occupied by the Americans along the road to Clervaux. These are now our nearest enemies, barely two miles from us.

Reliable rumor has it that elements of the Panzerlehr division under the command of General Bayerlein are arriving from the east and have passed through Benonchamp and Mageret. Our situation is such that the eastern defense of Bastogne must be reinforced. So far, the 501st hold Neffe, the 506th Noville, the 327th Marvie. The 502nd are en route "west of town." Since seven this morning the battle has been clearly audible with most sounds coming from the Neffe area and the Vanderesken château where Colonel Cherry is located, confronting the dense fog and the Panzerlehr Volksgrenadiers. It is all very confusing.

Having started to fall sporadically about 8:00 P.M., shells are now falling with regularity on the center of town. Men accustomed to similar situations calmly tell me they must originate from 105-millimeter German cannons. They do very local damage. The strong stone and brick buildings, unless hit directly, are resisting quite well. While we work setting up the medical center, the doctor tells me that most of his men will be needed to carry the wounded from the battlefield and that he will count on me to help provide care to the new arrivals.

With few supplies, he is worried. Supplies have not arrived and it looks as if they may never arrive. It is the same with his missing personnel. He asks me to tour the local pharmacies with a list of what is needed. Later I will go back with the proper requisition papers and fetch the goods. One large pharmacy owned by a Mr. Heintz is only a hundred yards up the street and faces the Catholic school. Further on down the street is the big church and the massive Trier gate tower. In this small town, nothing is far apart. Nowhere in my searches can I locate saline or lactate solutions. It is clear that we will not have enough sterile solutions to stabilize hemorrhaging wounds. The local civil hospital is also undersupplied and treating civilians wounded by shrapnel and flying debris.

Close to nine in the morning our own wounded begin arriving from the Neffe area. The worst has an extensive abdominal wound and would normally be sent to a very advanced trauma center. For lack of such a facility, the hospital has left him with us. There is little we can do beyond giving him massive doses of painkiller and wetting his lips to abate his thirst. We do not believe he would last long even if the best of care were available. His wounds are deep and contaminated. Our first day at the station passes in such constant activity that we do not notice the winter darkness creeping back upon us. I tour the pharmacies a second time and bring back a few drugs and other supplies, but not much. For the better part of the day, I have cleaned wounds, given shots, bandaged patients. From one who is only slightly wounded, I hear of the fighting. It seemed clear to him that the Germans lack transport. From a height in Luxembourg, overlooking the battle area, he has seen German infantry followed by ordnance carried on horse-drawn wagons.

The panes of our windows shake violently all day and we prudently secure them with strips of adhesive tape, the only thing at hand. As night comes on, the sounds of battle noticeably decrease. Only the shelling of the town continues unabated and the sky is reddened toward the east.

In the kitchen, the stove has been burning all day to provide sterile water. Tea has kept us going, enabling us to ignore our empty stomachs. After four years of ersatz beverages, my body must have become totally decontaminated, for now it responds with a vengeance to the frequent doses of black tea. It is only while eating that I realize how ravenous I am.

Being a first aid post we have few serious wounds at first. Most of our patients will return to their duties. Tonight we have few men to care for and most will sleep well. One has a fractured arm, another a deep bullet wound in his thigh. Others have less complicated problems and need only a little time to heal. Precisely at 10:00 P.M. a shell lands up the street where the school of the Notre Dame sisters is located. No one is injured. Shortly after midnight our abdominal patient passes away. It is calm again and I lie down to rest, hoping to be ready for what tomorrow brings. It may be a busy day.

Wednesday, December 20

I did not sleep well. Many shells exploded in our vicinity throughout the night. Several times I woke to respond to the requests of the men under my care. Most were simple needs and thirst. It is six-thirty and still dark. Unlike yesterday there is an early breeze. Will it break the fog or just blow in more wet weather? The temperature has dropped again over the frozen landscape. The doctor, an agreeable young man with a strong sense of humor, has seen D-day in Normandy and the battles through France. He has been tested under fire along with the rest of his division. My confidence grows in this young doctor barely my own age.

Radio messages for our ambulances begin to come in around seven. They are followed by many others. Those collecting wounded to the east are back fully loaded before eight. Our patients share their news from the front.

During the night, the Germans have crept forward and installed themselves in hastily dug foxholes. From there they shouted to wake our men at the very first crack of dawn and the battle was on, but to a new tune, a tune not heard before—American artillery, barely half a mile from us. The earth shakes with every shell fired. As the day progresses, the music grows louder. And louder. German cannons bombard both the town and its defenders. In the constant exchange of artillery, shells explode around us. The doctor orders us to move everybody downstairs to the basement. As the battle progresses, it becomes clear from the fragmentary news we receive that the Germans are determined to take the town. Bizory, Neffe, Mont, Marvie are all under attack. For a time, Marvie, slightly south of the Wiltz road, had been taken back into enemy territory. To do this the German panzers had to fight through O'Hara's tanks and they are now on the advance again.

Cleaning wounds, dispensing drugs, giving shots, time passes. The wind blows harder now, contributing to ever greater misery. Outside, in foxholes, twenty-year-old boys from Maine and North Dakota and southern states defend people they don't even know. Many of the southern troops have never even seen snow. German pressure increases to the north and in early afternoon, casualties from Noville began to flow in. Casualties, that is, who escaped, for Noville was retaken by the enemy around noon. The 506th could not withstand the sheer numbers of the Volksgrenadiers moving in behind the panzers, yet they resisted. One patient has a thick, bloody pad on his left ear. He's lucky. A German bullet took away the midsection of the ear lobe, barely scratching his cheek. An inch the other way and he would have stayed in Noville forever.

About three, a civilian from the outskirts comes asking for our help. His neighbor is trapped under the ruins of a barn, his leg pinned between the stone floor and a large oak beam. He implores our help. The doctor and I go. At the barn, we have to crawl under the battered walls and broken remnants of roof to reach the poor man. Under the ruins it is dark, but dry. The neighbor goes for candles as the doctor prepares his tools. When the neighbor returns and I light the candles, we see a man in his mid-forties lying before us. I cut his trousers away to mid-thigh, revealing an open fracture and much hemorrhaging, the lower leg hopelessly pinned under the collapsed beam. To save his life, we must remove his leg above the knee. Hurriedly the doctor assembles the necessary material while I suspend a bottle of saline solution from a peg overhead and insert the needle into the patient's

vein. When we are ready, I inject our patient with a massive dose of morphine, which is all we have to reduce the pain. As the drug takes effect, I
apply my weight across the man's upper body and Doc starts. The poor man
struggles against my restraint. Time passes so slowly that it seems as if the
clock has stopped and this poor man's agony will never end. Then the moan-
ing subsides slightly and Doc says it is over. Gently we pull the groaning body
from under the collapsed structure. An ambulance stands ready to take him
to the hospital. As Doc and I ride back to our post, I look at my watch: it has
taken less than twenty minutes.

Later that evening, during a battle lull, we hear that the village of Marvie
has been evacuated.

Our food reserves are getting low. Our medical supplies dwindle.

Taking advantage of the relative calm of late evening, Doc goes to the
college and then to the hospital to see what he can scavenge, but he returns
disappointed. Supplies are low everywhere. We must make do with what we
have until more arrive. At day's end, the firing of our cannons becomes spo-
radic. Are we wanting ammunition too?

It is only my second day at the aid station. Am I afraid? Yes. One single
shell or piece of shell can kill or maim. But men need help and we must
provide it. I am drained. I am dirty, and I need rest. Amazingly, I manage to
find sleep even as German shells continue to fall around us.

Thursday, December 21

My birthday! Thirty-two, in my prime, armed with my Ph.D. But, for the
last seven years, I have been either in the army or in other ways fighting
against the Nazis. I resent the waste of time, waste of energy. It is early, and
still dark. It is calm in the station. The men rest comfortably and there is
time for reflection. My parents must wonder where I am. There is no way to
let them know. Maybe that's better. We are not very safe.

I am preoccupied with the fog. The Allied air force is grounded. I pray for
the weather to clear. Getting out of bed, I go outside only to be greeted by
another freezing day without any visible signs of clearing. In fact, the visibility is the worst since I arrived. A passing soldier says that the town now seems
completely surrounded.

The men who came in yesterday will go back to their units after a dressing
change and I wonder how they will fare. Only a few will remain, resting.

Like yesterday and the day before, with the coming of light, the battle
resumes with an intense shelling of the city. The inhabitants have retreated
into the strongest basements. It is communal living, up to forty people in

some basements. The Franciscan fathers have opened a shelter under their chapel choir stand. There is another at the Récollets Convent. The first shelters one hundred, the other a hundred and fifty. Food is increasingly hard to come by and the college has opened its kitchen, serving three thousand Spartan meals a day. It is said that at the Soeurs de Notre Dame, the sisters are preparing a shelter in the basement corridors to accommodate up to six hundred people. We are under military authority and curfew is from 6:00 P.M. till 8:00 A.M.

By best estimates, there are about three thousand civilians left in town. The food situation is so bad that the military has requisitioned all available stocks and controls food distribution.

The city and battle zone remain blanketed in fog. The wind persists. Men brought in from battle complain mostly of being frozen and having wet feet. The numbing cold is lowering their pain tolerance. But all is not totally dark. There is good news from east of town. Our counterattacks have been somewhat successful and many small German units are surrounded near Neffe and Bizory.

In late afternoon the 101st has to abandon Sibret and Assenois to the southwest. Night is engulfing us. Just before curfew, I take the opportunity to step outside for a cigarette and for the first time I realize the extensive damage done by the shelling. I have been so busy with the wounded that there seemed no time to notice.

A few disabled military vehicles sit abandoned here and there. Many buildings show signs of battle. Luckily no fires are reported. The electricity has been off since this morning. Happily we have gasoline lanterns. A civilian, who like me is outside smoking, tells me that the mother superior of the Notre Dame sisters has been killed by shrapnel that entered the basement shelter through a narrow window at sidewalk level. The day ends with the sounds of distant battle. I go back inside to eat and attempt to comfort the men in my care, trying to induce some sweet thoughts and sleep.

Friday, December 22
The shelling of town did not completely stop during the night and the days and nights of fierce battle are taking their toll. And the cold. And the fog. But today would prove to be different. It is evident. I realize it as soon as I go outside to breathe the early morning air. It is still dark. A foot of snow has fallen during the night, a heavy, thick blanket of cold and dampness laid

down and blown about in drifts by the wind. How much more miserable can it get for our fighters?

But then it must also be miserable for the enemy. Will it be miserable enough to undermine their determination?

Visibility has improved over yesterday and the temperature is stabilizing just above freezing. After a few biscuits and some coffee, which I definitely prefer to tea, I set about another day of chores. Doc has already reexamined the wounded who spent the night with us. Medics prepare ambulances. I change dressings, get those who will be discharged ready, and make the others as comfortable as possible. With the onset of daylight, the noise of battle increases and mortar shells again fall on the town. The ambulances leave to bring in casualties. No moment is left for our minds to run. No time for personal thoughts. Barely enough time to treat the ever-increasing numbers of wounded.

This Friday I shall forever remember as the day we treated our first cases of frostbite. They range the scale from mild to severe. For the latter, we can do nothing. These we send to the hospital. The others we treat as best we can: mild morphine to ease the pain, gradual warming and light massage to help restore blood circulation. Most of the time it will take a day before the patient feels comfortable again.

At the front, incredible, harsh fighting continues in this cold, windy, fog- and snow-covered landscape, a sea of agony; of cold; of wetness. Our fighters use calories faster than they replace them. It is clear to Doc and me that army field rations are not suitable for harsh winter battle conditions. Additionally, they are rationed for want of supply. In late morning the soldiers are asked to spare ammunition. Soon this lack of supplies will act on our morale.

Early in the afternoon Doc returns from a quick trip to the hospital where he has heard an incredible story. Were it not for the source, General McAuliffe's headquarters, we would dismiss it as fantasy.

German plenipotentiaries presented themselves at Marvie in late morning. They asked Bastogne to surrender, promising in case of refusal a general attack and an increased shelling of the town. Surrender was declined. Later in the day, as it spread through the camp like wildfire, General McAuliffe's concise and laconic four-letter answer reaches us: "Nuts."

In Bastogne, our day passes without any increase in the shelling. In fact, the opposite. But as the number of shells decreases, their size increases. The Germans have begun using truly big guns, shooting projectiles of incredible power. Where they fall, entire buildings collapse and disappear into craters.

We simply pray not to be under an impact point. The blast leaves no window panes unbroken within a two-hundred-yard radius. These new shells must be of the size fired by battleships. But that's clearly impossible. Or is it? Nobody has any idea of the caliber or their origin.

The thermometer is falling again, and the cold is more bitter than ever. Light snow is falling.

At the end of the day, the army decides to make room at the hospital and medics are moving hundreds of patients into the Notre Dame sisters' underground corridors. Half the six hundred spaces are quickly filled with stretchers.

Night has long engulfed the battlefield, but the shelling continues. The town, however, is for once temporarily off the battlefield and relative safety has returned. The Germans, once again, are not true to their word. They had promised to shell us to death. Not yet! Bluff again? Or are they able to deliver?

Saturday, December 23
The sky is clear! The fog is gone. Only a cloud here and there. Our prayers are answered. A pale winter sun shines timidly over the snow-blanketed and desolate, wounded landscape. The cold persists. But in our camp, the excitement mounts. Does this promise help? Is it possible for the Allied air forces to take advantage of this new situation? One that may be only of short duration? Time enough to resupply or launch an effective assault, driving the Germans back? Questions breed questions.

The aid station is busier than usual. The clear night has caused much trouble. The number of frostbite cases increased as the temperature dropped throughout the night.

In the early daylight, the air force takes advantage of the weather change. Planes in force hammer at the German positions around us. At ten, a group of ten to twenty C-47s drop parachute loads to the west of town along the road to Marche. The Germans respond by intensifying their assault.

Bad news. The Germans have reached a point scarcely a mile from us between Remoifosse and Kessler's farm. An entire U. S. battalion may have been taken prisoner.

The pressure is kept on nearby Marvie.

Then, in the afternoon, an Allied air armada fills the sky. More than two hundred Dakotas are dropping a multicolored multitude of parachuted supply loads. A few fall in town and a few fall to the Germans near Assenois and Marvie. All together, we are told, the drop has brought in more than one hundred fifty tons of material and food, including nearly twenty thousand K rations. For the overstretched medical teams, no bandages, no drugs, no help! I must go begging civilians to give us bedsheets to be used as bandages. But how long will these last? We have no absorbent cotton left; no new medical personnel have arrived. Our need is critical. We hope that the weather will hold, allowing help to join us. Throughout the day and into the evening the wounded of the 327th Glider Division, who have been ferociously attacked near Chenogne, arrive. Throughout another clear night, the battle continues and many wounded make their way to us. There is no opportunity to sleep. There is work to be done, care to be dispensed. By midnight, the German attack on the south side of town dies down. The Arlon road for now seems secure. It is bitter cold!

Sunday, December 24
The flow of injured continues unabated throughout the night. I am exhausted. Living on "munch when you can" and coffee is catching up with me. I am using my reserves faster than I can replace them. Like all of us. Complaint? I am indoors by a roaring fire fed with wood scavenged from the ruins around us. I feel the cold only through the soldiers coming to us, each suffering his own ordeal.

The shelling of town continues. The weather remains clear. The Allied resupply effort begins anew. More than fifty gliders have landed in the Sans Soucis area alone. In all, 160 planes are attempting to bring in more than 160 tons of artillery shells, and, praise God, some medical supplies.

Another aid station installed in a three-story building has received a direct hit. Twenty of the twenty-six wounded there and a Belgian volunteer nurse have perished in the collapsed building.

In the afternoon, after another drop, our artillery no longer saves its ammunition. It is in full action. This day, the Sunday before Christmas, passes in suffering and unthinkable violence. It is a denial of all we cherish. It is worse than barbaric.

The Germans have parachuted a Christmas message on printed handbills over us. It is clearly designed to undermine our morale, but achieves the opposite effect. They emphasize the fact that we are trapped, that we will not return home to our loved ones. McAuliffe issues his own Christmas message, "What's a merry Christmas?" As we read it, something within us, despite the carnage, is proud to be part of this battle.

At 8:00 P.M., German airplanes blanket the town with incendiary bombs. They explode without much noise and disperse burning phosphorous, spreading an eerie yellowish green light around us. Surprisingly they create few problems, it is so wet. One casualty, the large Sarma food store to be south of us, is burning. But it is an empty place, the food long since distributed. By 10:00 P.M. we function like robots. Tired to the bone from yesterday, we lose our notion of time today. Night offers no respite. The German air force has rejoined the battle. They too are taking advantage of the clear sky, risking the few planes they have in reserve to further the misery of destruction. Ours have been busy all day strafing their positions and supply lines.

As Christmas mass ends, German planes again drop incendiary bombs along our street. An entire row of buildings from the sisters' school to the Sainte Thérèse Chapel is afire. There is nothing we can do, nothing whatsoever. We have no water. In 1917, so family legend says, Christmas night was celebrated with a truce in the Yser trenches. Packages were exchanged across the front. Songs sung. But then, those were Germans, not Nazis, not SS.

Christmas

Is it really Christmas day? I have been accustomed to spending it at home in a quiet, familial atmosphere, not on a battlefield.

My energies are spent caring for wounded bodies. Thinking about my safety is futile; I am the one who decided to stay. I could have ignored CIC advice and taken my chances on the Liège road. Who knows? I could be safely home by now.

I am dreaming. I am needed. I am up facing an aluminum army cup filled with hot coffee to help me through another day. Tanks are rolling down the street on their way to battle at the outside perimeter. Men are pouring in from all points, needing immediate attention. This Monday proves to be the heaviest action of the Battle of the Bulge.

In the very early morning, while I am still resting, fifteen German tanks have forced their way through the positions of the 327th, between Champ and Hemroulle, penetrating our line of defense to the west. They were allowed to pass our foxholes so that we would be able to attack them from the rear, where they are vulnerable to bazookas. Ten of them are destroyed. Hours of fighting follow. At nine in the morning it is announced that more German tanks have been destroyed. The few remaining have turned and fled. From HQ Doc has learned that Patton's men are moving north, approaching us from the south. There is already fighting eight miles south of us at Chaumont, on the Neufchâteau road. Could it mean that the iron circle around us will soon be broken?

Afternoon. More German attacks between Champ and Hemroulle. Colonel Chapuis' men are holding ground and containing the hordes. Buildings in the town around the college still burn from last night's air raids.

After dark, German planes again drop incendiaries on the southwest district near the Sarma general store on the Neufchâteau road—the store has been burning for more than fourteen hours. Another day under fire. They shell us. We shell them. The battle continues. Fewer shells fall on us tonight. Are they short of ammunition?

Tuesday, December 26
Under a clear sky, the battle has raged all night. The cold will not release its pitiless grip. Frostbite continues to plague the infantry. Some men now display purulent toes that will have to be amputated. We can only hope that help will reach us before gangrene or septicemia set in.

In midmorning, American planes arrive with more supplies, and finally, when we had nearly abandoned any hope of serious medical help, eleven gliders with surgeons and nurses and plenty of medical supplies arrive. We have received a flying hospital brought in by one of the three hundred C-47s that are also bringing us more food and munitions. Around noon, after the last drop, we hear that Patton's men have seized Remichampagne, a bare ten miles south of town. At four in the afternoon a Lieutenant Boggess has entered Bastogne with his tanks that have pushed here with great speed from the Saar. In four days, from their point of departure, these men of the Third Army, Fourth Armored Division, have forced a wedge between the German forces surrounding us to join us. Help has come from the outside and the inside has once more been provisioned. Headquarters made a head count and found that of the 101st Airborne, 711 officers and 9,500 fighting men are still on the field of battle. And what courageous men these are!

With the medical relief that has come in, we know we will be able to relax a little and I am already dreaming of the possibility of going home. Taking advantage of the last vestiges of daylight, I pay a visit to where I parked the Opel, along the side wall of a building. I have little hope of finding it intact; probably it has been crushed. Amazingly, it has only minor body damage from flying debris and is apparently in good enough shape to be driven. Tomorrow I will clean the rubble from around it and see if it starts. I return to the aid station, where I have a cot and some blankets. Doc is beaming. Help has finally arrived from his professional field. Truly expert care can now be given. There is hope of organizing the first convoy of ambulances to evacuate the wounded to rear field hospitals. Complicated cases will go first, thoracic and abdominal, to the Villers-devant-Orval hospital. With help at hand, Doc and I plan and organize a long rest, after having leisurely eaten to full-bellied satisfaction. The last news this evening was a tally of the air help received so far: 962 planes have brought 850 tons of supplies of various sorts and have flown more than a hundred gliders in. Before falling asleep I think about these vast quantities of supplies we have received and about the bombings and strafings the Germans have been suffering these last three days. To the sound of our pounding artillery, I doze off.

Wednesday morning, December 27
The night has passed differently from previous ones. Our artillery has been pounding the enemy positions with fierce rage, while the shelling of Bastogne has dwindled to very little. Doc and I each had a long night's sleep and feel more alert. The station is nearly empty. A new unit is caring for the wounded. After breakfast of C rations, Doc goes to headquarters to find out about evacuating the wounded. He comes back with positive news: a corridor roughly half a mile wide at its narrowest point has been created and an all-out effort will be made to enlarge it throughout the day. The men at the top are confident that by tonight, a Red Cross convoy will be able to leave the city.

At noon, more C-47s have reached us, another group of 164 from Châteaudun near Paris. Unfortunately 13 have been shot down on their way, as was a glider. With our additional matériel, the Germans are now caught between two fighting forces, one in town and one outside, to the south, with an open corridor joining us. The encirclement has been broken for us and begun for them. My decision is made to try to leave town tomorrow and the CIC men I speak with admit I may just make it. During the afternoon I take an extensive tour of the now dilapidated town. It is amazing how much damage has been done, the extent of the wanton destruction. Almost miraculously, the massive Saint Peter's church and the Trier gate are still standing nearly intact, continuing to offer symbols of fortitude and resistance, as they have resolutely done since the Middle Ages.

Among the townspeople, only a few report no dead or wounded among the members of their families. Luckily, most of the shelters have so far avoided a direct hit. But the town looks like a battlefield. Burned buildings are gutted and blackened by smoke. Here and there, huge craters engulf one, two, three houses at a time. Facades are pitted by shell bursts. Electrical wires hang from houses and from broken and splintered posts. Roads are being kept open by army bulldozers pushing debris into the craters to fill them and level the surfaces.

Everywhere I look is the absurdity of war.

Around 5:00 P.M. the news is that General Maxwell Taylor, commanding officer of the 101st, has arrived in town. He was on leave in the United States when his division was called up from Reims. He insisted on being parachuted in, but permission was denied. So he had to wait and only now enters behind Patton's forces.

There is great activity around the college and the Sisters of Notre Dame shelter where medics are preparing the wounded to be evacuated, some eighty men. German prisoners are assembled, 580 of them, and will be marched toward Neufchâteau and internment; they will leave ahead of the ambulances. Near sunset, a convoy of twenty-two ambulances and ten trucks leaves town toward Villers-devant-Orval. I watch them leave and then go back to the aid station where I have been since the nineteenth.

It seems impossible that I have been here for so short a time. The hectic days and the hard, miserable work I have been doing account for the impression that it has been much longer. One more night, I hope, and home. The sky is clouding, gray moving in. Before I retire for the evening, a soldier comes in with a printed sheet that he says explains the special clear weather we have enjoyed these last four days. It is from General Patton. It is a prayer Patton asked his chaplains to address to the Almighty just before Christmas. Whether the prayer had anything to do with the change in the weather is a question I will leave to wiser ones than I to answer. Here is the prayer that sent me to bed happy and full of confidence for what lay ahead:

Sir, this is Patton talking. The last fourteen days have been straight Hell, rain, snow, more rain. More snow—and I am beginning to wonder what's going on in Your Headquarters. Whose side are You on, anyway?

For three years my chaplains have been explaining this as a religious war. This, they tell me, is the Crusade all over again, except that we're riding tanks instead of chargers. They insisted we are here to annihilate the German Army and the godless Hitler so that religious freedom may return to Europe.

Up until now I have gone along with them, for You have given us Your unreserved cooperation. Clear skies and a calm sea in Africa made the landing highly successful and helped us to eliminate Rommel. Sicily was comparatively easy and You supplied excellent weather for our armored dash across France, the greatest military victory that You have thus allowed me. You have often given me excellent guidance in difficult command decisions, and You have led German units into traps that made their elimination fairly simple.

But now, You've changed horses in midstream. You seem to have given von Rundstedt every break in the book, and frankly, he's been beating hell out of us. My army is neither trained nor equipped for winter warfare. And as You know, this weather is more suitable for Eskimos than for Southern cavalrymen.

But now, Sir, I can't help but feel that I have offended You in some way. That suddenly You have lost all sympathy with our cause. That You are throwing in with von Rundstedt and his paper-hanging god. You know without me telling You that our situation is desperate. Sure, I can tell my staff that everything is going according to plan, but there's no use telling You that my 101st Airborne is holding against tremendous odds in Bastogne, and that this continual storm is making it impossible to supply them even from the air. I've sent Hugh Gaffey, one of my ablest generals, with his 4th Armored Division, North toward that all-important road center to relieve the encircled garrison and he's finding Your weather much more difficult than he is the Krauts.

I don't like to complain unreasonably, but my soldiers from the Meuse to Echternach are suffering the tortures of the damned. Today I visited several hospitals, all full of frostbite cases, and the wounded are dying in the field because they cannot be brought back for medical care.

But this isn't the worst of the situation. Lack of visibility, continued rains have completely grounded my air force. My technique of battle calls for close-in fighter-bomber support, and if my planes can't fly, how can I use them as aerial artillery? Not only is this a deplorable situation, but, worse yet, my reconnaissance planes haven't been in the air for fourteen days and I haven't the faintest idea of what's going on behind the German lines.

Damn it, Sir, I can't fight a shadow. Without Your cooperation from a weather standpoint I am deprived of accurate disposition of the German armies and how in hell can I be intelligent in my attack? All of this probably sounds unreasonable to You, but I have lost all patience with Your chaplains who insist that this is a typical Ardennes winter, and that I must have faith.

Faith and patience be dammed! You have just got to make up Your mind whose side You're on. You must come to my assistance, so that I may dispatch the entire German Army as a birthday present to Your Prince of Peace.

Sir, I have never been an unreasonable man, I am not going to ask You for the impossible. I do not even insist upon a miracle, for all I request is four days of clear weather.

Give me four days so that my planes can fly, so that my fighter-bombers can bomb and strafe, so that my reconnaissance may pick up targets for my magnificent artillery. Give me four days of sunshine to dry this blasted mud, so that my tanks roll, so that ammunition and rations may be taken to my hungry, ill-equipped infantry. I need those four days to send von Rundstedt and his godless army to their Walhalla. I am sick of this unnecessary butchery of American youth, and in exchange for four days of fighting weather, I will deliver You enough Krauts to keep Your bookkeepers months behind in their work. Amen.

▼

CHAPTER 17

New Year, 1945

It was early in the morning on December 27, 1944, and I had decided to leave Bastogne. Taking advantage of the corridor that Patton's men have opened to the south, I planned to take my chances. The day before, I had cleaned the rubble away from my car, and now I was attempting to get it running. The glass was intact, except for the rear window, which was shattered but holding. The body had suffered minor damage from flying objects but was functional. It took several attempts for the engine to come back to life, but finally it did. The battery must have been half-frozen. The CIC had advised me of the safest road to Liège and, from there, home. It would not be the shortest route, but much of the territory was still in German hands. First I would travel south to Fauvillers and from there navigate southwest and then north around the Bulge, according to the advice given me by the military authorities.

My progress was slow due to the road conditions. All were in terrible shape, rutted by heavy military traffic and tank tracks. At places I had to negotiate small detours around bomb impacts. At Fauvillers I was directed toward Neufchâteau, Beauraing, and at last Givet on the Meuse River. It was only when I had reached Dinant that I found a working telephone. Dialing 48-50-57 I got my mother, ecstatic to learn of my location. I told her I would probably be home before dinner. In few short words I told her of my Christmas in Bastogne and tried to prepare her for the condition I was in, dirty and unkempt. I was badly in need of a bath and a change of clothes. Would she or Dad call Special Forces and let them know I was on my way back? The trip to Liège was slow. The steady stream of military traffic was heavy and I proceeded cautiously, traveling against convoys on their way to the front.

Most roads were closed to civilian traffic and I was frequently stopped by MPs to show my papers in order to proceed. I was glad to see this new awareness of security. Traveling the right-bank road along the Meuse to Yvoir, I crossed the bridge and resumed on the left bank to Namur. This road had been "redballed," reserved for military traffic. Military police had these roads clearly indicated. At intersections large, bright red plastic balls hung from trees or posts, indicating the arteries feeding fresh battle blood to the front.

Traveling against the flow, I was passed by a column of heavy tractors pulling semis loaded with tanks. They traveled fast, ignoring ruts and potholes, plastering my car with thick mud. Several times I stopped along the side of the road to clean my windshield. Only then could I proceed upstream against those called "Hell on Wheels," the army suppliers.

Once I got to Liège, the traffic eased a bit and the road to Brussels became wider and less congested. As I neared home, I wondered at my mother's reaction to seeing me so dirty, ragged, and somewhat torn. I smelled bad! But I was unhurt. I had been lucky, having sustained only a slight skin wound from a protruding nail I did not see while helping to clear a bomb site.

At home, the joy of being together tempered the shock of how I looked. My smell was not mentioned, although after long minutes of tearful reunion, we all agreed it was time for me to take a bath. An hour later as we sat around the dinner table, I told them of my tribulations from Bovigny to Bastogne. According to the latest news, nothing much had changed on the German front. It was heavy winter in Russia, and the British and Americans were containing the onslaught at the Bulge. I could not keep my eyes open and could acknowledge at last how tired I really was. Tomorrow I would meet with Special Forces.

The next morning, freshly dressed, I was at their offices on the Avenue des Arts to see Major Malinson and Captain Simms and was received like a true soldier back from the front. My stay in Bastogne, though not glorious, had been dangerous. I thought of the thousands still there in the cold, trying to push the enemy back. For Special Forces I had to explain all over again what had happened in Bovigny, the barn shot that had missed me, the drop of German agents, the meeting at CIC Bastogne, and the days in that martyred city. I did not mince my words about the degree of esteem I had for American intelligence. I explained without restraint that, in my opinion, U. S. intelligence had failed and they were now paying a high price for that failure. Both officers listened to my diatribe without offering comments on my candid opinions. I could feel they did not totally agree with my views, but they kept a polite silence and did not discuss this delicate subject. The British are good listeners and good diplomats. They offered that I had done a good job and merited a rest, a few days of total freedom. They wished me a happy New Year, a year they confidently predicted would see the Germans defeated and this nightmare ended.

It was agreed we would meet again on January 2. Out of a drawer Major Malinson took and offered me a bottle of whiskey. Now, said he, I could propose a proper toast to the new year and drink to the German defeat. I went home for lunch with my precious possession.

December ended with the temperature dropping even lower. I thought often of those left behind in Bastogne. January, 1945, proved to be the coldest on record since 1917. The thermometer in Bastogne rose only twice above freezing. At night it dropped to an arctic seven degrees Fahrenheit. Thanks to our underground work, however, my family received coal by priority and would be warm.

At the Bulge the battle was far from over. It would take the Allies until January 25 to regain their preinvasion positions: German losses—120,000 men (35,000 killed); Allied losses—72,000 (12,000 killed). The civilians, the Ardennians, were devastated, their farms and towns in ruins. Their dead— cattle, hogs, horses; mothers, fathers, brothers, sisters, friends—gone. The SS and the Légion Wallonie under Degrelle's leadership perpetrated many atrocities. In Malmédy the SS executed about eighty American prisoners of war; at Bande, Degrelle killed former resistance fighters. But it was the last twitch in the death throes of the Nazi beast. Compared to Bastogne, the conquest of Germany was to be relatively rapid.

CHAPTER 18

▼

Victory

For most of western Europe 1944 was a year of suspense, accomplishments, and restored peace. Most of the occupied territories had been liberated, with the exception of Holland, and people could celebrate the new year dreaming of a rapid end to the conflict. We Belgians thought the ordeal was over until the Battle of the Bulge; the Ardennes people were suffering hell.

Food was still subject to ration coupons and many things were rare. Tea, coffee, sugar, and cocoa would still be rationed for several years, although gas, electricity, and coal were now available. At least we had light and heat while other things gradually improved. Antwerp, the largest arsenal in Europe for the armies that would soon destroy Nazi Germany, was heavily targeted by V-1 and V-2 bombs. Brussels was receiving only V-1s and Liège V-1s and V-2s, the new German weapons. In the fall of 1944 my parents' house had been heavily damaged and narrowly missed being demolished by a V-1. Five families close by had been nearly annihilated and their houses totally destroyed.

Our real celebration was about being alive and well. About having done what we had to do to bring an end to it all. The future was full of hope. We were all impoverished but eager to rebuild and resume the normal life of the free. Looking ahead, we saw the need to participate in the still great effort required to end the conflict, to punish those who had chosen the easy road of collaboration, and to help in rebuilding our shattered economy. We had reasons to rejoice and the energy to enter the new year with enthusiasm.

After a few days at home I went back to my British friends at Special Forces, where a surprise awaited me.

Supreme Headquarters was calling some fifteen former underground chiefs to a meeting. I went and met my friends and colleagues in counter-intelligence. For reasons of safety we had acted in isolation, independent of each other, so I knew only those I had met in September when the group had been assembled. Under the chairmanship of a U. S. major of the security branch, the meeting was called to order. The major first recognized us as a hard-working group that he said had provided very valuable intelligence and uncovered many German agents. The U. S. officer could not emphasize enough how valuable we had been. He then talked about the Battle of the Bulge, how they had been surprised and caught off guard. He said that had it not been for the weather, the Germans would never have gotten as far as Celle, near the Meuse River. The CIC fully appreciated what we had done and wanted us to know it. The Allied forces were confident that once the Bulge was eliminated they would be strong enough in men and matériel to chase the Germans without respite through the Eiffel while simultaneously crossing the Rhine and the Mosel.

To avoid a repetition of the German attack of mid-December, they realized now they had to perfect their intelligence gathering behind the lines and obtain accurate information, no matter what the weather. Aerial reconnaissance was simply not enough. Men on the ground with radios would be of the greatest help. Would we be willing to be parachuted behind the lines? There he paused and waited for reactions from the group. The reaction was one of silence, total disbelief! One of us finally recovered the use of speech and said a few words in French, a tongue the major did not speak. We all agreed with what he said and the man, now speaking English for us all, suggested that the officer should step outside for a few minutes so that we could discuss the proposal before giving him an answer. The officer obliged and left the room. The former freedom fighter then spoke to us in a few sentences defining his position, a stand from which he would not deviate and one he hoped we would all support.

His arguments were simple and based on a few well-taken points. We all had formerly worked for the underground. All of us were certainly known to the enemy. Practically none of us spoke fluent German. None of us had been trained for work behind the lines. We had all served loyally till now and had had time to form an opinion about how our information had been received and to what degree the army had responded to our warnings. The proposal before us was the equivalent of collective suicide. Let the army do their job as they saw fit, without us. We had risked our lives since 1940; we had done all we could; let them do the same. In ten minutes we had come to complete agreement: let us resign our commissions. Let us go back to our homes and civilian life. Let the army conduct matters their way. The major was called back and the same friend, speaking for us all, told him that our answer was unanimously negative and why. Also we were all known by the gestapo. We would have no chance to escape rapid detection or death if caught, and caught we would be soon enough due to our conspicuousness and our general lack of German language skills. We had been glad to serve in our own country where we could count on the help of all our former wartime connections. In Germany we would be alone and vulnerable.

The major understood we were in firm agreement when he saw us returning the documents we had been given months before. Simultaneously, we all arose and left him in the room facing a stack of General Eisenhower's passes. The meeting had lasted less than half an hour. On the way out one of us proposed we all have a beer and talk. We walked downtown to an old student café most of us from Brussels knew, La Mort Subite ("Sudden Death"). There in midmorning we could be alone and exchange impressions. Soon, facing glasses of well-aged *gueuze,* a potent Belgian brew, we talked. It was clear why we had all so quickly agreed on leaving: we had in common the experience of having faced intelligence officers imbued with their position and unwilling to comprehend the situation; unable to accept German trickery and Machiavellian behavior. The Americans with whom we had been in contact still believed the Germans possessed honesty, decency, and fair play. When we went to them with our improbable but all too true stories, we were dismissed as lunatics. The only way for American intelligence to learn was to let them go alone for the truth to Germany.

After lunch I was back on Avenue des Arts reporting to our friends at Special Forces. Those officers knew Europe and the German mind-set. They knew what those Germans were capable of—knew we would not survive long behind enemy lines. Both the major and the captain understood our unanimous reaction. Major Malinson made no comment. Later when I was alone with Captain Simms, to whom I now felt very close, he opened up to me and in a confidential way offered some remarks that confirmed what I thought. The Americans were overconfident, had little intelligence experience, and in his view were too confident of their superiority. But, he added, this was just his personal opinion.

Changing subjects, Simms asked where I would go from here. I said I had not the vaguest idea. From what I knew it would be months if not longer before our industry would be back at work. Prospects for employment were at best very shadowy, if not downright dark. Simms then asked if, as a man trained in chemistry, I would be interested in continuing to work in intelligence for a while, a year at least, in Brussels. When I expressed interest, he went on to explain about a branch of intelligence I knew nothing about: censorship. Since before the war, the British had been looking into the mail between South America and Europe. The system was now being modified and mail censorship units would soon open in Holland, France, and Belgium. The new offices were being staffed. Each office would need a specially trained chemist and the training would take place in London. The training would be sensitive and ultrasecret. They needed people they could trust completely. The Belgian Ministry of Defense had already presented a candidate but the British would have liked to keep the position "in the family." They wished to have someone they could trust, someone who would later go back into civilian life.

The position, under British Military Intelligence (MI-6) classification, would be equivalent to captain in rank and would have PX privileges. If I agreed, they would immediately enter and support my candidacy. Needless to say I was more than interested; I was enchanted. In a year, I was certain, I would be able to reenter the Belgian labor market and in between, I would have another interesting job with privileges not to be ignored in our still hard situation. The Belgian ministry fought hard to push its candidate, but the British fought even harder for me and finally won. Soon I learned I was going to London for a six-week intensive training period.

At that time civilian airlines had not yet been reestablished and people going to England had to fly RAF transport command planes. I would travel as a civilian with a Ministry of Defense order of mission. At the Brussels airport at Evere, immigration was controlled by a Belgian gendarme or state trooper, responsible for checking the few civilians passing through. He checked passports against a file of persons who were forbidden to exit the country. The man took my documents, looked into the card file, bypassed the letter B, then turned back to the beginning while the plane waited, its engines revving. I told the gendarme my name certainly was not in his file. He looked at me in surprise, looked again at my passport, and stamped it, apologizing for not having recognized me immediately. "I am sorry," he said, "I did not realize you were your father's son." I set off across the tarmac pondering what he had said. Obviously I was my father's son. Then it hit me as I climbed the boarding ladder: Botson was the name of the Belgian attorney general. Since the trooper did not even seem altogether familiar with the sequence of the alphabet, I figured that confusing a d with a t was a minor mistake that had played in my favor. More, could the son of an honorable person not have misbehaved?

I was on my way to London by a very special route. At that time, as the

Germans were still in Holland, Allied transport was operating over the route of invasion through Normandy and then over the sea. It was a well-protected and secure corridor. As I flew over the cratered landscape, the remains of the Atlantic sea wall, the destroyed villages and towns spoke for themselves of the terrible combat the landing forces had experienced only six months before in early summer.

Once in London, I was ushered through various military offices, both Belgian and British. A pleasant surprise was in store. The British offered me the option of replenishing my wardrobe using officers' shops offering military and civilian attire of the highest quality at affordable prices. I received the equivalent of four years of coupons. Then followed six weeks of intense training. Life in England was still operating on a war schedule. We worked on Saturdays and gone were the ten and three o'clock teas. Work was from eight until six, six days a week. On Sundays I took long walks through the devastated city, devastated by the German air raids of 1940 and now under fire by the V-1s and V-2s coming in from the Netherlands. I was living on Gloucester Road not far from Hyde Park. One Sunday early, around 8:00 A.M., I was walking near the Albert Memorial when a V-2 fell beside the Marble Arch. I was blown across a lawn, landing unhurt but dirty. The blast had thrown me over thirty feet! These V-2s, traveling at supersonic speed, were totally undetectable. First you heard the explosion and then the hiss of the incoming torpedo-shaped object.

The V-1s, by contrast, were nerve-wracking. They flew over with considerable noise. The moment they stopped making a noise, they had run out of fuel. That was the moment to watch for the falling bomb. The noiseless but potent V-2s were ten times more powerful than the V-1s and they came silently. You were caught or safe. For many years, all double-decker buses had had their windows replaced by a wire mesh coated in plastic that stayed pliable and transparent so that passengers would not be hurt by flying glass.

Almost unbelievably, London maintained business as usual, although the subway stations of the "tube" at night became vast dormitories. The streets of central London, nearly flattened in 1940, were all cleared and buildings were boarded up along the restored sidewalks. Only V bombs reached the city and the Germans failed to realize that with each bombing, they were only forging a stronger Britain, a nation ever more determined to annihilate them.

Weeks later I wandered again past Hyde Park Corner near Marble Arch on a Sunday morning. This is an interesting place where preachers or political rabble-rousers can address passersby from the top of a table or keg, some-

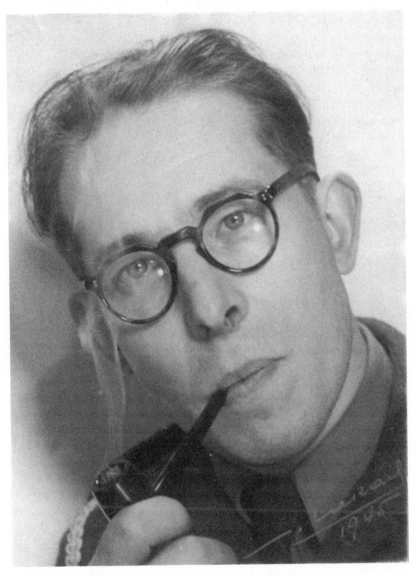

Bodson while serving as chief of the laboratory of Allied Censorship Belgium, 1945.

times drawing quite a crowd. The speakers' corner was popular even in time of war and I liked to go by and listen. Still at some distance, I thought I recognized a speaker in attire that made my blood boil. Perched on a three-legged stool was a Nazi Brownshirt in full regalia. Disregarding the rules of the park, I crossed a lawn to get a closer look. A London bobby addressed me, asking me not to cross the lawn again, as the Nazi continued to deliver his diatribe facing a disbelieving but smiling crowd, whose general reaction was, "Poor idiot! Go on, you poor fool." Only in England at war could a Nazi harangue folks under the very eye of the law.

Soon, my training at an end, it was time to leave. I asked for my bill at the hotel and told the cashier I had to go to Barclay's Bank to obtain the necessary cash. I returned with the proper amount in five-pound notes that the cashier accepted. While waiting for my receipt I felt a presence behind me. A bobby was asking me questions about the bills I had just laid on the counter. He asked politely to know the origin of the notes. I told him Barclay's Bank. Could I possibly accompany him to the bank? I was surprised, but what could I do but comply?

At the bank I identified the cashier who had helped me. The bobby went and spoke with him. He then came back to me and back we went to the hotel where he told the cashier that all was in order, apologized for the inconvenience, and left. When I asked the problem, the cashier did not volunteer any explanation.

The incident puzzled me for years after. It was only during the 1950s that, through reading, I finally put two and two together. The Germans had, in a concentration camp, a large counterfeiting operation that had flooded the world with five-pound sterling notes, as well as other foreign currencies. So everyone and especially foreigners, I suppose, using those denominations were suspect.

Back in Brussels, I found censors already up and running under the leadership of a small group of Allied specialists. I equipped my laboratory and went to work. Having been sworn to secrecy, I do not intend to describe my work in detail, but I may repeat what has since been published.

Even before World War II, England, feeling the menace of Hitlerism, had established a secret censorship station in Bermuda. South America was known to be a nest of German spies and a possible road to penetrate the United States and Canada. The British had some names and locations. These names were the first to go on the so-called "Black List." All letters and parcels from or to black-listed persons were intercepted, read, and resealed without leaving traces. The Black List grew as the names of the contacts of these spies were added. Most of the letters were innocent to the uninitiated, but to the British, they revealed the use of codes, secret ink, and even more sophisticated methods. My job was to learn about these and be able to detect them without leaving suspicious traces of my work. I also had to learn the use of codes, just enough to be able to detect their presence. If code use was suspected, the document was photographed or copied. Copies were sent to the decoding center for deciphering. Black List letters were handled with top priority, tested, resealed, and allowed to reach their destination. Rarely were they stopped. As the knowledge of spy networks grew, these could be watched or neutralized. Sometimes these spies were used to disseminate to Germany false information planted by the Allies. This was just one small part of the deception game played by the Allies to confuse the enemy.

Similar censorship stations were opened as soon as possible in the liberated countries of Holland, Belgium, and France. I was in charge of the laboratory at the Brussels station.

During the war, the liberated countries had done the same, trying to detect German agents who had stayed behind and were reporting to Germany using the mails. Our secondary function was to try to discover and stop unwanted dissemination of news of a military character innocently passed along by civilians as well as military personnel. Mail was read and unwanted news deleted. Some less innocent, incriminating letters were read, copied, and allowed to continue. We had received our Black List from the British. Mail from and to those on the list was treated with special care and would eventually lead to arrests. Spies and their contacts had to answer to the justices in the different lands.

General mail was read at random and from this portion of the work, eventually the Black List grew longer. At our Brussels station fifteen hundred people read the mail.

In the liberated territories the censorship had yet another role: the discovery of channels moving gems, precious metals, and currencies—all illegal activities in those days. Many people who had worked for the enemy or who had been war profiteers were trying to move their loot to secure places. It was in the Allies' interest to discover them and deprive them of the fruits of their dirty labor. The same was true for simple black market people who had lived off others' misery. They too would eventually have hard questions to answer.

I vividly remember a spring morning in 1945 when the head of the photo section entered my office with a film, still dripping wet, which he had just developed. The Allied troops were at that time penetrating deep into Germany. They were slowly discovering the somber truth about the concentration camps. One U. S. soldier had taken pictures while entering Buchenwald. The film showed trenches full of skeleton-like bodies, doors of incinerators where the bodies were burned, and a rank of survivors. The eyes of those prisoners still look at me today. Eyes without expression, eyes that could no longer express feelings, eyes that seemed larger for they were deeply sunk in shaven heads that seemed out of proportion to the emaciated bodies. Although these wretched souls had just met their liberators, their eyes were void of expression. Hope and spirit had been killed; only the bodies barely survived. These pictures are imprinted on my memory. These men had been ours, they had been the fighters for freedom, men who had risked everything for the cause we all believed in, men of courage and determination. They had been caught, tortured, interrogated, imprisoned. They had been, like animals, taken away in cattle rail cars to German concentration camps. There, outfitted in light striped cotton, they were forced to labor under the sun, the rain, in hot and freezing weather. Up at four, for a twelve-hour day's work nearly without food, they labored day after day, month after month. German intent was clear: use them, abuse them, reduce them from proud and fearsome people to servile machines, slowly abrading their will, wearing out their bodies, reducing them all to the level of obedient animals that would soon die and be replaced. When the bodies finally gave up, the Germans burned them.

The pictures of the living I saw that spring morning were those of people at the limit of endurance, empty living shells. Bodies yes, but bodies only; emptied of everything; bodies with dysfunctional brains so deprived of nutrients that they were walking corpses stripped of feelings, incapable of reactions.

I asked the photo section to print eight by tens from the film and took them to the staff of our censorship unit. We all decided that this story could not be released to the press without preparing for public opinion. The public needed to be gently and gradually informed. Our country had too many families anxiously awaiting news from husbands, brothers, sons known to be in concentration camps. Nobody was aware of the conditions. The press was carefully fed news worded to introduce these horrors gradually. In the meantime, teams of Allied doctors were attending the survivors, replacing the missing elements and nutrients in their bodies, and teaching them how to resume eating. Weeks after the discovery, some could be repatriated. For others it took much longer, but at least they were able to communicate with their families.

In December of 1945, months after the hostilities had ended in Germany, the censorship units closed their doors, having helped military security discover spies and deliver traitors, collaborators, and black marketeers to the courts. Seven and a half years of my life, since my conscription in 1937, I had spent at war or preparing for war, in uniform and in civvies, unarmed and armed, legal and illegal, paid and unpaid—mostly the latter—and finally repaid.

For at the end, for us, the underground survivors, hope had finally triumphed.

Epilogue—Fifty Years Later

Throughout this book I have often referred to the importance of hope. Hope gave us reasons to fight and to endure. Although an optimist by nature, I have had a few moments of discouragement that forced me into sobering introspection. I had to reevaluate world events and my participation in them. Nearly fifty years have gone by since the end of the war, and other events have taken place—some pass in a spark nearly unnoticed, some recur with insidious persistence, a few hold deep implications for profound and durable change.

From 1945 to 1951 I lived in Belgium reconstructing my life, getting married, and then having our first child. From 1951 until 1961 we lived in Zaire, the former Belgian Congo. Two more children were born to us on the high plateau of the Katanga province. From 1961 until now we have lived in the United States. I ended my career teaching in a U. S. college deeply involved in environmental sciences. I am still active trying to protect our physical surroundings.

Life on three continents, for prolonged periods, has greatly contributed to enlarging my horizons. It has forced on me studies and comparisons that have contributed to broadening my vision while forcing on me the realization that other cultures and environments are bringing forth different thinking and different ways to solve problems. My attitude forged during the war has enlarged and I have become more liberal, if not more radical.

Some four years ago I wrote my autobiography for my children. Out of the segment for 1932–45 has come this account. It has been a very burdensome task, this act of remembrance. Once it was almost complete, I was at last able to talk about the painful past and decided it would be good to go back to Belgium and the Ardennes, to revisit sites and try to reestablish contacts with former members of the old sabotage group while reevaluating Europe. Being only a few years older than most of my fighting men, I hoped to find many of them and collect their feelings and evaluate their reactions. How wrong I was. Out of twenty-seven members of my group, I found only two alive.

My wife and I spent two wonderful months in Europe, one in Belgium. The weather was fully on our side and we traveled unimpeded through all the little villages and woods that I had crisscrossed during my Ardennes years. I took with me only one document, the official roster of Service Hotton's Group East. From a friend's house in Liège I traced several names in my old sector villages and reached mostly younger relatives telling me that so and so was no more. Only two I could contact and visit: our nurse, Malou Hallin, who had moved from Vielsalm to Stavelot, and Léon Sadzot, who still lived at Forge à la Plez. I had hoped so much to see Laurence Joye. She too had recently departed, at the age of eighty-two, and I could talk only with her daughter, Marie Louise, who was two in 1944. She had heard of me through her mother. Her brother, who was seven at liberation, would probably remember me, but I did not meet with him; he had moved.

Meeting Léon Sadzot, long since married and with two daughters and a son, all full grown, was indeed a pleasure. He was still the same determined man, calm, resolved, sparing of words. I detected a note of bitterness about the war's events. This patriot had been asked to defend himself for having sold wood to the enemy. Farmers had to deliver food; he had to deliver wood. The state went so far as to block the family bank account and made life very difficult for them for years. They came close to bankruptcy. But neither the father nor Léon ever complained or said a word to us. They did not ask for the help we would have so gladly provided, as we did for many others. Rather they suffered morally and financially defending themselves, proud and secure in their clear conscience.

Forge à la Plez was still the quiet, isolated place I had known—the mill still operating, but with modernized equipment. Gone were the boiler and the steam engine; all was now electric. Some meadows seemed smaller, and some appeared at different places than in my recollection. Although the country roads were not all black-topped, throughout the Ardennes the old macadam or graveled roads were a thing of the past. The proliferation of cars has rendered the place less isolated, and there were numerous cars passing by.

Reminders of the Battle of the Bulge were still visible on many of the Sadzots' buildings. In a remote corner of a large shed filled with old equipment, Léon showed me the old 1939 Ford that had finished its days in service to the Secret Army before ending up in an accident that totalled it. But, said Léon, he could not let it go. He made room for it. I was glad to have seen the old car that had faithfully helped us so many times. Léon went upstairs and came back showing me the shotgun Charles, Christian, Noel, and I had offered him in 1945. It was his pride, and he showed me the engraved brass plate we had intended to have imbedded in the walnut stock.

When I had called him on the phone days earlier, I had detected a faint reserve. As soon as we arrived and Léon and I had a chance to be alone, I frankly told him of my impression. He told me he could not understand why I had kept silent and had ended my contact with him soon after the Bulge. I told him I had tried to put the war years out of my mind. They were loaded with too many painful memories. I had also married and had been trying hard to establish myself. I further explained the transformation I had gone through these last years while writing this account. He seemed to understand and quickly his former openness reappeared.

Léon and his wife now live in the new house that was started before the war and finished only long after. It is there that we sat for lunch. Later we visited the old farm house in which we shared the few quiet evening meals with Charles, Christian, and Noel. The barn in which our escaping U. S. airmen had spent time was still there, but smaller. During the Battle of the Bulge a shell had knocked part of it down. Repainted, what was left of it continued in use. With Léon's wife, we went into the nearby woods to see the enclosed park he had created for his herd of wild boars, some twenty-five of them.

There were no doubts in Léon's mind that our fight had been worth it. His only wish was that his father and his family could have been spared the harassment they had gone through after it was over, harassment that he said had been created by local jealousy. I had learned of many such instances. How I wished they had not been so proud and had asked for our help. We would have gone to great ends to prove their patriotism and vouch for them to the authorities, as we did on several occasions for people who had been less supportive and not as dedicated as these to the cause.

The woods and the countryside had not changed much, save the better roads. The villages had changed little. The solid Ardennes houses and farms had been repaired or rebuilt using the same traditional materials. Horses were still very much in use for logging. Only the old sturdy wagons which were used to carry logs to the mill had been replaced by modern diesel tractors and trailers. One place that had changed much was the once nearly deserted crossroads at the Baraque de Fraiture. A new super highway from Liège to Arlon now passed close by. The old crossroad was still there, but built up with cafes, restaurants, and service stations.

In Provedroux I met Thomas Laurent, son of Antoine. He, being sixty, remembered me well. He was twelve in 1944. Their old house received a direct hit during the Bulge, and they now lived in a bigger and newer one, quite modern for the area. Thomas reminded me of several actions we carried out with his father. Some I had not remembered during my writing: a theft in the early spring of 1944 in which we stole several drums of fuel oil from the Lierneux narrow-gauge railway station; a shed we built near Provedroux for a parachuted radio agent serving us and the Secret Army.

Those two small actions were executed for the Secret Army, whose men, at that time, did not own arms, except for the few they had salvaged in 1940 and had kept against German regulations. We helped them; they helped us.

Thomas had not himself participated in the underground, but he remembered well the things he had heard his father Antoine tell and retell. His father had died only a few years ago. For Thomas there were no doubts his father had done the right thing. The underground had been the organization to support.

From Provedroux we went to Honvelez by the back road and reached the house built for Jan by Mayor Faisant. The house was now occupied by a member of the Faisant family with whom I talked. I was very emotional as I stood in front of it, almost expecting to see some member of the Van der Borght family come to the door. My wife stood behind me, respecting this long moment of inner communion.

Then we went to the village and passed in front of the old milk cooperative. It had been transformed into a youth camp, and the flag floating in the breeze was blue with twelve yellow stars, the flag of the European common market. We went to Vielsalm by way of Salmchâteau, passing by what had been the property of Gustave Jacques. Remembrance piled upon remembrance. Souvenir upon souvenir. So many departed friends.

My wife was quite amazed at how I could, without the slightest hesitation, navigate through all those roads and streets after so many years of absence. I had traveled them by foot and bicycle—but not as fast as by car. Then I had ample time to notice all the details that an automobile driver would never notice. The features of the land were so deeply engraved in my memory that it was still easy. Besides, not much had changed except ownership.

In Vielsalm, after having passed former Notary Lambert's house, now the town library, we stopped at the Charles Legros house. It was no longer an

electrical store; the windows were now curtained for privacy. There we met
the son, Charles Junior, and his youngest brother, Hubert. Charles was six in
1944 and remembered me well. Hubert was only two then, but he had heard
of me through family conversations. They were both unmarried and teach-
ers. Their father had died at age sixty-five and their mother at seventy. The
two sons were quiet and well-educated. They had read about the local underground and were even able to lend me some publications by local amateur
historians. Having read those, I realized they contained a number of mistakes and omissions. How could it be otherwise? The active men at the fore-
front of the resistance were not taking notes and spoke only much later about
what they could remember. The story of the underground will never be
known in its totality, never with great accuracy. It was too secret, too com-
partmentalized, and no archives were left to consult.

In Baclain I had been surprised and altogether glad to see an engraved
memorial stone encased in the main wall of a house. The plate commemo-
rates the sacrifice of Omer Brasseur from Service Hotton. He had been a
part of the Oscar Cornet brigade in my group. The memorial did not mention Omer's connection to Service Hotton, but rather his membership in the
Secret Army Zone Five, Sector Four. Technically, it is accurate, since Service
Hotton was the engineers' group of the Secret Army. Omer died fighting
with us. I do not recall who mentioned to me the whereabouts of Oscar
Cornet's death. It took place shortly after the Bulge. Being a forester, he had
been called upon by local farmers who were clearing a forest road and came
upon a suspicious stack of trees piled over the road. While investigating it,
Oscar stepped on a mine and was killed.

I could not leave the Ardennes without paying another visit to Léon Joye's
place of burial at the Salmchâteau cemetery. High above the village, opposite
the railroad, with a splendid view of the Salm valley, lies the last resting place
for the village's inhabitants. I stood for a long moment facing my friend's
grave. The morning was calm and sunny, and I breathed in the serenity and
peace, the peace Léon had helped restore. I thought about this son of Flanders who joined the army as a career man and was later incorporated into
the Chasseurs Ardennais. I remembered how, after the defeat of 1940, he
brewed his rancor until 1942, when he decided to join the British, leaving
behind his wife and two children. How he died, executed by the Nazis at the
Liège Citadel in early September, 1944. How this man from the flatness of
Flanders had adopted the Walloon's hilly land and married a Salmchâteau
girl. I thought about his sense of duty, his longing for freedom. After having
paid my respects, I slowly toured the terraced hill. Again the Germans' bru-

Omer Brasseur, member of Group E, Service Hotton, killed in action.

tality hit me like a brick. So many tombs decorated with markers that spoke for themselves: killed in action 1914–1918, killed in action 1940, died in Germany 1942–1944, died in concentration camp 1942–1945, shot in Bandes during the Bulge, killed as civilians during the war. The complete story of a martyred village was written on its tombstones—the tragic ends of people who suffered unnatural death, death caused by human violence. It spoke personally to me because I had known these people, but it would have been the same in almost any other cemetery of Belgium or at the Bulge. Will this never end? Will we never learn?

In Liège, while visiting my cousin, J. Henniquiau, I noticed that he now walked with a cane; his old war wound did not make it easier on him. While we talked, exchanging war reminiscences, he told us about his breakfast in a German hospital. After being wounded in 1940, he was made prisoner and moved into an officers' military hospital, where for breakfast they all received a soft-boiled grade A egg decorated with a printed swastika! Officers only! To this day he still could not believe it. Was this part of Nazi propaganda, part of the party's belief in its superiority? Was it something out of the constant mise-en-scène needed to infuse and maintain the fanaticism of the Ubermensh? Was it related to the occultism that had permeated the whole of Nazi propaganda?

Since World War II has ended, in the nearly fifty years that have followed, the world has experienced many more wars. None as general, some not as harsh, but war nonetheless: the Korean war, the Algerian war, the Vietnam war where we erroneously acted alone without U. N. sanction, the Falklands war, the Afghanistan war, the Mid-East war, the Gulf war, and many conflicts of lesser severity, in addition to revolutions and liberations. But always there is use of force. Force used and abused. Time, money, and lives wasted to achieve goals that often could have been reached peacefully. Violence seems to be ingrained in human beings, and I wonder often if there is any reasonable hope that it will ever change.

I believe there is. After World War I there were mistakes. The biggest of all was the Versailles treaty, which literally made serfs of the Germans. There was also the demise of the League of Nations. Then fascism ignited Spain, Germany, and Italy, setting afire Europe, Japan, and the Asian world.

However, there have also been successes. After World War II the victors adopted a different attitude. Germany and Japan were allowed to live, and the world even helped them rebuild. Can we forget President Truman or the Marshall Plan? There has been the generous attitude of France and a serious willingness to pardon and forgive. The United Nations was created. Today, more than 160 nations are members and the U. N. carries some weight. This is somewhat encouraging.

Through rapid communication and the increase in international exchanges, we have created an international trade of unprecedented magnitude. Nations formerly contained within their borders have entered into commerce with their neighbors and with even more distant partners. Exchanges of raw materials contribute to creating new international ties. From their first timid partnerships, economically driven nations have signed trade agreements to further their common interests. We are fast becoming part of

a rapidly more populated, more active, more coherent, and more interde-
pendent world.

But there are greater reasons than economics for us to pull together. The
problems of world pollution and ozone depletion have already been at the
base of international conferences and multinational resolutions. Our meager
participation has to be reevaluated and amended. Population growth is ag-
gravating our problems faster than we can act on them. These are reasons
for all nations to adopt a stronger attitude of international cooperation and
to create new opportunities to bond and pull the world together.

Traveling through Paris and Belgium, talking about the underground with
people of different backgrounds, I realized the public at large knows or re-
members very little about it. Those who know, know more about traitors and
collaborators than about common heroes. Much publicity has been given to
the former, while many of the latter lie unremarked in village cemeteries
throughout the world; but then, true freedom fighters do not enjoy remembering. They try to forget and continue on with their lives, anonymously. We
realize we know little about what really happened. We know only a little part
of the vast saga in which we had participated, surrounded by secrecy. I, too,
had to realize that I was only a tiny part of a grand and vast effort.

Of those of us arrested and tortured, some died without revealing anything, some sent the enemy on a wild chase. But some talked. Some gave
little; some gave all, provoking mass arrests. How are we to be their judges,
knowing the kinds of tortures to which they were subjected? I long ago decided, if it was possible, not to be taken alive if I fell into enemy hands. Dying
under torture, even the bravest cannot predict his behavior. Nevertheless,
the story has to be written again and again so that the idea of freedom lives
and acquires deeper roots.

It is the same reason we erect monuments, put up memorials, leave permanent plaques at the sites where heroes have fallen, gun in hand or facing
the executioner. While such local memorials are practically unknown in
America, they appear all over formerly occupied Europe:

—A plaque at the Liège Citadelle with seventeen names, among them
   members of the Secret Army Zone Five, Sectors Two and Seven, and
   two members of the Special Forces, friends trained in Britain, L. Joye
   and A. Delplace;
—The plaque to Omer Brasseur in Baclain;
—The plaques in all the village cemeteries;

The monument to the fallen comrades of Service Hotton, in Bruly de Pesche's woods. Above the statue of Our Lady of the Underground, the cupola bears the names. Photo © Gerard Mathieu, Brussels.

—The plaques on city walls where freedom fighters fell
   during liberation;
—The Allied cemeteries in Europe where thousands upon
   thousands sleep forever in the earth they had come so far to
   help liberate.

These monuments are there to remember, so that following generations might think about values worth dying for. Because people need to be reminded that the freedom they enjoy today has been dearly acquired and needs defending.

I have lived and worked on three continents. I am no longer attached to any particular piece of land. I am more concerned about my rights to live the way I like among people that let me do so, people tolerant enough to respect my person for what it is. Do I consider myself a patriot? I suppose I could say I have been one of many in Belgium, but my vision has changed. The kind of patriotism I have responded to in the past I consider today narrow and obsolete. I have reached larger views. I have become an earth patriot. Only my ideas about freedom have not changed. In my thinking, patriotism limited only to one's own nation now borders on chauvinism. We now must move toward "world patriotism," going far beyond borders, creeds, races, or places.

I cannot listen to a bugle or a drum call anymore. I respond to the waving in the wind of the flag of planet earth.

I listen to the finale of Beethoven's Ninth, the hymn to joy, the chorus to brotherhood; to Sergei Prokofiev's Fifth Symphony dedicated to the Freedom of Man; to Verdi's Song for Liberty.

Agent for the Resistance was composed into type on a Miles 33 System and output on an Agfa Acuset 1000 in ten point New Caledonia with three points of spacing between the lines. New Caledonia was also selected for display. The book was designed by Pat Crowder typeset by Graphic Composition, Inc., printed offset by Thomson-Shore, Inc., and bound by John H. Dekker & Sons, Inc. The paper on which this book is printed carries acid-free characteristics for an effective life of at least three hundred years.

TEXAS A & M UNIVERSITY PRESS : COLLEGE STATION